D1002229

Edith and Winnifred Eaton

THE ASIAN AMERICAN EXPERIENCE

Series Editor
Roger Daniels, University of Cincinnati

A list of books in the series appears at
the end of this book.

Edith and Winnifred Eaton

Chinatown Missions and Japanese Romances

DOMINIKA FERENS

VILLA JULIE COLLEGE LIBRARY
STEVENSON MD 21153

University of Illinois Press

URBANA AND CHICAGO

© 2002 by the Board of Trustees
of the University of Illinois
All rights reserved
Manufactured in the United States of America
C 5 4 3 2 1

∞ This book is printed on acid-free paper.

Library of Congress Cataloging-in-Publication Data
Ferens, Dominika, 1964–
Edith and Winnifred Eaton : Chinatown missions and
Japanese romances / Dominika Ferens.
p.   cm. — (The Asian American experience)
Includes bibliographical references and index.
ISBN 0-252-02721-3 (cloth : alk. paper)
1. Sui Sin Far, 1865–1914. 2. Eaton, Winnifred, 1875–1954.
3. Novelists, Canadian—20th century—Biography.
4. Eurasians—United States—Biography. 5. Sisters—
North America—Biography. 6. Canadian fiction—
Asian influences. 7. Asian American women—Biography.
8. Eurasians—Canada—Biography. 9. Asia—In literature.
10. Asians in literature. I. Title. II. Series.
PR9199.2.S93Z68   2002
813'.409971—dc21   2001004000

The photo of Edith Eaton on page 47 was published in
Land of Sunshine, November 1900; the photo of Winnifred Eaton
on page 111 was published in *Frank Leslie's Popular Monthly,*
September 1899.

One summer when I was about six, my family drove to Maine. The highway was straight and hot and shimmered darkly in the sun. My sister and I sat in the back seat of the Studebaker and argued about what color the road was. I said black, she said purple. After I had harangued her into admitting that it was indeed black, my father gently pointed out that my sister still saw it as purple. I was unimpressed with the relevance of that at the time; but with the passage of years, and much more observation, I have come to see endless overheated highways as slightly more purple than black. My sister and I will probably argue about the hue of life's road forever. But the lesson I learned from listening to her wild perceptions is that it really is possible to see things— even the most concrete things—simultaneously yet differently; and that seeing simultaneously yet differently is more easily done by two people than one, but that one person can get the hang of it with time and effort.

—Patricia Williams, *The Alchemy of Race and Rights*

Contents

Foreword

ROGER DANIELS

TWENTY YEARS AGO, the names of Edith and Winnifred Eaton, born in Montreal in 1865 and 1875, respectively, to an English father and a Chinese mother, were all but unknown to students of literature, although each had a successful literary career. Both passed for "white"; each took an Asian pen name. Edith Eaton became Sui Sin Far and wrote largely about Chinese North Americans; Winnifred Eaton became Onoto Watanna and wrote of a Japan she had never visited. Most of the critical attention that has been paid to the sisters since S. E. Solberg and the late Amy Ling brought them to the attention of scholars in the early 1980s has focused on Sui Sin Far/Edith. Critics have tended to praise the "authentic" sister who wrote about her "own" heritage and to look down their noses at the "phony" sister who invented a "fake" Japanese heritage.

Dominika Ferens will have none of this. Her study of the sisters is both a literary study and a kind of ethnography; she refuses to value one sister above the other and, by dint of detective work of considerable ingenuity, has greatly expanded the literary corpus of both sisters and thrown new light on their lives. Ferens has not worked alone but has shared research findings with several other scholars who are exploring other aspects of the Eaton revival. Diana Birchall's biography of her grandmother, *Onoto Watanna: The Story of Winnifred Eaton,* appeared in this series last year. An as yet untitled collection of Winnifred's essays and stories edited by Elizabeth Rooney (also an Eaton descendent) and Linda Trinh Moser will join the earlier works, which began with Annette White-Parks, *Sui Sin Far/Edith Maude Eaton: A Literary Biography* (1995) and an edition of Edith's writings, *Mrs. Spring Fragrance and Other Writings* (1995), edited by White-Parks and Amy Ling.

Unlike some of the scholars with whom she has worked, Ferens is no blood kin to the Eatons. In fact, she is unlike any other active scholar working on the Asian American experience. Born and reared in Poland, she has two graduate degrees from the University of California at Los Angeles and is currently on the faculty of the University of Wrocław, where she has been vice chair of the Department of English since 1999. She is not the first continental European to examine the Asian American experience at length: Karin Meissenburg published her 1987 Free University of Berlin dissertation, *The Writing on the Wall: Socio-Historical Aspects of Chinese American Literature, 1900–1980* (1987); and Brigitte Scheer has been focusing her seminar at the University of Innsbruck on Asian American literature for a number of years, and at least two of her students have done Asian American dissertations. But none before Ferens has published a research monograph in the Asian American homeland. Surely she will not be the last. Asian American history and literature are finding an increasingly solid base in the academy, and transnational approaches will almost certainly become more dominant in the foreseeable future.

Acknowledgments

To Professor King-Kok Cheung goes the lion's share of my thanks. Her engagement in this project and her rigor, tact, and readiness to read and comment on multiple drafts literally overnight have brought me this far. I challenge anyone to say his or her mentor measures up to mine.

The chance to work with Diana Birchall, granddaughter and biographer of Winnifred Eaton, was a privilege. Our weekly "Winnying" sessions sustained me through a strenuous year of dissertating and made my research doubly exciting. Without Diana's networking skills and willingness to share her materials on the Eaton family, this project would have been much impoverished. Two other members of the Eaton family, Elizabeth Rooney and Paul ("Tim") Rooney, generously helped with research and bibliographic work. I am also deeply grateful to fellow-"Winnyer" Jean Lee Cole for reading and commenting at length on the drafts of several chapters and for her valuable reading suggestions.

UCLA graduate students Karen Keely and Lois Leveen worked with me every inch of the way. I thank them for applying their eagle eyes to first drafts and for helping me shape them into chapters. Our study group meetings became my measure of academic rigor and the mainstay of my writing process. Also my mother, Izabela Ferens, has been an untiring proofreader and commentator on my work.

Professor Jinqi Ling introduced me to Edith Eaton and guided me through the mazes of critical theory. Professors Valerie Smith and Henry Yu inspired and supported me throughout my course of studies. I am particularly indebted to Henry Yu for daring me to try an interdisciplinary approach to literature.

Many librarians assisted me in the archival search. I am grateful to Frances

Salmon of the University of the West Indies and Valerie G. Francis of the National Library of Jamaica for doing research on my behalf. At the University of Calgary Library, Apollonia Steele went out of her way to make my research productive, coming in early and staying after hours to give me as much time as possible with the Winnifred Eaton Reeve Collection. Finally, without the expertise of Jenifer Abramson of the UCLA Research Library, I would not have stood a chance of finding the microfilms of the Jamaican *Gall's Daily News Letter,* for which Edith and Winnifred Eaton worked as reporters.

I also want to thank the Fulbright Committee and the UCLA English Department for investing in my education and Roger Daniels for his staunch support of this project.

Edith and Winnifred Eaton

Introduction

> Especially when we live over here, we already know what people
> want, need to know, and what people should know about us. We
> offer something that they would not understand even though they
> may have lived there. They lived there as servicemen, journalists,
> politicians, and scientists.
> —Le Ly Hayslip in *Words Matter: Conversations with Twenty*
>   *Asian American Writers*

THIS PROJECT TRACES the crossovers between the practices of literature and ethnography, more specifically, between the work of Edith and Winnifred Eaton,[1] on the one hand, and nineteenth-century ethnographic discourses of race, on the other. Biracial sisters of British and Chinese descent, reared in Canada in the second half of the nineteenth century, Edith and Winnifred adopted the pen names Sui Sin Far and Onoto Watanna, respectively, and went on to pursue literary careers in the United States. One claimed Chinese descent, the other Japanese. In the early decades of the twentieth century, both were involved in the production of what I call ethnographic knowledge for popular consumption, yet they developed disparate subjectivities, ethnographic interests, epistemologies, narrative structures, and conceptions of the writer's social role. Those differences stemmed, in part, from their individual positioning in relation to their audience and their ethnographic subjects. Both sisters drew eclectically on available discourses of race and the Orient. But because they brought to their writing the experience of racialized subjects, they reproduced orientalism with a difference.

Past criticism has tended to polarize the Eaton sisters on ideological grounds and to use the commercially successful Winnifred as a foil for the more politically engaged Edith. By attending to the historical and discursive context in which the sisters wrote, I problematize such binaries as accommodation and resistance, repetition and innovation, reinscription and contestation. In line with recent reformulations of orientalism by Lisa Lowe, Dorinne Kondo, and Ali Behdad, this project assumes there is no uncompromised space outside discourse from which to contest it. Like the European orientalist writers, the nuances of whose work Behdad explored, the Eaton sisters could not have avoided the "'baggage' of orientalist knowledge that . . . mediated their desire for the Orient" (15). Undeniably, Winnifred's work is more heavily weighted with such "baggage," yet when criticism indulges in the "good sister–bad sister" paradigm, both Winnifred's subtle antiracist interventions and the muted orientalism of Edith's work go unnoticed. When applying a broadly defined criterion of subversiveness to literature, we are obliged to pass over or oversimplify texts that are perhaps ideologically dated and therefore less useful to us today, but without which we cannot begin to reconstruct the intellectual climate of their day. Fortunately, there is ample room in literary studies for texts that Asian Americanists dismissed as compromised in the fervor of historical recovery. To avoid teleological judgments and favoritism altogether is probably no more possible than to stand outside orientalist discourse. Aware of my own fallibility, I attempt a case study of the Eaton sisters' work that treads back and forth between teasing out received orientalist discourses and attending to what Kondo called "relative degrees of subversiveness" (53).

With the epigraph from Le Ly Hayslip in mind, I locate this project in the space between what turn-of-the-century readers "here" already knew and wanted to know and what Edith and Winnifred Eaton thought they should know about being "there." I map out the meanings that *here* and *there* had for the Eaton sisters and suggest where in relation to these imaginary spaces they situated themselves at various points in their careers. *Here* for both sisters would have stood for mainstream America, a space they inhabited more or less uneasily. *There,* in Edith's case, stood for the Chinatown ghettos into which she ventured as a teacher and sympathetic writer, though not as a resident. But what was *there* for Winnifred, who set her narratives against an imaginary though well-researched backdrop of Japan, a country she never visited? I propose that *there* was also a surrogate for *self-as-other,* a displaced biracial subjectivity, since the Eaton sisters' ethnographic vision was inevitably refracted by their own problems and preoccupations. Since both sisters also moved a good deal in geographic terms, a brief outline of their travels back and forth across North America and overseas to Jamaica is provided in the appendix.

This study is driven by a series of interrelated questions. If we use the term *ethnography* in its broadest sense—as a set of changing rationales for and styles of knowing and representing the other—how do the biracial Eaton sisters' practices alter our understanding of it? In what sense and from whose point of view were they ethnographers? Mine? Their own? Their readers'?

How did the literary marketplace shape their interest in the other? How did they claim ethnographic authority? What role did autoethnography and autoexoticization play in their literary careers? What epistemological assumptions did they make? What was at stake for each of them in the ethnographic project? And if white mainstream North Americans were in the process of defining themselves in opposition to their racial others, to what extent were the Eaton sisters able to disrupt this process?

Early assessments of Edith and Winnifred Eaton, written after S. E. Solberg and Amy Ling brought them to critical attention in the 1980s, highlighted Edith's commitment to the Chinese communities in North America and the value of her work for the emerging Asian American literary canon. Edith was read as a precursor of Louis Chu, Maxine Hong Kingston, and others who "claimed America" on behalf of the disenfranchised Chinese minority.[2] Recognized as a unique record of early resistance to racist discourses, her work was included in *The Big Aiiieeeee! An Anthology of Chinese American and Japanese American Literature* (1991) and the *Heath Anthology of American Literature* (1995) and is now being widely taught at American universities. By contrast, Winnifred's fiction attracted little attention, even though copies of her fifteen once popular novels are accessible. That Winnifred was not a politically engaged writer but a successful novelist "cashing in" on a Japanese fad made Edith seem all the more remarkable. Ling's groundbreaking work *Between Worlds: Women Writers of Chinese Ancestry* (1990) provided much-needed bibliographic and biographical material that gave an impetus to further research on the Eaton sisters. However, Ling's construction of Winnifred as an intriguing but lightweight novelist who failed to rise above the racist discourses of her day probably skewed scholarly interests toward Edith. Symptomatically, Xiao-huang Yin's 1991 dissertation and his book *Chinese American Literature since the 1850s* (2000) included detailed analyses of Edith's writings but made no mention of Winnifred's.

In 1995, Annette White-Parks published *Sui Sin Far/Edith Maude Eaton: A Critical Biography,* a meticulously researched study that has been an indispensable source of reference for me. With the growing interest in literary "tricksterism," the performativity of race and gender, and Mikhail Bakhtin's theories of "heteroglossia" and the "carnivalesque" in popular culture, an opportunity opened for the recovery of Winnifred's work and a reinterpretation of Edith's. Ling's articles on the Eaton sisters from this period complicated and enriched her initial response. White-Parks's use of the "trickster" trope added a new dimension to our understanding of Edith. In a reversal of earlier trends, some of the criticism that sprang from these theoretical breakthroughs, for instance, Lisa Botshon's analysis of Winnifred's autobiographical novel *Me: A Book of Remembrance* (1915), used Edith as a negative foil for the more adventurous Winnifred, who, according to Botshon, refused to be tied down by essentialist notions of race. Even critical texts that discussed just one of the sisters tended to imply a preference based on an ethical or political judgment. On the whole, however, Winnifred's "trickster-ism," unmediated by a sense of communal responsibility, continued to make readers uneasy.

More recently, the discourse of fluid cultural identity and heterogeneity has generated a slew of bold new interpretations of Winnifred's works. In 1997, Linda Trinh Moser edited a reprint of Winnifred's *Me*, offering a sensitive analysis in the afterword, and *Miss Numè of Japan* (1899), introduced by Eve Oishi, was reprinted in 1999. The dissertations of Noreen Groover Lape, Samina Najmi, and Carol Vivian Spaulding (each of whom devoted a chapter to Winnifred and some also to Edith), as well as the publications of Yuko Matsukawa and Pat Shea, credited Winnifred with having developed successful strategies of self-empowerment and for discussing such taboo subjects as miscegenation in ways acceptable to a broad reading public. But with the exception of Jean Lee Cole, who deftly reconstructed Winnifred's position in the contemporary publishing marketplace and in the film industry, critics have shown little concern for the material and discursive conditions in which her fiction was produced.

My study, much of which has been archival, attends to the historical and textual context. In reconstructing the Eaton family history, I have greatly benefited from a year-long collaboration with Diana Birchall, Winnifred's granddaughter and biographer, who introduced me to the family archives and shared her work in progress. One of the propositions of this project is that the mutually constitutive meanings of *China* and *Japan* that the Eaton sisters inherited—meanings they engaged creatively as writers—derive from two distinct discursive traditions: missionary and travel writings on the Far East. Reading these nineteenth-century texts, I found that ethnographic work on China was done most consistently by Protestant missionaries starting in the first half of the nineteenth century, whereas Japan was most energetically textualized by lay travelers in the last thirty years of the century. I explore the implications of these findings and link the two discursive traditions to the unconventional literary careers of the Eaton sisters.

I also contribute substantial new materials to the ongoing literary project of recovering primary texts: Edith's newspaper articles published over the course of five months in Kingston, Jamaica; several short stories and articles by Edith and Winnifred; and an important autobiographical piece by Edith, "The Persecution and Oppression of Me" (1911). Because Edith published this piece anonymously in the *Independent,* a New York political weekly, she was considerably more explicit here than in her other writings about the everyday experience of racism in its many guises. This is also the clearest statement we have of Edith's self-positioning in relation to the Chinese and Caucasians in North America.

Finding a cache of reviews of Winnifred's novels at the University of Calgary, as well as numerous articles about Winnifred in the popular press and several early responses to Edith's *Mrs. Spring Fragrance,* has allowed me to juxtapose current academic readings of the Eaton sisters with the initial reader response. This exercise occasionally tempered my impulse to read into the literature a subversive message that was simply not available to the first readers. Also by reading the scores of reviews that Winnifred collected in the early years of her career, I have been able to suggest ways in which her half-Japanese persona was shaped by the reader response.

I have adopted a cross-disciplinary approach that brings current theoretical concerns from anthropology into literary studies. To view the Eaton sisters through the paradigm of ethnography is useful because it underscores their shared biracial experience, as well as the commonalities of their literary practice. Until recently, critics have made a distinction between Edith's accurate representations of Chinese North Americans and Winnifred's phony portrayals of the Japanese. The assumption behind this type of criticism is that, being half-Chinese, Edith somehow had access to a more authentic cultural knowledge than did her sister, who only faked knowledge about Japanese culture. Thinking about their practice as ethnography forces us to keep in mind that both Edith and Winnifred grew up surrounded by English Victorian culture in Canada, knew no people of Asian descent besides their mother, who had left China as a child, and their encounters with the Chinese and Japanese, whether firsthand or vicarious, were mediated by orientalist ethnography. Their identification with Asians in North America was also complicated by class difference: the Eaton had been reared with the values and expectations of the middle class, whereas the majority of Chinese and Japanese immigrants in America were of working-class background. Over time, Edith may have become more of a "participant observer," with an extensive network of Chinese friends in Canada and the United States, and Winnifred more of an "armchair ethnologist," working from Japanese "fieldwork" done by white travelers, yet the difference between their practices is one of degree, not kind. Edith studied ethnographic works by China missionaries, borrowed heavily from one, and inherited from her mentors many thematic preoccupations and a didactic bent. Winnifred, however, may not have relied solely on book lore: Birchall has found evidence that Winnifred knew the Japanese immigrant poet Yone Noguchi in the late 1890s and that she later employed several Japanese students in her home. These "native informants" may well have supplemented her secondary sources.

Though Edith and Winnifred put their ethnographic knowledge to different uses, here, too, is a telling similarity: Winnifred is generally perceived as the shrewd businesswoman in the family, yet Edith never gave up the idea of making a living as a writer and competed alongside Winnifred for a share of the "local color" or "exotica" market. To break into a viciously competitive publishing marketplace, both sisters used similar strategies of claiming ethnographic authority. They took ethnically marked pen names and invoked a biological connection to the ethnic groups they fictionalized. Authenticity, then, or the semblance of authenticity, was crucial to their literary careers. Where Edith wore Western dress at all times, marking her cultural difference from her subjects, Winnifred went further in claiming racial authenticity, for she occasionally wore a kimono for publicity snapshots, wrote her autograph in Japanese characters, and altered the details of her vita to fit her public image. Though less flamboyant in her self-authentication, Edith also emphasized her Chinese descent for the benefit of the press, as did the editors who printed biographical notes alongside her stories.

Another reason for treating the Eaton sisters' fiction as ethnography is that although both women wrote literature using traditional Western genres, plots, and textual allusions, they were not read primarily as women of letters in the way that Sarah Orne Jewett and Edith Wharton were. My survey of the response to their writing suggests that mainstream readers approached Edith's stories and Winnifred's romances as "native" or "auto-ethnography," a source of authentic knowledge about the morals, manners, and mentality of an exotic "race." The editors of the *Chautauquan* showcased Edith's story "Aluteh" in a special 1905 issue on Chinese culture. A serious educational and self-improvement magazine, the *Chautauquan* also listed Onoto Watanna in the bibliographic appendix of an issue on Japanese culture. In the age of James Frazer's *Golden Bough,* Winnifred's reviewers, even when responding to her most fairy-tale-like plots and stylized settings, sought and found in her texts a certain anthropological truth. Finally, what better proof exists that Edith's fiction was read primarily for its ethnographic content than the fact that the most exhaustive review of her book *Mrs. Spring Fragrance* (1912) was published in the *American Antiquarian and Oriental Journal,* which specialized in Asian anthropology?

To call Edith's and Winnifred's interpretations of life "there" for people "here" ethnographic, I want to extend the conventional meaning of *ethnography* to the practices of travelers, missionaries, journalists, and fiction writers. Unlike the critic Sau-ling Wong, I draw no distinction between legitimate and "quasi-ethnography" (202). Relegating discredited areas of knowledge to "pseudoscience" has long been a way for science to defend its claim to objectivity (Stepan and Gilman 75); in effect, the distinction obscures more than it elucidates. I assume that knowledge, whether acquired by scientists or amateurs, is always historically located and that the boundary between different ways of knowing the other is permeable.

Conventionally, *ethnography* refers to a "research process in which the anthropologist closely observes, records, and engages in the daily life of another culture" and subsequently makes his or her "personal and theoretical reflections available to professionals and other readerships" (Marcus and Fisher 17–18). The understanding of the optimal length and nature of the "engagement" has changed over time. Franz Boas may have insisted that his students study their subjects' language before attempting cultural interpretation, but scholars have recently pointed out that Boas himself usually worked through native interpreters (Prus 106). Because of their lack of systematic methods and knowledge of their subjects' language, Edith and Winnifred would never have passed muster as ethnographers according to Boas's criteria. Yet Edith's "engagement" in Chinatown culture lasted half her lifetime, while Winnifred researched Japanese history and culture during the most productive decade of her career. But if Edith and Winnifred would not have qualified as ethnographers, neither did Boas's student Zora Neale Hurston.[3] For the purpose of this project, I therefore take *ethnography* to mean the production of knowledge about a subordinate ethnic/racial group for the dominant group and occasionally the defamiliarization of the culturally dominant group's practices for its own consumption. I also follow the standard usage of *ethnography* as the written text based on a study of the other.

To position Edith and Winnifred in the general debate about race and culture, we need to consider who the practitioners of ethnography were, what was at stake, and what the everyday uses of ethnography were in North America. When we look at the contents of the popular and scientific press from the turn of the century, it is apparent that the debate about the meaning of race became particularly heated in this period and that ethnographic materials were being supplied at a staggering rate to fuel this debate. Perhaps the most obvious catalyst for the rise of popular and academic discourses of race was the intensified drive to colonize the Third World on the part of western European nations, joined in the late nineteenth century by the United States. The need to tell people apart became particularly urgent in the United States as racial categories detached themselves from geographic spaces and preordained niches in the social hierarchy (see figure 1). Americanness, too, needed to be redefined now. As Henry Yu put it, "Maintaining a sense of difference, a boundary between 'America' and 'non-American' was essential for legitimating ideas about the nature of what was American. . . . Only with 'genuine,' unassimilated, 'un-Americanized' immigrants staring at you from the other side of the divide could the divide exist" (280). Even when laws defining whiteness as the right to own property and blackness as the mark of property were struck off the books, the underlying prejudices remained

		Ideal Negro Type [1]	Ideal Mongol Type	Ideal American Type	Ideal Caucasic Type [2]
Hair		a. Short, jet black, frizzly, flat in transverse section, little or no beard; b. Reddish brown, woolly	Coarse, black, lusterless, lank, round in transverse section; beardless	Very long, coarse, black, lank, nearly round in section; beardless	a. Long, wavy, soft, flaxen; b. Long, straight, wiry, black; both oval in section; both full-bearded
Color		a. Blackish; b. Yellowish brown	Yellowish	Coppery, yellowish	a. Florid; b. Pale
Skull		a. Dolichocephalous; b. Brachycephalous	Brachycephalous	Mesaticephalous	a. Dolichocephalous; b. Brachycephalous
Jaws		Prognathous	Mesognathous	Mesognathous	Orthognathous
Cheek bone		Small, moderately retreating	Prominent laterally	Moderately prominent	Small; unmarked
Nose		Very broad, flat, platyrrhine	Very small, mesorrhine	Large, bridged or aquiline, mesorrhine	Large, straight or arched, leptorrhine
Eyes		Large, round, prominent, black; yellowish cornea	Small, black, oblique, outerangle slightly elevated, vertical fold of skin over inner canthus	Small, round, straight, sunken, black	a. Blue b. Black; both moderately large and always straight
Teeth		Large (macrodont)	Medium (mesodont)	Medium (mesodont)	Small (microdont)
Stature		a. *Above the average; 5 ft. 10 in.* b. Dwarfish; 4 ft.	Below the average	Above the average	a. *Above the average; 5 ft. 10 in.* b. Average; 5 ft. 6 in.
Speech		Agglutinating of various prefix and postfix types	Agglutinating chiefly with postfixes; isolating with tones	Polysynthetic mainly	Chiefly inflecting; some agglutinating
Religion		Non-theistic, nature and ancestry worship; fetishism and witchcraft prevalent	Polytheistic; shamanism; Buddhism; Transmigration	Polytheistic; animism; nature worship	Monotheism; Judaism; Christianity; Mohamedanism
Temperament		Sensuous, indolent, improvident; fitful, passionate and cruel, though often affectionate and faithful; little self-respect, hence easy acceptance of the yoke of slavery; science and art undeveloped	Sluggish, somewhat sullen, with little initiative, but great endurance; generally frugal, thrifty and industrious, but moral standard low; science slightly, art and letters moderately developed	Moody, taciturn, wary, deep feelings masked by an impassive exterior; indifference to physical pain; science slightly developed, letters scarcely at all developed	Active, enterprising, imaginative; a. serious, steadfast, solid and stolid; b. fiery, impulsive, fickle; science, art and letters highly developed in both
[1] a.=Negro; b.= Negrito				[2] a.=Xanthochroi; b.=Melanochroi	

Figure 1. Classification of racial types in A. H. Keane's *Ethnology* (1895).

largely intact and were extended to other people of color (C. Harris 1709).
Yet old systems of marking and containing other races faltered in the face of
successive waves of immigration from southern and eastern Europe, Asia, and
the Pacific Islands and the migration of African Americans out of the post-
Reconstruction South. Anthropology stepped right in, rolled up its sleeves,
and with notebook, camera, and tape measure in hand set out into the field
to seek definitions of racial difference.[4]

Just how intent white Americans were on telling people apart becomes
apparent when we find artists making a science of racial portraiture. In a 1900
article entitled "Painting Racial Types" that appeared in *Century Magazine,*
the journalist Charles de Kay discussed a new genre in painting. The art of
the Dutch painter Hubert Vos, he suggested, was fit to be shown at a "museum like the National at Washington, that of Natural History in New York, or
the Ethnological in Berlin." De Kay did not hide his ambivalence about the
notion of the "racial type" itself, for he pointed out that "when looking at . . .
professed works on ethnology, it is always amusing to reflect on the type
chosen to represent the Aryan" (167). But if he recognized that types are an
illusion, he was also aware of the usefulness of this illusion to such institutions as the Emigrant Bureau—a place where racial categories were used daily
to exclude undesirable immigrants:

> While examining [Vos's] collection one can scarcely fail to reflect how few are
> the faces among these Oriental folk which would not pass muster for those of
> Europeans if they appeared at the Emigrant Bureau in New York, provided their
> owners dressed in the ugly clothes of our civilization. The Hawaiian would pass
> for a Provençal, or a Neapolitan; the Panjabi for a Turk, an Armenian or a Gip-
> sy; the Javanese for a man from the Basque provinces; and the Chinese damsel
> for a jolly Finland girl, a Swede, or a Samoyed, but an uncommonly pretty one.
> (168–69)

De Kay's sympathies seemed to be on the side of the Asian immigrants, whose
exclusion was just then being hotly debated.[5] At the same time, however, the
connection he made between racial types and immigration is symptomatic
of the American public's anxiety about the unfit and unassimilable "passing" into the country. Type-casting people of color remained problematic for
de Kay, yet he decided that so long as the public perceived the need for typical representations, it was the job of professionals like Vos to satisfy it: "All
honor to him if he have the endurance and enthusiasm to supply a lack that
is felt as well by the layman as by the scientist!" (167).

Belief in the value of observing and defining America's racial others generated a vigorous, self-perpetuating industry, with paid jobs for academics,

respectable occupations for lay men and women like the Eaton sisters, and publishing opportunities for both. For instance, in the 1880s, employees of the newly established Bureau of American Ethnography represented their work as both a means to ensure more efficient and humane government policy toward Indian tribes and a quest "for better knowledge of civilization through the study of its antecedent forms" (Hinsley 54). After the United States annexed the Philippines, squadrons of anthropologists descended on the native tribes, bringing away from the islands materials that filled scholarly and popular journals for years. Edgar L. Hewett, a scientist writing in the *American Anthropologist* in 1905, went so far as to propose that the colonial authorities responsible for education in the Philippines should withdraw for several years until extensive professional studies of the Filipino's "ethnic mind" were conducted to determine how to "make him a better Filipino" (10).[6] Some anthropological studies were publicized as thoroughly utilitarian. According to a review in the *American Anthropologist,* H. N. Hutchinson's motive for writing *The Living Races of Mankind* (1902) was "a new one in ethnology, namely that the most profitable markets for British wares may . . . be found in places which are now the darkest corners of the world. . . . The half-clothed savage just emerging from the brute condition is a human being capable of education, in the near future, into a customer for British trade" ("The Living Races of Mankind" 305–6).

Hutchinson's utilitarianism, though endorsed by the academic community, was not typical; most anthropologists saw their work in a more altruistic, romantic, or even heroic light—but useful nonetheless. At the turn of the century, there emerged what present-day scholars call the "narrative motif of salvage"—the impulse to record the lifeways of "primitive man" before they are eroded by modernity, so that they might then be relearned by the West (Marcus and Fischer 129). Academic anthropologists were the group most committed to "salvage," but popular fiction writers also embraced this ideology. As I suggest in chapter 3, the "Chinese" stories Edith wrote for Charles Lummis, amateur ethnographer and editor of the *Land of Sunshine,* functioned in the context of his magazine as a record of an exotic culture about to be eradicated from the West Coast by the exclusion laws. Similarly, for many of Winnifred's enthusiasts, her romances of Japan captured the essence of a fragile, archaic culture caught in the grip of Western civilization.

Though Edith's work was commonly read through the narrative of "salvage," her ethnographic approach had roots in a very different ideology, one oriented toward the future rather than an idealized past. She aligned herself with North American middle-class churchgoers who came together under the auspices of missionary societies to support the work of their emissaries among Third World peoples—work that included ethnographic research. Throughout the nineteenth century, written reports of non-Christian cultures were printed and circulated to raise funds for further mission work. "Native" converts (such as Grace Trefusis, Edith and Winnifred's mother) were sent to the West to study and testify. Within this Protestant movement organized around saving the racial other, women like Edith cut out for themselves some of the first socially acceptable professional careers. They raised funds for and operated missions and "rescue homes" in areas inhabited by America's others: Native Americans, Chinese, and, interestingly, Mormons. According to Peggy Pascoe, "[M]issionary groups were the largest women's organizations in the [United States] from the 1870 to 1900; larger than their close cousin, the Woman's Christian Temperance Union, and far larger than the more thoroughly studied suffrage organizations" (xviii). On the American frontier, as in the colonial world, "white women became the excuse for— and the custodians of—racial distinctions" (Georgi-Findlay 240). For instance, female missionaries in China in 1900 constituted a group powerful enough to hold its own conference in Shanghai on "The Home Life of Chinese Women" (Stuart 31). For the participants of this event, the chance to exercise moral authority as they analyzed the disadvantages of women's lives in traditional Chinese culture (low social status of women, footbinding, arranged marriage, and the like) was surely a moment of self-empowerment.

If studying the other races reinforced the meaning of whiteness, if it meant jobs, publishing opportunities, and, for white middle-class women, also a rare experience of agency and moral authority, how did the biracial Edith and Winnifred fit into the picture? Did they experience the practice of ethnography in the same way their white counterparts did? A single woman often on the move, Edith sought out Chinatown missions wherever she went, finding in them a welcome support network, a respectable occupation, and opportunities to meet Chinese Americans in whom she was interested as a politically conscious biracial writer. While still a novice to both writing and mission work, Edith dwelled on the evils of footbinding, gambling, and marriage by proxy, much as her contemporaries who attended the women's conference in Shanghai did. Soon, however, she must have realized that representations of the sensational and the exotic legitimized anti-Chinese sentiment, for most of her Chinatown fiction highlights the analogies between Chinese and American culture and downplays the differences.

Underlying this shift away from the exotic was a refusal to see Western Christian culture as superior. The Chinese American life Edith portrayed is organized around such domestic concerns as love, marriage, and the rearing of children—the way it might have been had white racism, manifested in immigration laws, not created the anomaly of the virtually all-male Chinatown ghettos. That she mostly elided such daily concerns of the Chinese in America as work, exploitation, racism, solitude, and alienation was probably deliberate rather than caused by ignorance or lack of empathy. Some of her earliest articles in the *Montreal Daily Star* were frank and well-informed treatments of the problems that plagued Chinese men separated from their families. Ethnography is as much about someone as for someone, and Edith's was addressed to a white middle-class audience that responded most readily to domestic themes in literature. As a mature writer, she also used her knowledge of Chinese lifeways as a springboard from which to critique American values and institutions.

For both Winnifred and Edith, writing ethnographic literature had the power to turn the stigma of race into an asset. By becoming observers of non-Western cultures, they could briefly step out of the prescribed role of the observed. It was also a way to affirm and valorize their ethnic origin, albeit on terms dictated by the dominant culture.[7] Those who reviewed their work frequently remarked that, being biracial, the Eaton sisters were ideally suited to the role of cultural translators or go-betweens. Such opinions would surely have been an incentive to investigate the very side of their family heritage that disadvantaged them in everyday life yet proved a valuable commodity when turned into reading matter. Even when writing with the expectations of their mainstream readers in mind and limited by the popular genres, narrative conventions, and stylistic devices of the day, the Eaton sisters did create a space within ethnographic fiction for their unconventional views on the racial hierarchy, miscegenation, and cultural difference.

Edward and Grace Eaton's interracial marriage resulted in the family's loss of social status and probably led to their emigration from England to Canada. Unwilling to experience her "Asian blood" as a mark of inferiority, Winnifred discovered that by posing as a Japanese writer rather than as a Chinese, she acquired charm and an exotic mystique in the eyes of white Americans and that used strategically, those assets could be turned into a steady source of income, social status, and personal agency. Edith never attained the giddy heights of fame, and she did pay the emotional cost of "coming out" as Chinese whenever the Chinese were being maligned in her presence. Yet she, too, managed to write herself out of the working class. In subsequent chapters, I explore other subtle differences between the way the Eaton sisters and their white counterparts "in the field" understood and used ethnography.

Though I borrow from the rhetoric of ethnographic fieldwork, the scientific accuracy of Winnifred's and Edith's accounts is not my main concern.

On the contrary, this project is informed by the recent critiques of anthropology from within the discipline that focused on the constructedness of the
ethnographic text and on the rhetorical strategies used to bridge gaps in
empirical knowledge. I have found the framework of ethnography useful in
that it led me to focus on the complex relations between the biracial author
and her others: the ethnographic subjects, on the one hand, and the editors
and readers, on the other.

Since the mid-1980s, ethnographers have been borrowing the critical tools
of literary criticism to revitalize their discipline and get a better understanding of ethnographic accounts as historically determined cultural texts. Once
ethnographers began to foreground the narrative structure of fieldwork accounts, the sacrosanct authority of the researcher to represent Third World
cultures came under close scrutiny. Not only did cultural anthropologists
begin to reread classic fieldwork accounts in a new light, but also some turned
their attention to texts not normally classified as ethnographies. For instance,
the anthropologist Michael Fischer wrote on the fiction of Maxine Hong
Kingston, Frank Chin, and Shawn Hsu Wong, while his fellow professional
Vincent Crapanzano usefully juxtaposed J. W. von Goethe's 1789 account of
the Roman carnival, an 1833 account of a Mandan Indian ceremony by George
Catlin, a painter and traveler, and Clifford Geertz's celebrated "Notes on the
Balinese Cockfight" (1973).

Literary scholars, in turn, have demonstrated pluck and versatility in an-
alyzing the rhetorical structure of classic ethnographies: Ruth Larson, Vincent Pecora, and Marianna Torgovnick have taken on such leading figures in
cultural anthropology as Michel Leiris, Clifford Geertz, and Bronislaw Malinowski. The same questions asked of literary texts are being asked of ethnographies: questions of voice, authorial stance, narrative strategies, ruptures,
elisions, overarching tropes, underlying assumptions, and, most important,
stakes. But only a handful of literary critics have used the paradigm of ethnography to examine fiction. Significantly, critics are more comfortable with
interpreting as ethnography those fictions that defamiliarize the customs and
rituals of the dominant culture. Thus Martha Banta, in her 1994 introduction to *The House of Mirth,* attributed an ethnographic impulse to Edith
Wharton. Alvina Quintana interpreted Ana Castillo's *The Mixquiahuala
Letters* as a literary ethnography of U.S. and Mexican cultures written from
the vantage point of a traveling Chicana.

But to read the work of ethnic American writers as ethnography or autoethnography is problematic, for, as David Palumbo-Liu pointed out, "the
dominant other mediate[s] the very manner in which its subjects . . . represent themselves even in the relatively free space of the fictive" (121). Not only

have writers of color historically been expected to produce "insider" accounts of their ethnic communities, preferably in the autobiographic mode, but also the publishing industry made it very difficult for them to publish anything else. For writers of Asian descent, the imperative to dwell on cultural differences to satisfy reader expectations has meant a reification of their communities' foreignness, which then justified discrimination. Little wonder, then, that the word *anthropology* is a highly charged one for Asian Americans. It was with the utmost contempt that Frank Chin accused Maxine Hong Kingston of indulging in "pop cultural anthropology" in *The Woman Warrior* (Kim 198). Writers whose work smacked of this genre were excluded from the influential anthology of Asian American literature *Aiiieeeee!* (1974). Yet the demand for ethnographic fiction has continued to draw Asian American writers to "armchair ethnology." Amy Tan, Gus Lee, Aimee Liu, D. H. Hwang, Belle Yang, and many others have produced fictional accounts of the long ago and far away or of contemporary Asian/Asian American communities with which they have had little contact. From the point of view of the mainstream press, the "factuality" of these fictional works is authenticated by the author's ethnicity.

In recent decades, critics have pointed out that ethnography and ethnographic fiction have tended to represent non-Western people as dehistoricized and essentially other. Such representations are easily commodified because they appeal to larger audiences than does work that problematizes interracial relations. The fiction of Zora Neale Hurston is an interesting case in point. The critics Beth Harrison, Françoise Lionnet, Benigno Sánchez-Eppler, and many others have praised Hurston's self-reflexive stance, as well as the narrative strategies she developed to reflect those aspects of African American and Caribbean cultures that elude formal ethnographic description. Hazel Carby, however, rightly questioned the ease with which Hurston's representations of rural black folk were embraced in their day and have since been absorbed into academic syllabi, to the exclusion of urban black mass culture represented by more militant figures, such as Richard Wright. In overexposing Hurston's ethnographic fiction about black folk "who are outside of history," publishers and academics unwittingly suppress the memory of what Carby called the "conditions of aggression and antagonism" (41–42) that gave rise to such books as *Native Son*. Edith Eaton's place at the head of the Asian American literature canon is now ensured. Her work is increasingly taught in American literature seminars as well as in women's studies classes. Far more politically engaged than her contemporaries Yone Noguchi, Sadakichi Hartmann, or Yamei Kin, Edith has displaced no Asian American Richard Wright. Yet because critics so often stop at contrasting her work

with Winnifred's popular and supposedly "inauthentic" fiction, the authenticity of Edith's vision goes unchallenged.

The audience's predilection for exoticized ethnography reflected in publishers' choices is one of many factors to impact the production and marketing of literature by Americans and Canadians of Asian decent. In the case
of Edith and Winnifred Eaton, geographic location played a major role, giv-
en the marginalized position of Canada in the production of English-language culture,[8] as well as East Coast and West Coast politics. Edith, who for
twelve years lived and wrote on the Sinophobic West Coast, had virtually no
local outlets for her writing, while Winnifred found an enthusiastic audience
in middle-class easterners stricken by *Japonisme*. Edith's fortunes finally
turned when she moved to Boston, where, despite occasional encounters with
racism, she found an audience sympathetic to China's republican aspirations
and efforts to modernize.

That people of Asian descent in the United States continue to be treated
as perpetual foreigners means that their work is impacted by international
events and shifts in U.S. foreign policy to a greater extent than the work of
European Americans. The upswings and downswings in the Eaton sisters'
fortunes were correlated with American responses to three major events that
took place in Asia around the turn of the century: the Sino-Japanese War of
1895, the Russo-Japanese War of 1904–5, and the Chinese Revolution of 1911
(see my discussion in subsequent chapters). Waves of intensified racism
prompted by wartime propaganda, domestic economic crises, and fear of
immigration also left their mark on Edith's and Winnifred's careers and on
subsequent generations of Asian American writers. King-Kok Cheung observed that "the self-hatred induced by the psychic strain of being denied
American civil rights and of having to choose between being Japanese and
being American are graphically depicted in John Okada's *No-No Boy*" (*An
Interethnic Companion* 5)—a novel whose 1957 edition was ignored by mainstream and Japanese American audiences alike and thus was not reprinted
until twenty years later. Hence the double bind: mainstream audiences and
editors expect of Asian American literature what Cheung called "a strong
'ethnic' quotient," as do some members of the writers' ethnic communities,
yet the same "'ethnic' quotient" accentuates the writer's foreignness, exposing the work to the fluctuations of public sentiment toward foreign nations.
Even though the intersection of ethnic American literature and ethnography
is a tense and troubled one—and in some sense because of it—I believe that
we have a good deal to learn about the work of Edith and Winnifred Eaton
by bringing to it our current understanding of the racial and textual politics
of ethnography.

To give equal weight to each of the writers, this book is structured symmetrically. The first chapter sets up the discursive context; it is followed by two chapters on Edith and two on Winnifred, organized around clusters of key issues at the intersection of literature and ethnography but sequenced to preserve a general chronology of Edith and Winnifred's literary careers. The first chapter, "Two Faces of the Oriental(ist)," surveys two interrelated literary traditions, missionary and travel ethnography of China and Japan, to show how these two groups of texts contributed to the shaping of oppositionally constructed images of the Chinese and Japanese in the nineteenth century. From these texts, the chapter reconstructs an image of the Chinese from which Winnifred recoiled and the image of the Japanese that she embraced. I argue that what drew Edith to missionary writings on China and Winnifred to tourist representations of Japan was the respite these writings offered from overtly racist nativist discourses. I also suggest that in choosing to study the Chinese and Japanese through the discursive frameworks of missionary and travel writings, respectively, Edith and Winnifred encountered disparate rationales and epistemologies for studying the other. My survey of nineteenth-century Far Eastern orientalist ethnography provides a much-needed discursive context for the writings of the Eaton sisters. It lays the groundwork for the subsequent discussion of Edith's and Winnifred's choice of literary persona and allows me to reference what they borrowed and what they creatively rewrote, what they accommodated to and what they resisted.

The second chapter, "A Journalistic Mission," which is largely based on new archival materials, reconstructs the beginnings of Edith Eaton's career as a reporter in Montreal, Canada, and Kingston, Jamaica. I discuss the formation of Edith's professional identity around the presence of a Chinese minority in Montreal and show how involvement with mission work enabled her to develop personal relationships with Chinese immigrants, which, in turn, provided interesting story material for her newspaper work. It was in the missionary circles that Edith acquired a lens through which to read Chinese culture, as well as an ethic of responsibility toward this particular immigrant group—an ethic that manifests itself in the themes she chose to write about and those she evaded. In the second segment, I show how Edith's identification with white mainstream culture had to be renegotiated when she entered Jamaican society. While working in Kingston, Edith was required to write not for the dominant white majority about its racial others, but for the small white elite about itself. Neither a member of that elite nor able to identify fully with Jamaica's marginalized working-class black and Asian population, Edith alternately aligned herself with and distanced herself from both. By uncovering her multiple, unstable, and often conflicting positionings, I draw attention to the vital role played in ethnographic writing by the location of one's self in relation to one's audience and ethnographic subject.

In the third chapter, "Subjects of the Gaze," I first consider the ways in which Edith's representations of the Chinese in California were shaped and put to use by Charles Lummis, editor of the *Land of Sunshine*, a regional progressive magazine. Viewed in the context of the *Land of Sunshine*, Edith's work reveals the role played by representations of people of color in the white middle-class project of promoting California to outsiders and reinventing the region's past and present for its growing cultural elite. I read Edith's stories from this period as parables designed to do the reverse of missionary tracts: not convert Chinese to Christianity but win Christians over to the cause of interracial harmony. In the second part of the chapter, I show how Edith went on to articulate her own ideas on the epistemology of cross-cultural investigation, diverting the ethnographic gaze away from the Chinese to interrogate race, class, and gender relations in the United States. Unlike many of her white contemporaries who engaged in Chinatown ethnography assuming a unidirectional, objective gaze, Edith posited in her later stories that ethnographic interest may be mutual.

In contrast to Edith, who openly claimed Chinese descent but emphasized her genteel Euro-Canadian cultural background, Winnifred made her name as a writer by "going native." The case of Winnifred Eaton/Onoto Watanna exemplifies the nexus of authority, authenticity, and performance. In "Strategies of Authentication," the fourth chapter, I lay out the historical circumstances in which Winnifred became "Japanese" and ask why her way of claiming ethnographic authority to write about Japanese culture was so effective at the time. Since Winnifred's entry into the popular magazine and book market was facilitated by the writers of travel narratives about Japan, her authority as a writer was premised on her skill at approximating reader expectations set up by such amateur ethnographers as William Griffis and Lafcadio Hearn. But more important, her authority rested on her "Japanese blood," which, readers believed, guaranteed a more genuine insight into Japanese culture than any white writer could offer. By examining reviews of her work, I show how readers perceived—and helped construct—Onoto Watanna. Then, using a series of her fictional works that thematize such issues as performance, the assumption of authority, and originality versus mimicry, I consider how Winnifred theorized her own position.

While the fourth chapter seeks to explain how Winnifred performed a Japanese identity to authorize herself, the fifth chapter, "Decoupling Race and Culture," shows how she used her ethnographic authority to explore ideas of difference. I argue that in mimicking the predominantly male-authored orientalist travel narrative, Winnifred shifted its thematic focus and took advantage of the fictional space afforded by the genre to interrogate race and redefine miscegenation. When Japan's exotic aura began to wane in the wake of the Russo-Japanese War, Winnifred sought difference in other places: inside the "white" home where lines of class divided the kitchen from the parlor, on the closing western frontier, and even among those socially stigmatized by illegitimacy or prostitution. With race out of the picture, Winnifred was able to concentrate on cultural constructions of difference. Exploring the tensions between a dominant group and its others was, I suggest, more than an intellectually and psychologically satisfying practice for a writer deeply conscious of her own otherness; such scenarios were also highly marketable, and Winnifred often balanced precariously between exploring and exploiting difference.

This account of Edith and Winnifred Eaton can be summed up in the trope of hand-me-downs and alterations. I want to consider not just the physical features, clothes, habits, and beliefs that are handed down within families but also the larger cultural networks through which we inherit discourses that define who we are and what we do. Hand-me-downs often need alterations: a faded collar may have to be turned inside out, seams taken in, pockets darned, the lining replaced. Pride sometimes keeps us from accepting a hand-me-down at all, for there is a hierarchy implied in the transaction. The fascination of studying literary siblings is that they inherit what appears to be a similar package of looks, clothes, habits, beliefs, and even memories, yet what they do with that inheritance may be surprisingly different—which is precisely the case of the Eaton sisters.

1. Two Faces of the Oriental(ist): Missionary and Travel Ethnography in China and Japan

She sits afar on flowery isles,
To Europe's frowns gives beams and smiles,
Softly uncovering China's wiles:
Gentle little Japan.
—Margaret A. Brooks, "Japan, the Youngest Born"

EDITH AND WINNIFRED EATON grew up in the same household, in a biracial Chinese-English family, just ten years apart, yet they traced the genealogies of their literary personas to different homelands: China and Japan, respectively. This chapter probes the context underlying the two writers' self-constructions by looking at meanings that accrued to the words *China* and *Japan* over the course of the nineteenth century. Defining Asia, I argue, was largely the province of missionaries and lay travelers—two groups of writers through whose eyes Edith and Winnifred caught the first glimpses of their imagined homelands.

Around the time the Eaton sisters began writing, the North American press, spurred by the Sino-Japanese War in 1894–95 and increased Asian immigration, carried an unprecedented number of stories on things "oriental." The *Montreal Daily Star,* for which Edith worked as a correspondent, was filled with articles on Japanese aesthetics and military prowess, Chinese trade and diplomacy, and the doings of Chinese workers in Canada: their border crossings, church attendance, criminal activities, births, and funerals. Such writings tended to represent the Chinese as antithetical to the Japanese and explained China's war losses and Japan's gains in terms of cultural superiority and inferiority (see figure 2). Direct comparisons of China and Japan were very common, and, like the epigraph, tended to elevate the Japanese while denigrating the Chinese.[1] The author of this poem, published in a popular magazine, painted an obliging geishalike Japan divesting China of the last shreds of her dignity on behalf of Europe, who stands frowning in the wings. That "Japanese" romances would sell better than "Chinese" stories in such a climate is obvious. But how exactly did China become "wily"? And how "gentle" was Japan in at the turn of the century?

There are, of course, many reasons for this discursive split: China's economic and political decline in the second half of the nineteenth century, paralleled by Japan's technological and military advances, and the differences in how the two governments regulated foreign traffic within their territories and imposed emigration restrictions on their own citizens. Even the size of Japan and China contributed to the disparate images: one was smaller and easily accessible by sea, the other loomed large and impenetrable; one, though

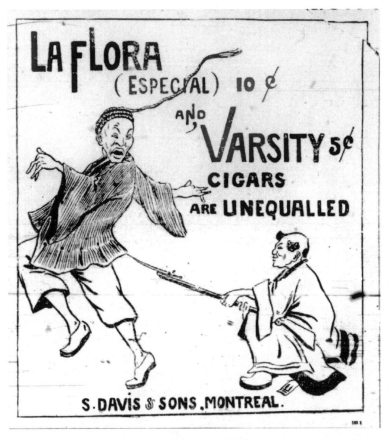

Figure 2. Cigar advertisement from the *Montreal Daily Star*, August 6, 1894, playing on popular stereotypes of the Chinese and Japanese during the Sino-Japanese War.

densely populated, restricted emigration and focused on colonizing its Asian neighbors, the other seemed ready to spill its "untold hungry millions" across the world. My intention is not to displace these well-documented geopolitical explanations but to show that nineteenth-century ethnographic knowledge of China and Japan provided westerners with ways of understanding geopolitical change. Critical interpretations of orientalism have focused heavily on the Near East, the Middle East, and Southeast Asia (Said; Lowe; Behdad). Although interesting work has been done on Japan (Iriye; Kondo) and on representations of the Chinese in American popular culture (Chin et al.; Moy), orientalism's Japanese and Chinese facets have not been treated comparatively in any depth. Yet such a juxtaposition is in order if we are to understand the Eaton sisters' entanglement with orientalism.

To give a sense of the knowledge of China and Japan available to Edith and Winnifred, this chapter introduces a range of amateur ethnographic writings from the 1830s through the end of the century. There is direct evidence that Edith and Winnifred studied some of these texts. Edith, who had close contacts with Chinatown missions throughout her life, relied heavily on the Reverend Justus Doolittle's study of Chinese customs and manners, and much of her writing can be read as a polemic with various aspects of the missionary ethic. Winnifred, in turn, drew freely on the work of William Griffis, John Long, and Lafcadio Hearn, while one of her earliest stories is a wry commentary on Pierre Loti's *Madame Chrysanthème*.

Bible and Baedeker

When academic ethnography began to define its goals and methods in the last quarter of the nineteenth century, China and Japan fell outside its purview. Professional ethnographers were primarily interested in cultures that had had little or no contact with the West, and neither China nor Japan qualified as "primitive." Consequently, what ethnographic writings we have on China and Japan from that period are by missionaries, diplomats, and tourists. For reasons I discuss below, two of these groups—Protestant missionaries and lay travelers—wrote a great deal, each generating something of a tradition. Around those traditions, I construct my argument that the split of orientalism into polarized discourses of China and Japan derives, in part, from the fact that English-language ethnography in China was first and most influentially done by Protestant missionaries starting in 1807, whereas the most widely read ethnographers of the Japanese were lay travelers in the last quarter of the century. Although I argue for the predominance of a missionary ethnographic tradition in literature about China and a distinct strand of secular travel writing on Japan, I have consciously set up my two camps in a heterogeneous terrain covered by many writers, some of whom would not pitch their tent in either camp. My two provisional categories do not, I hope, obscure the wide range of genres and perspectives within each group. But while I draw out individual differences between the texts, I intend to do so without losing sight of the two persistent approaches or discourses.

Missionaries and lay travelers went to both China and Japan, but there was historically an asymmetry in their numbers, the timing of the two enterprises, and their purposes: proselytizing and tourism. British and American Protestants designated China as a "mission field" very early: 1807 is traditionally taken to be the date of "first entrance." By the end of the century, Protestant missionary societies were supporting over twenty-seven hundred white religious workers in China and as many "native helpers" (Dwight, appendix I).[2] As a rule, British and American missionaries of all Protestant denominations worked noncompetitively; Asia was large enough for all of them (Latourette 410–15). Significantly, they all labored in the shadow of the more firmly established Roman Catholic missions active since 1581, which had claimed thousands of converts. While I focus on the writings of Americans, I also refer to several British works whose American editions came out shortly after their publication in England.

Unlike China, Japan remained more or less closed to foreign traffic until 1856, when, by means of a show of power, Commodore Matthew Perry, an American, "opened" the port of Yokohama to foreign trade. Japanese government edicts banned proselytizing until 1873, and as late as 1878, the Englishwoman Isabella Bird traveling in Japan reported that the government obliged missionaries to preach within the limits of treaty ports. By the 1880s, tourism began to flourish. Japan rapidly modernized its tourist infrastructure to cater to Western capitalism's new leisure class; steamer lines to Yokohama multiplied in the last quarter of the century; and people flocked to see "ancient Japan" before it succumbed to modernity. For a brief moment, it seemed, one could enjoy a "Medieval" experience in modern comfort and safety.

Missionaries and tourists were not the only westerners to write about the Orient for Western audiences.[3] Yet no other groups made the printed word so central to their enterprise or enjoyed the publishing opportunities that missionaries and travel writers had. John K. Fairbank noted that in nineteenth-century China "only missionaries sought direct contact with the common people in the *two* civilizations [Chinese and Western]," since merchants and diplomats communicated and collaborated only with their "opposite numbers." Missionaries were "the principal if not the sole link between village China and small-town America [and] wrote almost as much as they preached" (2). To cope with the enormous flow of polyglot writing, mission societies operated presses throughout Asia and in the West (Latourette 437–41). Tourists came to Asia later in the century, when the commercial press was already large enough to absorb their texts. Writing transformed their experience into a valued commodity that could be sent in installments to a popular magazine or consolidated into a book. Judging by the outpouring of orientalist travel writings published in London and New York at the turn of the century, few tourists left Japan without a written trace. The operating principles behind the two types of presses—one run by charitable organizations, the other commercial—coupled with the different expectations of their readerships—one open to a call to Christian endeavor, the other looking to enjoy a little vicarious travel—made for two distinct literary genres.

For both missionaries and travelers, writing was a way to ensure the continuity of their respective enterprises. Few ventured into a foreign land without reading in the vast tradition of geographical and ethnographic texts; in fact, reading often served as a catalyst for travel and a call to Christian duty. Missionaries would occasionally write books and articles on China for their home constituencies in order to maintain the financial support of mission boards and draw new recruits. Travelers, leaving trails of landmarks and practical advice in their writings, likewise envisioned readers as following in their footsteps. Travel was textualized, circulated among readers, and reenacted.

Throughout the nineteenth century, missionaries went "into the field" from a deep conviction that non-Christians needed to be saved from a fate worse than death. When studying an ethnic group, they tended to perceive a "lack" to be filled or a cultural difference to be modified. As the verb *convert* suggests, their purpose was to initiate change. Once in Asia, missionaries had to resolve dilemmas about how much of the foreign culture they should change before it became Christian. Some were exceedingly attentive to local sensibilities and lifeways; others worked to eradicate "paganism" at any cost. Resistance to conversion was frequently interpreted as "wiliness." Consequently, missionary ethnographies conceived as both a call to Christian duty and a tool for others "in the field" emphasized those aspects of Asian cultures that were incompatible with Christian morality and, conversely, those that might make Asians receptive to change. As Susan Stewart proposed in discussing anthropology's "missionary connections," the writings of missionaries relied on "the rhetoric of transformation projected as a rhetoric of writing—the conversion of 'experience' or 'spectacle' into detail, the conversion of 'the scene' into form, and the conversion, ultimately, of 'other' into self, 'self' into other" (67).

Lay travelers may have observed those same foreign cultural practices and even imagined change as imminent, but they usually wished only for the kind of change that would improve their own comfort on the road. While a handful were as concerned about the introduction of Western moral, hygienic, and educational standards as were the missionaries, the majority savored exotic difference and moved on. For instance, of the French sailor and novelist Pierre Loti, one critic wrote that "although he was always receptive to new sensations and experience [he] wanted to maintain conditions in all the countries he visited as they were or, preferably, to turn the clock back to a more traditional state" (Szyliowicz 119). In the nineteenth century as much as today, lay travelers actively pursued the exotic, expecting themselves to be changed in some way by the encounter. Loti articulated this attitude succinctly in the preface to his *Madame Chrysanthème* ([1888] 1985): "Although the most important role may appear to devolve on Madame Chrysanthème, it is very certain that the three principal personages are myself, Japan, and the effect produced on me by that country" (5). If, like the missionaries, lay travelers exaggerated or exoticized racial and cultural difference, they did so using a vocabulary of "fullness," not "lack." Japan consequently emerged as a country from which to draw aesthetic or spiritual inspiration and take home a trunkful of precious collectibles.

Whereas travelers to Japan often sought instant gratification of the senses, missionaries accepted China as a locus of responsibility, long-term commitment, and delayed gratification. For morally responsible Christians, China functioned as a vast receptacle into which the Word of the Gospel and the fruits of Western progress must be poured. Edith Eaton was evidently drawn to the missionary ethic of responsibility when she volunteered to do what today would be called "community outreach" in Montreal; she was, however, deeply ambivalent about the imperative to convert.

Travelers might come across as more tolerant of difference and more receptive to the non-Western thought, yet the fact that they were "just passing through," often without learning the language, precluded all but the most superficial exchange of ideas. Goods, particularly artifacts, were the most common objects of exchange. Bodies, too, were objects of commerce. Winnifred Eaton's early writings show that she was at once attracted to the rhetoric of "fullness" and deeply concerned by what she perceived as the objectification of Asian women by white male tourists. When practicing autoexoticization and creating sexually irresistible Japanese heroines, she took full advantage of the fact that westerners valorized the Japanese female body. The exchange of goods and services within the tourist economy is very much a part of her fiction, but the focus on the exchange of meaning through cross-cultural communication distinguishes her approach from that of many contemporary travel writers.

Unlike tourists, whose need to communicate with the locals was often minimal, missionaries were charged with conveying a complex philosophical message to potential converts, which forced them to acquire a linguistic and cultural proficiency seldom matched by lay travelers in Asia. To persuade effectively, they had to collaborate with Chinese "ghostwriters," study local rhetorical conventions and literary genres, and shed their cultural naïveté. While they invariably assumed Western cultural superiority, the precariousness of their position in Asia pushed some missionaries to study Chinese and Japanese ways seriously and grant intellectual sophistication to those they would convert.[4] Perhaps more important, when addressing Western readers, they countered scientific efforts to equate race and culture with what George Stocking described as "the optimistic and embracive egalitarian humanitarianism" of the late eighteenth century, which assumed all races to be capable of cultural progress (*Race, Culture, and Evolution* 28). For missionaries and their sponsors, the belief that culture is not essentially tied to race remained an important way of justifying the project of religious conversion. At a time when westerners were gradually being swayed by the racial essentialism of physical anthropology,[5] such an "egalitarian humanism" must have appealed to Edith Eaton as an alternative.

No matter how much travelers and missionaries diverged, their paths constantly crossed, and in times when knowledge on Asia was scarce, each group read the other's writings. Such publishing houses as Rand McNally initially printed both missionary and travel accounts. Travelers sought refuge at mission stations, bringing welcome news and relief from the mundane. Missionaries with seniority in the "field" produced dictionaries and handbooks invaluable to lay travelers. The anthropologist in the metropolis appropriated the work of both.

The Deserving Heathen: Missionary Ethnography of China

Prior to the rise of Far Eastern tourism and *Japonisme,* westerners tended to write about the Chinese and Japanese in much the same terms, without casting them as polar opposites. An example is the two-volume anthropological study entitled *The Uncivilized Races* by the Reverend J. G. Wood, which came out in England in 1868 and in the United States in 1870 (see figure 3). Wood's Chinese and Japanese are all of a kind, neither "wily" nor "gentle," differing only in customs and dress. Similar things about the two cultures interested Wood, including social ranks, military tactics, war machinery, and manner of treating prisoners.

Wood's material on China is arbitrarily divided into three groupings. In

Figure 3. "A Representation of Uncivilized Islanders and Indians," frontispiece of J. G. Wood's *Uncivilized Races* (1870).

the first section, most of the data concern male and female grooming and footbinding, but there are also digressions on the educational system, lanterns, and birds'-nest soup. The second begins with weapons and methods of torture and ends with the administrative structure. The final section contains a miscellany that fits under neither "grooming" nor "weapons and torture." Here "Mode of Using the Opium Pipe," "Boat-Life in China," and "Chinese Music and Instruments" are discussed side by side.

The two chapters on Japan are very similar in tone and content, except that Wood had to improvise to cover the evident lack of information. This he did by redundantly narrating scenes from the woodcuts that illustrate the text. He even resorted to describing at length a troupe of Japanese acrobats whose dexterous performance he saw in England. Wood's Japanese are not little, gentle, or quaint—adjectives most commonly used to describe Japanese by the end of the century. "Their stature is about equal to that of ordinary Europeans, and their limbs, though not large, are often very powerful," he wrote (1449). Englishmen, Portuguese, and Italians furnished Wood with many analogies for the Japanese. A chapter on Japanese weapons and modes of torture parallels the one in the China section. Though Wood knew of teahouses and geishas, the lore of the beauties and graces of Japanese women had not yet taken hold in the West at midcentury. Neither did he dwell on the artistic skills of the Japanese. China, in contrast, comes across as a land where music, fine arts, and skilled artisanship flourish. Soon these attributes would adhere to Japan alone. The encyclopedia describes both nations in terms of what they do rather than what they are. If it does not demonize the Chinese as would many later texts, neither does it glamorize the Japanese.

When Wood began to research his section on China, he faced the problem of selection. This he acknowledged at the start: "We now come to China, a country of such extent . . . that justice could not be fully done if an entire volume were devoted to it. We will therefore restrict ourselves to a selection of those particulars in which the Chinese appear to offer the greatest contrast to Europeans" (1426). Amateur ethnography was plentiful, largely through the labors of missionaries, who, in Fairbank's words, "penetrated farthest into Chinese life and became among the foreign invaders the most deeply involved in the local scene" (2).

Among the first book-length works was one by W. H. Medhurst. In 1816, Medhurst was sent by the London Missionary Society to the Malay Peninsula, the British outpost closest to China. There he studied Chinese, was initiated into mission work, and was ordained in anticipation of the "opening" of China.[6] His book *China: Its State and Prospects,* published in Boston in 1838, was the direct result of the need to communicate to English congregations the enormous extent of work to be done in China and its potential benefits. What Medhurst wanted to establish in the minds of his readers was the concept of a great and deserving nation, one that "rises superior to every unevangelized country" (14). To this end he devoted over fifty pages to various estimates of China's population. Using available statistics, he presented a dismal vision of one-third of humanity unenlightened by the gospel, a full million Chinese dying every month with no hope of salvation. The hundred pages Medhurst allotted to China's technological and cultural achievements presented a positive image of a country that possessed "as much civilization as Turkey now, or England a few centuries ago" (87). As something quantifiable, civilization could and should be shared—poured through the presses in the form of Chinese-language Bibles and tracts. Rude or polite, suspicious or trusting, indifferent or eager, these are the terms that limited Medhurst's study of the Chinese as he encountered them on his evangelical mission. But whether ignorant, shy, or prejudiced against foreigners, the Chinese were invariably imagined as needy, capable of change, and deserving.

An 1864 missionary text tapped into the same discourse, though it painted a much less flattering portrait of the Chinese. The Reverend Justus Doolittle's two-volume *Social Life of the Chinese* took up where Medhurst's left off: it is virtually all ethnography. The eight hundred or so pages are divided into chapters on such topics as "Betrothal and Marriage," "Superstitious Treatment of Disease," "Death, Mourning, and Burial," and "Meritorious and Charitable Practices." Emphasizing rituals and traditions for which even his Chinese informants seemed to have no rational explanation, Doolittle delineated a whole sphere of activities and beliefs that, interesting as they are, beg to be eradicated. The effect of absurdity is magnified by the piling on of endless detail, the more peculiar or sensational the better. Reading Doolittle, one begins to understand that his goal was to compile a catalog of sinful practices on an unprecedented scale, both as a manual for future missionaries and as a way of convincing readers back home of the importance of mission work (see figure 4). Thirty years after it was first published, Doolittle's book was Edith Eaton's primary source of information on Chinese culture, which suggests that no equally exhaustive study was available. The section to which Edith referred most frequently, "Betrothal and Marriage," required fifty small-print pages. She also made use of his exhaustive data on gambling, fortune-telling, and the system of competitive literary examinations.

The lasting popularity of Doolittle's study may be because no matter how unsympathetic its treatment of Chinese practices, it bore no trace of racial determinism. In the opening, he argued that Chinese were held back by Buddhist and Taoist beliefs but were otherwise remarkably receptive and

WORSHIPING THE ANCESTRAL TABLET IN ITS NICHE.

Figure 4. Illustrated examples of Chinese superstitions in the Reverend Justus Doolittle's *Social Life of the Chinese* (1865).

BRINGING BACK THE SOUL OF THE SICK INTO HIS CLOTHES ON THE BAMBOO.

FATHER TEACHING HIS CHILD TO WORSHIP.

advanced. Ending the book, Doolittle returned to his antiracist argument. He attacked American congregations for their inability to sympathize with China while "their interest, and sympathy, and prayers are freely bestowed on many other lands." It was inhumane, he argued, to withhold prayer (and begrudge donations?) merely because China appeared to us as "an uninteresting field" and its people as "unattractive" (2:430–31). Alluding to his own vivid description of tea production, Doolittle attempted to infuse tea with a symbolic value, making it a daily reminder of Western obligations to China, whose cheap labor it exploited: "May the connection between tea and missions—between the drinking of tea and the offering of prayer for the heathen tea-picker—in the experience of Christians, be very evident and intimate. May the tea-drinker become a constant and ardent prayer-offerer in behalf of the Chinese, as well as a liberal supporter of the missions among them" (2:436). Doolittle attempted to make the Chinese real to his audience, to bind the reader of ethnography in the metropolis to the ethnographic subject on the imperial periphery, to make the tea-drinker aware of the economic and moral ties that bind him or her to the tea-picker—and make the missionary an indispensable link between them.

By the late nineteenth century, missionary discourse had absorbed the anthropological theories of race. Arthur H. Smith's *Chinese Characteristics* (1894), a text that essentializes the "wily" Chinese, is an example of this shift. Much had happened since the 1860s to alter Western attitudes toward China. The accelerating industrial development gave Smith and his contemporaries a sense of cultural and technological superiority that his predecessors were still able to keep in check. Smith quoted freely from British and American secular thinkers, referred to Matthew Arnold's cultural theory and Herbert Spencer's "survival of the fittest," and employed the fashionable notion of "race decay." His chapter "The Absence of Nerves" (see figure 5) was informed by George M. Beard's popular scientific study *American Nervousness* (1881).

Smith's psychological portrait of Chinese society is organized in terms of racial traits. Each trait is amply illustrated with anecdotal evidence and linked to a set of others, showing how as a result Chinese institutions fail to function. Twenty of Smith's twenty-six chapter headings carry negative judgments ("Intellectual Turbidity," "Contempt for Foreigners," "Absence of Sincerity," and the like), and even the chapters in "Economy" or "Benevolence" tend to stress the absurd lengths to which the Chinese take these virtues. Despite his initial claim to a morally neutral standpoint, Smith ended the study with these conclusions: "What the Chinese lack is not intellectual ability. It is not patience, practicality, nor cheerfulness, for in all these qualities they greatly excel. What they lack is character and conscience" (317). By character, Smith

Figure 5. "The Absence of Nerves," chapter head from the Reverend Arthur Smith's *Chinese Characteristics* (1894).

meant a chivalric-Christian moral code, or, in the words of Matthew Arnold, whom he quoted, "the banner of righteousness" (329). Incapable of modernizing alone, the Chinese needed assistance but not from self-serving diplomacy and commerce or from amoral science. The lack that Smith's text constructed for us—that glaring absence of character—could be filled only by the "Christian civilisation" (330).

Representations of the Chinese were shaped by the writers' goals, assumptions, and the prevailing orientalist discourse more than by any characteristics inherent in their subjects. To demonstrate this, I briefly look at a text on the Japanese written in the heyday of *Japonisme*. The Reverend R. B. Peery's *Gist of Japan* (1897) provides insight into what was probably a common missionary experience of displacement and alienation, feelings that were occasionally projected onto the "natives." Few missionary writers, perhaps with the exception of Smith, dwelled on the hardships they encountered "in the field," perhaps not wishing to discourage others from following in their footsteps. Peery, however, produced a long chapter on the "Private Life of the Missionary" in which he speaks openly of the missionary as a man "who must go on year after year among people from whom an impassable gulf separates him" (225). Because he cannot make meaningful contact with the "natives," his life "is full of disappointments" (226). The chapter is a twenty-page lament, followed by one-and-a-half pages of "Pleasures." Although Peery had positive things to say about his daily work, the grievances refuse to be suppressed and surface in two more chapters: "Hindrances" and "Special Problems."

Little wonder, then, that the Japanese he represented had more in common with Doolittle's and Smith's Chinese than with the Japanese as lay travelers saw them.[7] Peery seemed not in the least affected by the fashion for things Japanese that drew westerners by the thousands to the oriental fairyland. There are no teahouse entertainments to be found in his account, no cherry-blossom festivals, and no effusions over Japanese art. The common sight of nudity, which prompted many a lay traveler to reflect on the delightful innocence of the Japanese and on the merits of a simpler life, had no appeal for Peery. "Many of the people," he wrote, "do not realize the necessity of burdening themselves with clothes on a hot summer day, and wear very little. The government has been constrained to make laws against nudity, but these are enforced only in the cities" (82). Under the heading "Japanese Characteristics," we encounter the familiar Oriental, subordinated to the principles of family and national loyalty, meek and unquestioning, more practical than speculative, lacking in steadfastness and fixedness of purpose, inconsistent, wanting in originality, and dishonest in private (though not in public) dealings. Peery's praise for the patriotism, thirst for knowledge, and cheerfulness of the Japanese do little to counterbalance the national flaws (51–106).

Whether Peery had styled his text on Smith's *Chinese Characteristics*, he clearly worked within the same discursive tradition, organizing his description around behavior patterns and beliefs that his Christian duty obliged him to identify and counteract. *The Gist of Japan* and other missionary narratives could not but follow this rhetorical structure if they were to justify the missionaries' presence "in the field." Missionary ethnography of the Orient consequently stands out as a coherent and self-conscious tradition. Missionaries went to school on their predecessors' works, corrected one another's biases, often recycled the same ethnographic material for different effects, and, above all, had similar reasons for studying and representing Asians. Complicit with Western imperialism and perhaps even conscious of being its avant-garde, missionaries nonetheless often had their own agendas that conflicted with the dominant ideology.

Because missionaries observed their subjects through the lens of evangelism, the orientalist discourse they constructed was ambivalent. On the one hand, to move fellow Christians to charity, they called up images of absence and lack, of vast spaces and innumerable souls deserving of attention. On the other, they filled those spaces with manifestations of vice, folly, and superstition, all of which could fortunately be eradicated through prayer and mission work. Unlike many of their contemporaries, they constructed a racial other capable of change, not a creature arrested in an inferior stage of development or regressing on the evolutionary scale. This attitude toward potential converts allowed missionaries to differentiate between race and culture in times when science tended to collapse the two. When, as in the case of Smith and Peery, their personal experience of evangelizing had been a disappointment, they did tend to project that sentiment onto their subjects, constructing them as obtuse or unfeeling. But for the most part, the function of the missionary narrative as an advertisement kept ethnographic sensationalism to a minimum and required that the Oriental have a recognizably human face.

The Desirable Heathen: Travel Ethnography of Japan

As industrial capitalism proceeded apace, more westerners acquired the income and leisure to travel. By the 1880s, steamship lines made travel cheaper and faster, and Europeans and Americans visited the Far East in greater numbers than ever. Because the Chinese economy was failing and internal unrest made travel unsafe, few stopped for long in China's ports. Meanwhile, the "young Japan" became a fashionable tourist destination. In the 1880s and 1890s, the country acquired powerful meanings for westerners, who touted its ability to absorb and adapt Western political principles and technologies. At the same time, Japan's cultural difference was tamed, romanticized, aestheticized, and commodified.

For the middle class, there emerged many respectable ways besides chaperoning or making travel pay for itself. A quick survey of *Harper's Magazine*, *Chautauquan*, *Independent*, or *New England Magazine* from the period indicates that countless travelers roamed the world either fully or partially financing their ventures as correspondents. Travel journalism and fiction launched the careers of many men and women, including Winnifred Eaton and John Luther Long (author of *Madame Butterfly*, the novella), both of whom were vicarious travelers. Other westerners found long-term employment in Japan. Under the government's aggressive policy to modernize all aspects of life, advisory positions opened up for Americans and Europeans.

Educational reform created jobs for English-language teachers, philosophers, and scientists as early as 1870. William E. Griffis, whose book *The Mikado's Empire* Winnifred used, was among the first Americans to teach in the interior of Japan. He was succeeded by many men and women who worked for state schools and colleges.

Few of Peery's cares and concerns were shared by Western tourists and lay sojourners in Japan. If sponsored by the Japanese government, they were generally given salaries and retinues exceeding what they were used to at home. If traveling independently or with organized tours, they would have had sufficient income to live comfortably in Japan, associating mainly with upper-class Japanese and expatriate communities. Unlike the missionary who had the prospect of working for a decade or more abroad, the sojourner usually had a limited time to savor to the fullest. It is hard to imagine Peery exclaiming after a day's preaching, "As the day began, so it closed. I should like to have detained each hour as it passed. It was thorough enjoyment," words used by the traveler Isabella Bird in her *Unbeaten Tracks in Japan* (2:129). Clearly, then, a foreigner's perceptions of a country and its people may be colored by the prospective length and purpose of stay.

Going to the Orient to convert others to their own creed and way of life, Protestant missionaries invested Western living standards with a moral value. According to Peery, "The mission home should be a Western home transplanted in the East. It may not become too much orientalized. It should have Western furniture, pictures, musical instruments, etc., and should make its possessor feel that he is in a Western home. It should be well supplied with books and newspapers, and everything else that will keep its inmates in touch with the life of the West. The missionary must not be orientalized, else he will be in danger of becoming heathenized" (212). The imperative constructions and repetitions in this passage suggest how seriously the church treated cultural boundaries. By equating "oriental" with the negatively charged adjective "heathen" instead of "exotic" and "desirable," Peery defined himself against his pleasure-seeking compatriots. They, in turn, often poked fun at the missionary.[8] Winnifred Eaton found the travelers' vision of Japan decidedly more appealing. Though she wrote a short story and two novels featuring missionaries, she portrayed them satirically, as a tourist might have done. To market her fiction, she "went native"—wore kimonos in publicity snapshots and presented herself as Japanese-born to interviewers—a strategy that contributed to her well-earned popularity as a writer of romantic fiction.

"Going native"—living, eating, and occasionally dressing like the locals—does not guarantee the best vantage point for observing them. It does, however, make for texts that valorize other lifeways, whereas a missionary account might hold such practices up to a supposedly superior Western standard. For many sojourners, including William Griffis, Ernest Fenollosa, John La Farge, Henry Adams, Lafcadio Hearn, Pierre Loti, and Arthur Tracy, "going native" was a delightful game, a way of enjoying the exotic flavor of Japan. Some, like Hearn who immersed himself in Buddhism and Shintoism, wished for nothing better than to become "heathenized." Several of the writers discussed below found a comfortable degree of "going native." A fair number came to Japan seeking an alternative to modernity, with its standardized mail-order furniture and bric-a-brac that Peery found so important for keeping his identity intact. Some wore kimonos and slept on futons; others stuck to corsets and brought their own beds along. The "natives" themselves became a source of fascination, their difference reified but no longer sinful or threatening. Particularly in male-authored texts but also in texts by women, desire increasingly mediated representations of the Japanese, and Japanese culture as a whole came to be both feminized and eroticized.

The American lecturer William Elliot Griffis spent four years in Japan (from 1870 to 1874) and witnessed some of its most dramatic political, social, and economic changes.[9] The result of his stay was *The Mikado's Empire* (1876), a hybrid book that combines history, geography, mythology, ethnology, and diary entries. Winnifred Eaton owned a copy of *The Mikado's Empire* (its flyleaf is preserved among her papers), and her novel *Tama* (1910) closely follows Griffis's adventures in northern Japan. The novel's male protagonist is a composite of Griffis and Lafcadio Hearn, whose writings are discussed below, while several of the minor characters are borrowed directly from Griffis's diary.

Among Griffis's first comments on arrival is a critique of Western manners in Eastern lands, particularly British expatriates' brutality toward their Japanese servants. Relieved to get away from the racially mixed crowds of Yokohama, he crossed the countryside on the way to Tokyo in an ecstatic mood: "I am in a new world, not the Old. Everything is novel. I should like to be Argus: not less than a hundred eyes can take in all the sight. I should like to be a poet to express, an artist to paint all I see. I wish I knew the language to ask questions. What a wonderful picture book!" (354). As this passage suggests, Japan for Griffis is an aesthetic experience, often filtered through images seen in books of Japanese prints that began to appear in large numbers in the West. It is also an experience best expressed in heightened, dreamy prose.

To the Western observer, Japan offered ample opportunities for voyeurism. Because much of what Griffis regarded as private was conducted in public, the country appeared to him open, transparent, and innocent. "Here is the human form divine bare to the waist, while its possessor laves her long black hair in warm water," he exclaimed soon after his arrival (364). Almost everywhere except in the college lecture halls, Griffis foregrounded women. Most memorably, on his first overland journey "pretty girls come out to wish us good-morning. One, with a pair of eyes not to be forgotten, brings a tray of tiny teacups full of green tea, and a plate of sweetmeats, begging us to partake. . . . The fairest sights in Japan are Japan's fair daughters" (359).

Griffis, writing in the 1870s, was among the first writers to feminize Japan. Edwin Arnold's *Japonica* and *Seas and Lands* (1891) fuse Japan and Japanese women in language so that for several decades it would be difficult to think of Japan in any other way. If others before Arnold began to describe the Japanese as "little," "dainty," and "gentle," his texts are certainly the most densely studded with such adjectives.[10] The first Japanese subject represented in *Seas and Lands* is a woman. "Little" and "small" appear fourteen times in that first descriptive passage; "pretty," "demure," "soft," and "white" fill out the picture. The photograph of a girl that accompanies this passage is one of thirty-three studio photographs of girls and women, singly, in pairs, threesomes, and foursomes, doing things Japanese (see figure 6). Three of the pictures show women naked to the waist, bathing or breast-feeding. By contrast, there are only seven pictures of men, all of them laborers.

Figure 6. "After the Banquet," illustration for Edwin Arnold's *Seas and Lands* (1892).

Because of the booming trade in orientalia, Western visitors to Japan tended to describe the scenes around them as if they were representations of the
more real figures painted on lacquer or porcelain. Arnold's first glimpse of
the Japanese in *Seas and Lands* is also filtered through a painted image:
"Plunge into the cheery, chattering, polite, and friendly crowd going and
coming along the Benten Dori, and it is as if you were living on a large painted
and lacquered tea-tray, the figures of which, the little gilded houses, the dwarf
trees, and the odd landscape, suddenly jumped up from the dead plane into
the living perpendicular, and started into busy being. Here, too, are all the
pleasant little people you have known so long upon fans and screens" (175).
Everything in Japan is in its proper place. Nothing is lacking. "We will not
take the *kuruma* to-day, but will walk instead, down the Kuboi-cho," Arnold
beckons in *Japonica* (63), as he leads the reader through the city in a single
paragraph that stretches over six illustrated pages teeming with street-life and
exotic commodities for sale (63–68).

Perhaps in reaction to Arnold's *Japonica* and other "surface" studies of
Japan—and yet lured there by the very same texts—Lafcadio Hearn,[11] an
influential latecomer to orientalism, set himself an ambitious task: he would
seek out the "invisible life" of the nation, its spiritual and intellectual pulse.
In 1894, he published the first of many books on Japanese subjects, *Glimpses
of Unfamiliar Japan,* part travel narrative and part philosophical meditation.
Winnifred Eaton was aware of his much publicized life story as far back as
1897; in 1910, she borrowed elements of it to construct the figure of O-Tojin-
san, the white teacher in *Tama.*

Hearn experienced Japan on both a spiritual and aesthetic level. He extolled the artistic skills of the people and found them to be innately aesthetic subjects. As a teacher, he wrote, "The average capacity of the Japanese student in drawing is at least fifty per cent higher than that of European students.
The soul of the race is essentially artistic" (436). He also never tired of describing the diminutive charm and beauty of the Japanese. They are "the sil-
very-laughing folk who now toddle along beside me in their noisy little clogs"
(137), the maid who runs across the street half-dressed, "with a bosom like a
Naiad" (225), people straight out of an old print: "Hokusai's own figures
walking about in straw rain-coats" (10).

For both Hearn and Arnold, the involvement with Japan proved to be more
than a passing fad: both married Japanese women, and Hearn stayed in Japan as a citizen for the remainder of his life. It is tempting to claim that their
desire for the exotic was distinctly masculine; the texts of two female authors
discussed below does suggest that women's experience of the interracial encounter was distinct from their male counterparts'. But I would also argue

that white women's relations with Japanese men were complicated by the women's purchasing power and a sense of membership in a more advanced culture. The desire for the exotic other thus appears to be more closely correlated with relations of dominance than with masculinity, and the erotic gaze is present in women's writings, too.

"It is so good to have got beyond the confines of stereotyped civilization" (52), exclaimed the British writer Isabella Bird in *Unbeaten Tracks in Japan,* a celebrated double volume of "letters" published in London in 1880 and New York the following year. Travel, particularly for unchaperoned women of the 1870s, was liberating. In her attitude toward the Japanese, Bird had more in common with the Reverend Peery than with such lay orientalists as Arnold and Hearn. Though curious about the Japanese, she saw them as "a nation sunk in immorality" and ended the book by expressing the hope that they might soon be Christianized (2:357). Her ethnographic observations consequently often tend toward brutal naturalism. Tumbling shacks, nakedness, flea bites, men's sweaty backs, women's dirty hands, and scabby scalps often caught her journalistic eye. Hers is an intensely physical account as she repeatedly commented on the short stature of the Japanese, the yellowness of their skin, and their plain features.

Unsentimental about the people, Bird frequently aestheticized the land and inserted herself into it as a romantic figure galloping on horseback across a moor or poised before a sweeping view, her guide Ito nowhere in sight. "The breeze came up from the sea," reminisced the narrator, "rustled the reeds, and waved the tall plumes of the *Eulalia Japonica,* and the thunder of the Pacific surges boomed through the air with its grand, deep bass. Poetry and music pervaded the solitude and my spirit was rested" (2:39). Exhilarating interludes such as this break up the prosaic narrative full of ruts and potholes.

Although as a lone explorer Bird usurped some of the traditional attributes of masculinity, she feminized Japan in somewhat different ways than did the male orientalists. Traveling with minimal luggage, professedly "to recruit [her] health" (1:vii), she seemed to tread lightly—a vulnerable persona who negotiated her passage mostly with men: officials who issue travel documents, innkeepers, horse owners, porters, Ainu headmen, and, most prominent, her guide, Ito. It is not the cultivated (feminine) Japan that draws her but what she calls "primitive" or "savage" (masculine) Japan. Being in a position to purchase manpower and doing so on a daily basis clearly empowers her, as it does other Western women in the Third World. In recounting the details of a trip to Yezo, she savored the relation of dominance and the very physicality of her contacts with the Ainu, the aboriginal inhabitants of Hokkaido, a northern island of Japan. On crossing a river one day, she wrote:

Then the beautiful Aino [sic] signed to me to come back and mount on his shoulders; but when he had got a few feet out the poles swayed and trembled so much,
that he was obliged to retrace his way very cautiously, during which I endured
miseries from dizziness and fear; after which he carried me through the rushing
water, which was up to his shoulders, and through a bit of swampy jungle, and
up a steep bank, to the great fatigue of body and mind, hardly mitigated by the
enjoyment of the ludicrous in riding a savage through these Yezo waters. (2:40)

Besides providing the license to possess and command men, the scientific
nature of her expedition also allows her to gaze freely at male bodies. The
account abounds with descriptions of male backs and calves straining between the shafts of her *kuruma* (rickshaw) and of the naked bodies of Ainu
men, whom she repeatedly calls "magnificent" yet likens to animals. Her own
virtue is above suspicion so long as the men around her are depicted as her
social inferiors, either because of their status as scientific objects (Ainu) or
because of their racial degeneracy (Japanese).

Women interested her little. She described aristocratic women's arts and
pastimes in the conventional language (1:131–40) but refused to appreciate
the teahouse entertainment that her male counterparts found irresistible. A
girl twanging a samisen in her text is a nuisance rather than entertainment—
a discordant noise beyond the paper wall of Bird's hotel room keeping her
awake. After an encounter with Ainu women, she related, "They asked me a
number of questions regarding *their own sex* among *ourselves*, but few of these
would bear repeating" (2:68, emphasis added). So different are these wom-
en from Western notions of the feminine that Bird does not identify them
as "our" sex, and so alien are their patterns of thinking that their inquiries
are brushed aside. It is the men who provide valuable information and make
Bird's progress possible.

If white male travelers sought contacts with Japanese women and took
pleasure in writing about them, such early feminists as Alice Mabel Bacon
did so for entirely different reasons.[12] When Bacon arrived in Tokyo in 1888,
she had already consulted her mentor, William Griffis, and resolved to write
a study of Japanese women: "What unexplored corner can I enter? While
Japan as a whole has been studied . . . one half of the population has been
left entirely unnoticed, passed over without mention, or altogether misun-
derstood" (*Japanese Girls and Women* v). In the fervor of claiming her sec-
tor of the "field," Bacon found a lack where there really was an abundance,
yet she rightly questioned the accuracy of the available representations. Griffis
and Arnold had stopped at glimpses of high-born ladies and teahouse en-
tertainers. Even Bird, Bacon's most imposing female forerunner, had left the
"woman's sphere" largely unexplored.

Japanese Girls and Women (1891) and *A Japanese Interior* (1893) were the product of two years, during which Bacon held a full-time teaching position in a Tokyo high school. Because of her students' class status, she had contacts with the ruling elite and attended official court functions. Her salary allowed her to maintain a cook, a groom, a horse, and a dog. Her relations with her two male servants and the occasional *kuruma* runner were similar to the ones Bird had with the men who surrounded her. She had even less sympathy for the upper-class men at court, whom she described as "effeminate" (*Japanese Girls and Women* 199). She particularly disparaged their efforts to adopt Western ways, as on the occasion when she referred to the partnerless Japanese men in a ballroom as "wallflowers" (*Japanese Girls and Women* 200). In singling out the women as her focus, Bacon contributed to the dominant orientalist discourse. For the most part, however, she emphasized the normalcy of Japanese home life, writing with an eye for the things in Japanese middle-class life that might empower women readers at home and make their work easier: the "rational" dress, housekeeping simplified by the uncluttered interiors, and useful child-care tips. What fascinated her most were the alternative female role models, such as the warrior women of the feudal era and even the female porters who carried her trunks up Mount Fuji.[13]

The feminization of Japan in travel writing, coupled with a bias toward the sensuous and the picturesque, led westerners to brush aside contemporary political developments, most notably Japan's militarization. Dominant discourse made it difficult for writers to imagine the island nation as a potential aggressor. In Arnold's *Seas and Lands,* for instance, the chapter entitled "Militant Japan" is randomly illustrated by the photo of a woman "In Winter Dress" (see figure 7). Her image reinforces the general air of peace and goodwill that pervades Arnold's report on the Imperial Army maneuvers at Nagoya. Even if Arnold had little to do with the placement of the illustrations in the text, it is interesting that his American publisher considered such a juxtaposition appropriate.

Similarly, Hearn's impulse to aestheticize Japan was so strong that when he watched soldiers march through an idyllic country town, their passing did not ruffle the smooth flow of his meditation:

> round the corner of the last temple come marching a troop of handsome young riflemen, uniformed somewhat like French light infantry, marching by fours so perfectly that all the gaiters move as if belonging to a single body, and every sword-bayonet catches the sun at exactly the same angle. . . . These are the students of the Shihan-Gakko, the College of Teachers, performing their daily military exercises. . . . And they are none the less modest and knightly in manner for all their modern knowledge. (157)

Figure 7. "In Winter Dress," illustration for Edwin Arnold's *Seas and Lands* (1892).

Just as Arnold failed to see the military maneuvers at Nagoya as anything more than a brilliant spectacle that "could not have had a more picturesque *mise-en-scène*" (*Seas and Lands* 417), Hearn did not see the soldiers as part of the Imperial war machine. Neither did he ask why future schoolteachers were being trained for war. Another manifestation of the war machine did unnerve Hearn, however. While he was visiting the traditional fishing village of Mionoseki, an Imperial man-of-war anchored offshore. Everyone in town, including Hearn, crowded onto fishing boats to visit the ship. The excitement of the moment lent itself to the narrator, whose emotions changed minute by minute.

> The host of quaint craft hovering and trembling around that tremendous bulk; and all the long-robed, wide-sleeved multitude of the antique port,—the gray and the young together,—crawling up those mighty flanks in one ceaseless stream, like a swarming of ants . . . and they wonder like babies at the walls and the turrets of steel, and the giant guns, and the mighty chains, and the stern bearing of the white-uniformed hundreds looking down upon the scene without a smile, over the iron bulwarks. Japanese those also, yet changed by some mysterious process into the semblance of strangers. Only the experienced eye could readily decide the nationality of those stalwart marines. (241)

A little further, the narrator described the ship as "a magnificent horror of steel and steam and all the multiple energy of death" (242) that dwarfed the child-like villagers. What Hearn dramatizes is the encounter of old Japan with modernity. It is the machine that deprives the marines of their racial features and national character (the marching riflemen were all the more Japanese for their French-style uniforms and gleaming bayonets). Evidently Hearn does not mind imperialism; he minds technology. Thus the discourse of "gentle little Japan" would persist in Western popular writing into the twentieth century, even after Japan had won victories against Korea, China, and Russia.

When reinscribing the positive, nonthreatening image of Japan, travel writing often used China and the Chinese for comparison. For instance in *The Mikado's Empire*, the position of women in society plays a crucial role in Griffis's distinction between progressive Japan and China, a nation that tolerates "Asiatic despotism." "No [Japanese] woman's feet are ever bound, and among the middle and lower classes she is almost as much at liberty to walk and visit as in our own land. An amount of social freedom among womankind prevails in Japan that could hardly be expected in a country at once Asiatic, idolatrous, and despotic. . . . the educated, the enlightened, the rising men of Japan loathe the words. The writer who applies these stinging epithets to them will receive any thing but thanks. They do not like to be called Asiatics" (554). Griffis was so anti-Chinese that he made an elaborate argument that the physiology, culture, language, and intellect of the Japanese are of Ainu and Malay origin, emphatically not Chinese (26–35). In 1907, Griffis would expand this claim into a book entitled *The Japanese Nation in Evolution*, arguing that the Ainu are an Aryan race and that the Japanese, their descendants, are white. In Griffis's narrative, as in most of the travel literature I discuss here, despotism, superstition, and other negative modifiers no longer applicable to the modern Japanese are projected onto the Chinese.

Nowhere is this strategy more apparent than in the Arnold's *Seas and Lands*. Traveling to Japan in 1889, Arnold made a stop in San Francisco. His impressions of Chinatown figure prominently in the narrative as a prelude to Japan. Though Chinatown filled Arnold with revulsion, he investigated this "hideous and uncleanly quarter" with relish, returning to it "again and again" by day and by night (133). Not satisfied with the view of its "thirty streets choked with Chinese" (139), Arnold penetrated the private quarters beyond and insisted on taking the reader with him:

> You enter any one of these [tenements] and plunge down a rotten staircase into a dark, narrow passage, on either side of which are ranged double bunks, one above the other, like those on board the most crowded emigrant ship. In the passage-way some are frizzling absolutely repulsive articles of diet over lamps or charcoal fires: in the bunks, stretched on bits of matting, others are lying asleep, or mending their unwashed clothing, or smoking tobacco and opium. There is no air, nor any attempt to provide it. (139)

So dehumanized are the Chinese laborers in the text that nothing about them could possibly arouse the reader's sympathy: "they do not live in this extraordinary quarter, but rather wallow like pigs and burrow like rats" (138) and are "packed away at night like sardines" (139). Chinatown, "lodged in the very heart" of "young" San Francisco, would not be tolerated for long, Arnold declared, in unison with California nativists. It is clear that different attitudes and methods of investigation underlie the representations of Chinatown and Tokyo. Whereas in Chinatown Arnold tirelessly inspected the back alleys and "underground burrows," once in Tokyo he was satisfied with the surface image: *kuruma* rides through major thoroughfares, shopping trips in the commercial district, and leisurely walks through formal gardens punctuated by stops at teahouses.

The writings of Griffis, Arnold, Hearn, Bird, and Bacon may appear to have more differences than similarities, partly because each author sought to carve out a different niche in the publishing marketplace. Bird roamed rural Japan "off the beaten track"; Arnold stuck to the "beaten track" and extolled the already famous sights, smells, and sounds; Bacon revised popular representations of Japanese women by focusing on the culture of the middle- and upper-class home; and Hearn turned his back on what he perceived as a superficial fixation on material culture, seeking Japan's spiritual core among the shrines and "simple folk." Yet all these writers participated in the Western ideology of salvage at a time when Japan was rapidly becoming an industrialized nation, even as they themselves acted as catalysts of change. To all of them, the Japanese embodied an essential difference. Fixing and valorizing that difference is what made tourism and writing about it worthwhile.

Unlike missionary ethnographies, nineteenth-century travel narratives tended to foreground the narrator's subjective experience and emotional response to the exotic. Bird's elation or distaste upon seeing a particular view, Arnold's musings about falling asleep in the comfort of a country hotel, and Hearn's response to sacred Shinto and Buddhist rituals placed the Western self squarely at the center of the narrative. This narrative framework particularly favored the aestheticization and objectification of Japan, an approach marked most strongly in the work of Ernest Fenollosa, Alfred Parsons, and John La Farge, men who interacted little with the Japanese but studied Japanese landscapes, art, and physiognomy. Finally, most travel writers aimed to give their audience a pleasant reading experience.

Pleasuring the reader was not the top priority for missionary ethnographers. Neither were they dependent on a market-driven publishing industry. The production of missionary texts was largely financed by people who already believed in mission work but sought reassurance that their money was going to a good cause. Such ethnographies as Medhurst's, Doolittle's, and Smith's served as a call to Christian duty. Written in the spirit of long-term commitment to Asians, these texts were usually based on many years of cross-cultural contacts. Where most secular writers regretted or were ambivalent about the modernization of Asia, the purpose of missionaries was precisely the opposite: to effect cultural change and make the racial other more like the self. Given this aim, their writings tended not to glamorize indigenous cultures.

As I show in the following chapters, the two distinct traditions that helped produce "wily Chinese" and "gentle little Japanese" had a good deal to do with the sober, moralistic tone of Edith Eaton's stories, as well as with Winnifred Eaton's narrative style, plots, settings, and characterizations. Borrowing eclectically from missionary and travel writers, Edith and Winnifred occasionally wrote counternarratives: Winnifred challenged the hedonism and self-absorption of Western travelers, while Edith questioned the assumption of "wiliness" and the rationale of converting the Chinese. Neither sister felt comfortable with the inherited tradition; both made complex alterations to accommodate their eccentric viewpoints.

Winnifred inherited from Arnold, Bacon, and Hearn an audience fascinated by things Japanese and, for the most part, warmly disposed to the Japanese people. She stepped into the role of exotic entertainer, humoring those who sought a pleasurable reading experience even as she chipped away at their understanding of "race," miscegenation, and racial "hybridity." William Griffis, Pierre Loti, Edwin Arnold, and Lafcadio Hearn were to Winnifred what the "man in the field" was to the nineteenth-century "armchair anthropologist": gatherers of ethnographic material that could be refashioned into

new texts. Edith found her gatherers of ethnographic data among missionaries to China and initially relied on their fieldwork. Only when she began
collating it with her own Chinatown fieldwork did their interpretations loos-
en the hold on her imagination. Emphatically not an entertainer, Edith continued to write didactic, politically engaged stories throughout her life. If she
managed to place them at all, she did so because of such like-minded magazine editors as Charles Lummis of the California *Land of Sunshine,* William
Hayes Ward of the New York *Independent,* and editors of children's periodicals and columns.

PART 1

Edith Eaton

2. A Journalistic Mission

THIS CHAPTER FOLLOWS Edith Eaton on her forays into the Montreal Chinatown and then, further from home, to Kingston, Jamaica, to see how her sense of self evolved when she first located her Chinese other and how her identity had to be renegotiated when she entered Jamaican society. In the first instance, the growth of a Chinese community in Montreal in the 1890s created for Edith a double social role: that of reporter who made the life of the Chinese minority visible to the dominant white majority and that of Sunday school English teacher who was able to affirm the stigmatized half of her racial heritage by helping integrate Chinese immigrants into her own larger community. The move to Jamaica, however, complicated her allegiances: she landed in Kingston as an outsider but immediately took up a job that required her to identify with the dominant white minority against a "colored" majority. While being a reporter in the Caribbean put her in a position not unlike that of an ethnographer entering an other community, her audience was not in a distant metropolis but right on the spot. Furthermore, as a person of color (albeit passing for white), she could neither fully identify with her white readers nor fully dissociate herself from the island's black and Asian population. By uncovering Edith's multiple, unstable, and often conflicting positionings, I draw attention to the vital role played in ethnographic writing by locating one's self in relation to one's audience and the ethnographic subject. While the distinction between Edith's self and other is relatively clearcut in Montreal, her Jamaican writings show a shifting allegiance, expressed alternatively as an enjoyment of the outsider's perspective and a discomfort with her role of reporter.[1]

Familiarizing the Unfamiliar

> The two men within the store are uncouth specimens of their race,
> drest in working blouses and pantaloons, with queues dangling
> down their backs. I recoil with a sense of shock.
>   "Oh, Charlie," I cry. "Are we like that?"
>   "Well, we're Chinese, and they're Chinese, too, so we must be!"
> —Edith Eaton, "Leaves from the Mental Portfolio of an Eurasian"

In 1912, soon after the publication of Edith Eaton's only book, *Mrs. Spring Fragrance,* a *New York Times* reviewer berated the author for the formal short-comings of her prose but suggested that these were more than compensated by Edith's novel subject matter and above all the "unusual knowledge she undoubtedly has of her theme" ("A New Note in Fiction" 405). For the reviewer, that authoritative knowledge constituted the chief value of *Mrs. Spring Fragrance.* In the same vein, a *McClurg's* advertisement claimed that *Mrs. Spring Fragrance* would "open an entirely new world to many readers." This "new world" had, through the agency or acquiescence of most Americans, remained contained and segregated as undesirable for fifty years. Yet in marketing the book, the advertisers recuperated American Chinatowns as a novelty, claiming that they "make as desirable reading as the title suggests."

Mrs. Spring Fragrance was also reviewed a year later by an anthropologist writing for the *American Antiquarian and Oriental Journal,* who treated it as a contribution to ethnographic knowledge.[2] The questions that interested the reviewer most were whether "the stories are accounts of actual experiences"; what the book contributed to the knowledge of Chinese character; to what extent the Chinese were capable of assimilation; and, finally, what the status of "half-breed American-Chinese" was. The reviewer had full confidence in Edith's ethnographic authority and her "insight into the thought and feeling of the Chinese who are with us, but not of us" ("Mrs. Spring Fragrance" 181–82).

"With us, but not of us" is a crucial distinction for the anonymous reviewer, one that led him or her to interpret Edith's text as evidence that the Chinese could not assimilate in anything but appearances, for even "the most Americanized . . . must feel, now and again, the pull of the old life, the force of old customs, the power of the old beliefs." "With us, but not of us" also justified the reviewer's assumption that the "half-breed" was doomed to extinction, "disadvantaged" and "handicapped for life unless he remains in Chinatown." The reviewer's sympathy for the exploited and humiliated minority was tempered by the conviction that the Chinese "are in our country for a definite purpose" (182). Since the reviewer did not explain what that "purpose" might be, presumably every reader would know that the Chinese came in search of vulgar financial gain. Because of its focus on assimilation, this anthropological reading of *Mrs. Spring Fragrance* managed to elide the intra- and interracial love and marriage plots, the child-rearing plots, and the "claiming America" plots so central to Edith's fiction. Though the reviewer recognized Edith's Chinatown as a site of both romance and tragedy, he or she assumed that, like its inhabitants, Chinatown may be in "our country" but not of it.

As the epigraph from "Leaves" suggests, Edith was unable to adopt the "with us, but not of us" stance that came so naturally to the reviewer. For Edith, the Chinese other could never be positioned safely outside the self, no matter how culturally alienated she may have felt from the inhabitants of Chinatown. In the light of this, Edith's case is particularly useful for discussing the construction of ethnographic authority and the racial hierarchy assumed in ethnographic studies. By borrowing from the vocabulary and tropes of ethnography, I make apparent some of the unspoken assumptions that accompany the reading of "ethnic" literatures and thus begin to reevaluate Edith's works, which, despite the author's literary ambition, were and still are read primarily for their ethnographic content. Among the issues I consider are the effect of Edith's ambivalent racial status on her positioning vis-à-vis the ethnographic subject and the reader, the function that ethnographic work performed in Edith's self-construction, and how her work may have reflected back on the Chinese communities she studied.

That she came to study them at all was neither natural nor inevitable: at the age of twenty-five, she was still writing poetry and prose on conventional subjects for the glossy *Dominion Illustrated.* There were no Chinese to speak of in Montreal. It was only through her subsequent involvement with the home mission movement that in 1894 the twenty-nine-year-old Edith turned her attention to the Montreal Chinese. At the time, Edith was doing occasional reporting for local papers, and she seems to have combined missionary work and journalistic investigation. Aside from the fact that she was brought up in a Presbyterian home, what would have attracted Edith to mission work? How did missionaries' attitudes toward China and Chinese immigrants differ from those of the general public? What did Edith mean by saying in an autobiographical piece she wrote for the *Boston Globe* in 1912, "From that time on I began to go among my mother's people, and it did me a world of good to discover how akin I was to them"? ("Sui Sin Far" 293). And can we say unequivocally that her work did the Chinese "a world of good"?

That the Presbyterian mission needed her precisely because she was half-Chinese would have allowed her to affirm the stigmatized half of her hereditary baggage. Also, if in their daily lives the Eaton siblings were under the strain of passing for white, Edith may have welcomed a community where her racial identity could be made public and where it perhaps even counted in her favor. The very fact that missionaries sought direct contact with Chinese immigrants and tried to open channels of communication (for instance, by holding free language classes) firmly distinguished them from the working-class nativists and upper-class eugenicists, even if the goal of converting and acculturating the Chinese was premised on Western cultural superiority. The rhetoric of universal humanity and the duty to share the gospel, used so effectively by the missionaries discussed in chapter 1, would have presented an appealing alternative to Edith, who was used to dealing with acute Sinophobia in everyday life and in print. Through the Sunday school network, she met Chinese on a regular basis and secured introductions to other members of the Chinatown community that proved useful in establishing her reputation as a Chinatown reporter.

Edith's early ethnographic method was strongly influenced by the tradition of missionary writings, particularly the Reverend Justus Doolittle's *Social Life of the Chinese* (1865). She began by exploring those cultural practices that had long enjoyed special status in missionary ethnography: the treatment of women in patriarchal society, footbinding, idolatry, gambling, and opium smoking. What distinguished missionary fieldwork from journalistic investigation was the long-standing tradition of interviewing native informants to get at cultural knowledge. As I demonstrate below, journalists were more likely to stop at observing the Chinese or interviewing white authorities, such as government officials.

Edith adopted the missionaries' style of investigation, yet she absorbed their ideology selectively. For instance, she was not altogether convinced that the desire to learn about "heathen" cultural practices ought to be motivated by the impulse to eradicate them and substitute one's own. Moreover, she exercised considerable discretion as to where and how to represent her findings, in ways that show she realized the potential consequences of the printed word for Chinese Montrealers. The rhetoric of lack associated with Chinese culture was an insidious one that Edith had trouble rejecting outright since it was the imagined lack in the world's spiritual economy that moved white Canadians to charity and goodwill toward the "heathen." Without going so far as to say that Christianity had little use value for most Chinese Sunday school students, Edith often wrote against the rhetoric of lack in Chinese culture. Without denying the need for cultural change or syncretism in immigrant communities, she insisted that the immigrants themselves should determine the pace and extent of that change.

Edith's motives for doing Chinatown ethnography, then, must have been complex. She admitted to engaging the Chinese in an effort to recognize her self in them. The chance to associate with white Canadians who both patronized and felt a responsibility toward the Chinese must have been an important motive. Also the Chinatown mission provided her with a line of work in which she could become an authority—an important motive for someone with "pen and ink fever" as she described herself in her December 30, 1896, article, "Woman about Town: The Horse Car, Sarah Bernhardt"—in a day when there were few fields in which women could professionalize. To "do the right thing" by educating the white reading public about things Chinese was surely not the least of her motives. Without question, as a home missionary, Edith did identify with the dominant Christian ideology and work within the power structure that objectified the Chinese. Nonetheless, she used the occasional space the papers allowed her to question the dominant uses of power.

My reading of Edith brings out the dexterity with which she balanced the needs and interests of her readers and subjects with her own writerly prerogatives and aspirations. The celebratory story of Edith Eaton has already been told by others. To tell that story, critics have tended to focus on her resistant and contestatory practice while eliding texts in which the author aligns herself more closely with dominant norms and discourses of power. In *Between Worlds* (1990), Amy Ling constructed Edith as a precursor of Maxine Hong Kingston's word-warrior persona. Annette White-Parks's literary biography rendered Edith in heroic proportions. Yet there are other, no less interesting stories to be told that account for a greater range of Edith's writings. I therefore suggest that instead of weeding out her "compromised" texts, we pay attention to them. To use David Palumbo-Liu's formulation, those moments of compromise or accommodation may be "indices to the boundaries of both containment and resistance at particular historical junctures" (99). Edith's newspaper and magazine stories, framed on all sides by the dominant discourses of the day, are particularly useful for contesting the boundary we draw between accommodation and resistance.

In a 1990 essay, James Clifford did a memorable reading of a poem by James Fenton, "The Pitt Rivers Museum," in which Fenton playfully lists a jumble of natural objects and cultural artifacts from a museum, as remembered by his childhood self. To this, Clifford no less playfully responded, "Do not encounter these objects except as *curiosities* to giggle at, *art* to be admired, or *evidence* to be understood scientifically" (142). Though Clifford wrote about cultural artifacts and Edith about the ethnic Chinese in North America, he articulated the standard options available to Edith for dealing with Chinese subject matter. Her readers were accustomed to observing Chinese immigrants as curiosities, being amused by Chinese characters on the stage, and having them represented scientifically as an inferior race. To turn the Chinese into art posed serious problems for Edith. In this section, I juxtapose her China-town journalism from the years 1894–96 with mainstream reporting and then read her articles against the stories she published in American literary magazines in roughly the same period. I show that not only the choice of genre but also the place of publication and Edith's understanding of various audiences' expectations inflected her representations of the Chinese minority.

The Chinese population of Montreal grew rapidly in the 1890s, the decade when Edith began to write poetry and short fiction for the *Dominion Illustrated* and do Chinatown reporting for local newspapers. Annette White-Parks cited statistics that show an increase from 36 Chinese in 1891 to 1,030 in 1901 (74). On May 8, 1894, the *Montreal Daily Star* reported that the city's eighty Chinese laundries employed some 250 men. Part of the population was transient, because Montreal was a stopover for thousands of laborers traveling to and from the United States. Short notes on the movements of migrant laborers and crime in the Chinese quarter appeared regularly in the *Daily Star*. These alternated with longer reports on the smuggling of Chinamen across the border. Evidently the Chinese aroused much interest. "To peer into the abode of a Chinese community is almost a chance privilege," confided a reporter, "yet a representative of the *Star* was admitted just recently to play the part of 'Peeping Tom of Coventry.' What follows is a standard tour through cramped living quarters, opium dens, and gambling houses" ("The Celestials in Montreal" 9).

Against the largely white immigrant population of the city, the Chinese were visibly different. But the preoccupation of local papers and magazines with things "Celestial" suggests they were not visible enough. An interesting example of how the *Daily Star* represented the Chinese to its readers is a full-page illustrated report by a journalist and an accompanying artist who watched a group of Chinese go through customs ("The Chinese Land of Promise"). Among the drawings (see figure 8) are scenes of interrogation, measurements of "the Mongolian," and identification by means of scars and moles. The largest and most sensational exhibit is a series of "type sketches." Since Chinese were required to travel in bond,[3] the artist had himself locked up with them in a railway car bound for Richford and reported:

As matters go, ordinarily the Chinaman is very patient, but if there is one thing more than another he detests, it is to have his picture taken. It may be superstition, it may be ignorance, it may be part of his religious scruples, but all the same, he hates the idea and resists it with all his power. On this occasion the inmates of the car were in blissful ignorance of the outrage which was being

perpetrated on their feelings until it was too late. One Chinaman, however, more
alive than his comrades, finally grasped the situation. Arising in his seat he
delivered some forceful expletives in the purest Hong Kong, at the same time
denouncing the *Star* artist with significant gestures. His warning cry was immediately responded to. The twenty-three rose as one man, and turning their
backs to the white man left him at liberty to take a rear view and that only.
However, the mischief had been done, and sufficient material collected to satisfy the artist's yearnings.

The passage makes it clear that collecting "material" on behalf of the reader
is the reporter's license and duty, and he will go to great lengths to get the best.
That the white reading public has a right to examine the Chinese is assumed.
Only if the reader is complicit with the journalistic voice does this exercise in
amateur ethnography seem humorous. Only if the reader agrees that no outrage has really been perpetrated can he or she smile at the rearview sketches
of Chinese heads. Only because the reporter is "at liberty" even when in bondage can he ignore the power dynamics inside the train. As is often the case in
ethnography when the fieldworker does not speak the language of the observed, a historically situated act—in this case one of protest against the abuse
of power—is interpreted as a curious custom or superstition.

The other group of Montrealers who made it their business to "examine"
the Chinese and had access to the press as well as the pulpit were Presbyterian activists. Work with the Montreal Chinese was initiated in 1884, to bur-
geon ten years later under Dr. Joseph C. Thomson, a missionary to China on
furlough after ten years "in the field." By the end of 1896, according to Edith,
there were thirteen Chinese Sunday schools in the city.[4] Interviewed by the
Daily Star, Thomson attempted to diffuse alarmist speculations that with the
growth of the Chinese population Montreal would have a "Chinese problem
upon its hands." The population estimates, he argued, were much overrat-
ed, but he did warn Montrealers against ghettoizing the Chinese, for "scattered as they now are, they can be no menace to the civilization of the day"
("Will Montreal Have a Chinatown?"). That Thomson's operation had such
widespread public endorsement was partly due to the rhetoric of converting the innocuous scattered heathens before they became a public threat.

Unlike the journalists who generally pursued the shady and sensational,
mission workers "made it a matter of duty to find out every Chinaman in
the city and outskirts and advise them on matters spiritual" ("Will Montreal Have a Chinatown?"). Texts by such workers, including Edith, contrast
starkly with such articles as "Peeping Tom's" guided tour of Chinatown and
the border-crossing reportage. In general, mission workers attempted to paint
a nonthreatening, orderly Chinese community; they implied that the manners

CHINESE LAND OF PROMISE—CAPTAIN GATES AND SING BOO EXAMINE A CHINAMAN.

CHINESE LAND OF PROMISE—CHINESE IN-
SPECTOR TIPPETT MEASURES THE MON-
GOLIAN.

CHINESE LAND OF PROMISE—TYPES OF THE HEATHEN CHINEE.

CHINESE LAND OF PROMISE—CANADIAN CUSTOMS OFFICER DUPUIS' PERFUNCTORY
EXAMINATION.

Figure 8. Illustrations for "The Chinese Land of
Promise," an article on a group of Chinese cross-
ing the Canadian-U.S. border in bond, *Montreal
Daily Star*, June 23, 1894.

and customs of the Chinese left a lot to be desired, but they were more likely to show Chinese in well-lit public places, assimilating.

Whereas the newspaper sent out reporters to serve as the reader's vicarious eye, roaming where the average citizen could not, Sunday school work brought scores of white Montrealers into direct contact with their Chinese neighbors (see figure 9). We know from Edith's autobiographical article "Sui Sin Far, the Half Chinese Writer, Tells of Her Career" (1912) that she and her mother Grace were brought into this fold by Dr. Thomson to teach Sunday school and visit the few Chinese women living in Montreal (292).[5] According to the *Daily Star,* Sunday schools were held in large halls, where, for an hour a week, each Chinese student would be assigned his personal English tutor to teach him basic language skills ("Chinamen at Sunday School"). Although the language barrier and the tutors' assumption of Christian cultural superiority would have stood in the way of much meaningful cultural exchange, there was at least a chance of building mutual trust and respect.

As White-Parks demonstrated in her discussion of Edith's Montreal writings, Edith was active in exposing racial discrimination, which took such forms as head taxes, travel and immigration restrictions, and random harassment by government officials. It would, however, be misleading to exaggerate Edith's achievement as a chronicler of the Montreal Chinatown. Instead of being an accurate reflection of Chinatown life, Edith's texts were inflected by her understanding of reader expectations and her personal interests, ambitions, and moral code. As Miss Edith Eaton, stenographer, reporter, and Sunday school teacher, she aligned herself with the dominant majority that valorized genteel domesticity, individualism, and Christian values. Throughout her career, she tended to counteract negative stereotypes of Chinese laborers by representing primarily middle-class Chinese, and she occasionally informed her white readers that many Chinese laborers in the United States were respected scholars or merchants in their homeland. By focusing on Chinese family life in her early fiction, she also marginalized the problems of the predominantly male-uprooted Chinatown society.

Moreover, Edith was a fledgling reporter who followed the rules—to the extent that her conscience allowed. She often covered the hottest topics of the day, such as illegal border crossings, miscegenation, or the subjugation of Chinese women. To borrow the formulation of the critic Dorinne Kondo, I would argue that by specializing in Chinatown reporting, Edith found a way to "assert a marketable difference" (125), a strategy particularly useful to an ambitious, self-educated woman in the male-dominated world of reporting. Newspaper editors who hired her services trusted her authority on

CHINAMEN AT SUNDAY-SCHOOL—ON THE WAY TO THE CHURCH.

CHINAMEN AT SUNDAY-SCHOOL—A CLEVER
TEACHER AND AN APT PUPIL.

Figure 9. Images of Chinese immigrants attending Sunday school, *Montreal Daily Star*, November 24, 1894.

CHINAMEN AT SUNDAY-SCHOOL—HARD AT WORK.

things Chinese, an authority she worked hard to establish. Edith's early writings on Chinatown indicate that from time to time she resorted to guesswork and popular stereotypes and was initially no less a stranger there than were her white counterparts. But through long-term commitment, participant observation, and questioning of English-speaking Chinese, she seems to have evolved a double sense of responsibility: to her readers and to the subjects of her investigations.

When Edith's fiction and journalism are viewed side by side, it becomes apparent in several cases that although the stories are extended readings of motifs and images from her newspaper reports, Edith firmly distinguished between what was appropriate for each genre. It is also apparent that her journalism addresses immediate social and political concerns of both the Chinese and white Montrealers and works against the volatile anti-Chinese sentiment. The stories tend to be more archetypal, detached from the local context, and less overtly political. By comparing the two types of writing, we see an author whose positioning in relation to the Chinese minority and the white majority was unstable and who vacillated between endorsing and contesting orientalist discourses.

"Girl Slave in Montreal: Our Chinese Colony Cleverly Described" (1894) is the title of an early article by Edith. Given the public outrage over reports that Chinese slaves and prostitutes had been disembarking in large numbers at Victoria, a "slave girl" would have made an eye-catching headline. The title was undoubtedly supplied by the editor rather than by Edith, for contrary to reader expectations, she denied there was anything going on in the Chinese quarter that would warrant moral outrage. In fact, the slave girl is a marginal figure in the text; all Edith said about her is that "her face is by no means her fortune." Her status in the household is that of a younger sister, for "it is a custom in China to look upon slaves as family."

At the center of the article is the narrator's visit to a Chinese hotelier's home and her encounter with the only three Chinese women living in Montreal. (As White-Parks and other have noted, Edith omitted her own mother from the count). Whereas the men, through their business dealings and Sunday school, have become more or less integrated into the larger community, the three women have no contacts with Canadians. Their seclusion and traditionalism make them all the more interesting as ethnographic subjects. The visit opens and ends with news of the daily activities of Chinese men in the public sphere, a structure perhaps suggested by the fact that to obtain access to the women's quarters the narrator has had to negotiate with the men.

For all the temptation to exoticize and dehistoricize her subjects, the narrator deliberately preserved a balance between the normalcy of "business as

usual" in the public sphere and the strangeness of the Chinese women seclud-
ed in their private realm. Even in that realm, she foregrounded the ordinary
Western furniture and a sewing machine, "proof that the Chinese do march
forward in the van of civilization." The menfolk speak English and lead intelligible, well-regulated lives. By contrast, the women's daily activities have
to be investigated and interpreted for the reader. The narrator could not speak
with them, but she made up for the communication problem by intently observing and describing the details of the person and apparel: "Mrs. Wing Sing
received me very graciously, her round face beaming with smiles. She is considered by her countrymen to be quite a beauty. . . . She wore the Chinese costume, pyjamas and blouse of dark stuff, a combination of silk and cotton.
From out the bell sleeves hung pretty little hands, which were somewhat
spoiled, however, by long nails. . . . Her feet are of natural size." The description echoes a common preoccupation of nineteenth-century texts with Chinese women's bound feet and long fingernails.[6] Though Mrs. Wing Sing's feet
are unremarkable, the narrator felt obliged to make reference to them. Since
to white readers the practice of footbinding symbolizes the enslavement of
Chinese women, the hostess's unbound feet mark her as a modern woman.
Silence hung heavy over the entire episode as the narrator's eyes darted from
the painted bamboo panels to the sewing machine and back to her amiable
but self-conscious hostess who "laughed at every sound we uttered."

Unable to ask what Mrs. Wing Sing thought of her life in Montreal, the
narrator had to hypothesize about what the Chinese woman was thinking—
or rather what she was *not* thinking:

> I looked around the four walls within which her life is spent and I wondered
> how it was she could laugh and be merry. Is it custom or nature that makes her
> contented with a life that to the daughters of Europe and America seems worse
> than death? Obedience, never-failing obedience, is the characteristic of the
> Chinese woman. She loves her parents and those who are put in authority over
> her because she is taught to do so. . . . No question of 'woman's rights' perplexes
> her little brains. She takes no responsibilities on herself, and wishes for none.
> She has perfect confidence in her man.

Edith did not hide the fact that her lack of Cantonese was an obstacle to the
investigation; she nonetheless sketched an authoritative psychological portrait of Mrs. Wing Sing—one based on ethnographic representations of
Chinese women in missionary handbooks. In constructing the Chinese woman as trained to unthinking obedience, Edith cast Western women—herself
included—as independent thinkers concerned with women's rights. It is in
passages such as this that we get a sense of the empowerment Western women

experienced in working with people of color, whether as missionaries, journalists, or trained ethnographers.

Edith anticipated most of the questions her readers might have posed: Do the women have bound feet? Should they be liberated from bondage? Are the Chinese receptive to Christianity? What kind of neighbors will they make? The overall effect of the article is one of reassurance. Contemporary Montrealers needed to see that all was above board in Chinatown; even the Chinese women were reconciled to their own confinement and had many a good laugh over a bowl of crisped rice.

But as Edith put before the reader this sanitized image of Chinatown, she seemingly retained some doubts about the situation of Mrs. Wing Sing with the round, beaming face and unbound feet. She also must have given the slave girl more thought, for wife and slave reappeared as a pair two years later in a tragic tale entitled "Ku Yum." Significantly, this tale, which thematizes the psychic cost of arranged marriage and patriarchal authority over children, was published in a California magazine, *Land of Sunshine.* There were few publishing opportunities in Canada, which may be one reason all of Edith's early Chinese stories were sent out of the country. There may, however, have been other reasons.

Because racism toward the Chinese in North America has always been aggravated by orientalism—a discourse that feminizes Asia and Asian men in particular—the ethnic and gender loyalties of men and women of Chinese descent have been conflicted. Put simply, when claiming a Western model of liberated womanhood, women of Chinese descent need to position themselves against a traditional patriarchal order and hence against the men of their ethnic group; meanwhile, men of Chinese descent reassert their masculinity in ways that may be oppressive to women (Cheung, "The Woman Warrior"). Edith's treatment of the three Chinese women is undeniably patronizing. Yet her decision as a Montreal journalist to refrain from voicing moral concerns—about the patriarchal order, for instance—can be interpreted as a mark of her responsible reporting. Had she assumed a more conventionally moralistic stance, she would have further undermined the precarious position of the city's six hundred Chinese men. Instead, we find Edith's concerns displaced into such tales as "Ku Yum," in which she permitted herself to probe aspects of Chinese culture that conflicted with her construction of Chinese as progressive.

"Ku Yum" can be read as a fictional reconstruction of how Mrs. Wing Sing and her nameless slave girl might have found themselves in the United States. The story turns on the reversal of identity between a well-born girl, whose face is her misfortune, and a beautiful, round-faced slave girl with unbound feet. To marry off their plain daughter to a Chinese American, Ku Yum's parents resort to deceit and present A-Toy, a slave, to the matchmaker. Ku Yum accidentally learns of the ploy and is so thoroughly humiliated that on the boat to the United States she trades identities with the slave girl. Abused by her new mistress, Ku Yum commits suicide, and her body is shipped back home, where her parents recognize her by the bound feet.

The story turns on both gender and class conflict. The male figures for whom Ku Yum is a "chattel" are preoccupied with female beauty; to have a modicum of control over their bodies, the women in the story can only use their beauty to build alliances with the men against other women. Since Ku Yum's mother was powerless to protect her from the proxy marriage, Ku Yum exercises her limited agency, first to avoid the marriage proper and then to remove her body from bondage through suicide.

That in the same year Edith published two more stories on arranged marriage and one on the destruction of a love match is surely not accidental. In one of these, "The Story of Iso," Edith projected her own experience of oppression onto a fictional Chinese character. As the oldest female child, Edith shared with her mother the upbringing of all the younger children, a fact she mentioned in her autobiographical essays with pride as well as resentment. In "The Story of Iso," she has the young Chinese protagonist criticize her parents before a white stranger for their irresponsibility in having more children than they can support. By representing the problem in Chinese trappings, Edith inadvertently rehearsed the popular views that the Chinese multiply recklessly, exploit women and children, and enforce absolute obedience to the patriarchy.

The proliferation of such themes in Edith's early work suggests that she had demons other than white racism to fight. Like many Western women who lacked the language to talk about their own oppression, Edith found oriental patriarchy a clearer target. Furthermore, her knowledge of traditional Chinese culture was limited to issues Western evangelists dramatized for the benefit of Christian readers. Finally, the bulk of popular fiction—a genre Edith hoped to succeed in—turned on love and marriage. A novice in the field would have had little choice of subject matter even if there were other plots on her mind. It would take Edith many years to find ways to turn the humdrum daily lives of Chinese in North America into literature.

But why would Edith, who worked so hard as a journalist to desensationalize Chinatown life, resort again and again to melodramatic plots such as the above? For an answer, we may consult Edith's opinions on the role and power of art—opinions she would have shared with many late Victorians. In her article on Sarah Bernhardt written for the Jamaican *Gall's Daily News*

Letter, Edith described the hold that Bernhardt, whom she had twice seen perform, exerted over the audience:

> Many a woman moved by the great Tragedienne's art sat crying in her seat; many a man turned pale with emotion. As for myself, though the tears did not fall, they were behind my eyes as I turned and said to my companion— "Sarah Bernhardt is well on in years and her character has been reviled, but she is the greatest genius of the age, and if I were the richest woman in the world, possessed of youth and beauty and the love of many friends, I would exchange all and more to be a Sarah Bernhardt. One can defy age and the carping of envious tongues when one wields the power to move the hearts of hardened, worldly wise men and women." ("The Woman about Town: The Horse Car, Sarah Bernhardt" December 30, 1896)

Cathy Davidson (1986) and Jane Tompkins (1985) have written persuasively on the "power of sympathy" and the discourse of sentimentality in the eighteenth and nineteenth century. Claudia Tate (1992) enriched our understanding of the social role of sentimental fiction by theorizing about African American women's novels of the post-Reconstruction era. Many women writers embraced the "power of sympathy" in the absence of more direct means of effecting social change. Melodrama—the much maligned genre that seeks to evoke a spontaneous emotional response—was one that Edith understood to be most useful for communicating deep social problems to a less than sympathetic audience.[7]

The tragic ending has never been an unproblematic choice for Asian American writers. Asian immigrants and their descendants have long been expected to produce personal narratives of success, reflecting the spirit of individualism rather than community and highlighting economic and social mobility rather than the impediments created by racism. Edith's choice to write tragic stories, particularly ones in which Chinese inflict suffering on other Chinese, does pose a problem. If Chinese patriarchy, superstition, and traditional animosities between rival clans are the culprits, then the white readers' cultural prejudice is validated, no matter how much they sympathize with the stories' victims. Why Edith, who was more than sensitive to racial representations in the Montreal context, should have fallen into this orientalist trap as soon as she moved from reporting to art can perhaps be better understood with reference to the literary context.

Orientalist literature in contemporary magazines appealed to an audience hungry for exotica. Readers expected such "novelty" fiction to reaffirm existing notions of the East as a timeless, unchanging place ruled by a despotism that feeds on ignorance and superstition. Projecting anxieties about gender, race, and class inequalities in the West onto a fictional Orient was, and still is to some extent, standard practice. When the Chinese were not represented to reassure westerners of their own moral superiority, they appeared as figures of fun in poems, plays, and musicals. I would argue, then, that Edith saw in tragic fiction a way to counteract the pervasive tendency to ridicule and trivialize things Chinese. Much popular ethnography in the latter part of the nineteenth century posited the Chinese as a desensitized race that neither valued individual life nor felt the grief of bereavement. Such writers as the Reverend Arthur Smith, discussed in the preceding chapter, made this the central premise of their ethnographic work. For Edith to insist that the Chinese were capable of feeling—whether romantic passion, indignation, humiliation, grief, or heroism—was an important way to contest dominant discourse.

Establishing in the popular consciousness an image of the Chinese as sensitive people was one of Edith's priorities in the *Daily Star* writings. Aware that white Canadians had trouble empathizing with the Chinese, she opened an 1895 Christmas article with the following words:

> This is the season when the thoughts of absent ones turn towards home, and friends and relations meet to spend the hours in happy social intercourse; this is more than any other season a home season—a time for children to make merry and rejoice without restraint, a time when mothers, wives, sisters and sweethearts are made happy by thoughtful remembrances and grateful attentions, and husbands, brothers, fathers and sons forget that business is before pleasure. A glimpse into the Chinese laundries in this city sets one musing. How do these men who are far away from home and children and women spend their Christmas? ("The Chinese and Christmas")[8]

In this passage, Edith plucked her readers' tenderest heartstrings by asking them to position themselves as members of families and as lovers; she evoked conventional images of home, community, and celebration; and she elicited a gender identification from the reader before mentioning the Chinese at all. The Chinaman, Edith continued in the same vein, "might like to see his mother as much as you would . . . he might like to have by his side the girl to whom he was wed the day before he started for Canada." Those relationships, she implied, were what the white Canadian reader shared with the Chinese. Since in Montreal the Chinese were mostly male, Edith realized it was important that readers imagine them in social roles other than those they performed in the city. Countering the stereotype of the cold-hearted heathen, Edith offered a cultural explanation for the absence of emotional display among the men she represented. "The Chinaman does not carry his heart on his sleeve; he has affections, but he betrays them in actions, not words . . . he sends home every month a cheerful letter and, if possible, some of his earnings."

The proximity of Christmas and the New Year in the popular imagination allowed Edith to collapse Western and Chinese holidays into one long season of merrymaking. "The Chinaman in China is Sabbathless and Christmasless; the Chinaman in Canada respects the Sabbath and for all his loneliness rejoices when Christmas draws near. . . . So in many a Chinese laundry in this city are Christmas preparations being carried on. . . . The Chinese do not need to come to Canada to learn how to celebrate the New Year. . . . The Chinese New Year in Montreal is like their Christmas. They spend it resting and eating and playing games." In restating over and over the significance of Christmas for Canadian Chinese, Edith seemed to be deliberately confusing or blurring the differences between the supposedly conflicting traditions. Rest, rejoicing, gift giving, good food, and a general spirit of goodwill, she implied, are not specific to Christianity.

But writing about sameness does not sell—difference does. Occasionally Edith shifted the focus to features that distinguished Chinese celebrations from Canadian merrymaking. For one thing, the traditional gifts differed (and here Edith provided a catalog of exotic goods). As befit a Sunday school teacher, she also mentioned "ceremonies too numerous to be particularized [the names of which] would cause a humorist to smile and the sober-minded to sigh." Nonetheless, at the risk of writing a dull piece, she foregrounded the safe, ordinary pastimes, such as storytelling, theatergoing, or visiting.

In the long, cheery article there is only one darker paragraph that a mainstream reader primed by years of Chinatown reporting would expect:

> Gambling and opium smoking are somewhat indulged by our black sheep Chinamen on Christmas Day. Gambling is not considered unlawful during a holiday season in China, and it may be that our Chinamen have not changed their minds on legal matters since becoming natives of Canada. A few confirmed desperate gamblers are said to have an image made of wood on which is a painted tiger with wings. This image is of the God of Gambling, and is called "His Excellency, the Grasping Cash Tiger." The gamblers light incense and candles before it and cast lots with bamboo sticks.

While Edith knew of such practices from missionary handbooks and may even have visited a similar establishment with other Presbyterian activists, oddly enough, the language of the passage is devoid of the negative modifiers one would expect. "Our" Chinese gambler is neither immoral nor dissolute: he is simply unfamiliar with the law of the land. As for opium smoking and idol worship, Edith refrained from commenting on them altogether. These were marginal practices, she implied, indulged only by a handful of "our black sheep Chinamen."

Whereas laundrymen were an appropriate subject for reportage, they were clearly less so for fiction. As far as we know, Edith wrote only one fictional piece about a Chinese laundryman ("The Coat of Many Colors" 1902), and even here the protagonist's workplace is not shown. There are remarkably few references in her stories to working-class Chinese: she represented the merchant class or idealized laborers with middle-class aspirations. I would suggest, however, that for Edith the *labor* Chinese perform in America is incidental and does not define who they are. What defines her Chinese protagonists are their *family* relationships: the ability to love parents, spouses, and children, as well as to maintain family bonds while in exile. Disaster strikes when these bonds are severed and the memory of family, once central to the exile's consciousness, cannot hold. Thus, instead of a story about laundrymen, we get one called "The Gamblers" (1896), the first piece of Chinatown fiction Edith ever published.

An expanded version of the paragraph cited above, "The Gamblers" contains all the elements of the earlier piece: the confirmed desperate gambler, the opium, the Tiger God, and the gambling sticks. But this time there is no sympathetic voice to explain the Chinaman's inner world—only a dispassionate eye that registers his movements and an ear that picks up snatches of dialogue. The narrator takes Ah Lin from a rain-drenched street down into the underworld: through an opium den into a gambling house, where he loses his last quarter and then provokes a brawl. At the crucial moment, the light goes out. "Someone struck a light. The owner of the place picked up the fallen God and placed it on the table. It calmly looked upon two dead men" (18).

Perhaps the most important thing for us to learn from "The Gamblers" is that it was difficult for a Victorian woman to embrace a community of Chinese men as her own. Here, as in other fiction from this period, Edith seemed to be working out her anxieties about Chinese masculinity, male violence, and cultural practices she found disturbing yet was unwilling to discuss in the newspapers.

Of all of her writings, "The Gamblers" comes closest in style and thematic focus to naturalism. It is clear from the start that Ah Lin is buffeted by forces beyond his control, clutching at false hopes, about to sink. The effect of Edith's storytelling technique is one of emotional distancing of the writer from the protagonist, which also creates a distance between Ah Lin and the reader. By the end of the narrative, both the Tiger God and the reader "calmly look down upon" the body of the protagonist. The story's determinism, coupled with the stereotypical portrayal of Ah Lin—a man with a "bald face [whose placidity] one could not penetrate" (14)—may account for the fact that "The Gamblers" has received no critical attention. Edith herself did not return to like themes or create another male Chinese character with Ah Lin's shambling gait and expressionless eyes. In the future, she would people her fiction with the best of men: kind, faithful, brave, liable to err but quick to change old ways of thinking in the New World.

Personal accountability was, I believe, at the core of Edith's journalism. Montreal was not a large city so the two or three regular Chinatown reporters could not have remained anonymous even if their articles were. In addition, far from being all-white, the readership of the *Montreal Daily Witness* and the *Star* potentially included the wealthier English-speaking Chinese, many of whom Edith knew personally, as well as the adult members of the Eaton family. Whatever she wrote about the Chinese could have had immediate material consequences for their community. Moreover, she could be held accountable by those who knew her.

By contrast, the American magazines Edith wrote for were divorced from the local context. Their editors, W. B. Harte of the *Fly Leaf* and *Lotus* and Charles Lummis of the *Land of Sunshine,* had literary aspirations. This meant that politics had to be muted, subject matter aestheticized, and a certain degree of timelessness and universality assumed. Occasionally, the aestheticization was outside Edith's control, as in the case of her "The Story of Iso," which was published with illustrations copied from Japanese prints. Also, since there was a time lapse of at least several months between the writing of the story and its publication, a current concern might become dated. Edith aimed, not surprisingly, for broader and more generalizable themes. This was particularly important in the case of the California *Land of Sunshine;* here Edith's stories written in Montreal implied or claimed the West Coast as their setting. In transforming Chinatown material from reportage to literature, then, Edith all but erased such facts as exclusion laws, borders, and racism—of whose existence, as we have seen, she was acutely aware.

But I would contend that Edith was led to partially dehistoricize her material as much by the demands of art as by the conventions of ethnography. Out of the raw stuff of reportage came the refined product: a record of culture understood as something that has a life of its own, beyond historical events. Thus in her early fiction Edith drew on Doolittle and other missionary writers whose understanding of culture was organized around Chinese rituals, beliefs, and traditions that appeared to them anachronistic.[9] For instance, "The Story of Iso" contains a typical missionary catalog of rites and superstitions that the spunky heroine must outgrow with the help of a nameless "red-headed stranger"—possibly a missionary. "A Love Story of the Orient," published in October 1896, introduces a series of characters who become disillusioned with Buddhism, the Five Classics, civil service examinations, and arranged marriage. Like the missionary writers, Edith spoke out against popular and scientific discourses of Chinese as a morally and intellectually inferior race, locating their difference in culture alone. But while she denied that Chinese were stuck in a timeless, alien culture, they were interesting to her because they carried in them the seeds of modernity that allowed them to grow away from the exotic Orient toward the neutral West.

Defamiliarizing the Familiar

> In terms of its own metaphors, the scientific position of speech is that of an observer fixed on the edge of a space, looking in and/or down upon what is other. Subjective experience, on the other hand, is spoken from a moving position already within or down in the middle of things, looking and being looked at.
> —Mary Louise Pratt, "Fieldwork in Common Places" (1986)

Late in 1896, Edith replaced her younger sister Winnifred on the staff of *Gall's Daily News Letter* in Kingston, Jamaica.[10] In going as a reporter from North America to the Caribbean, Edith reenacted the classic journey of the ethnographer from the Western metropolis going to a South Sea island. For the next six months, she would document the daily comings and goings of "native" Kingstonians, study the workings of their institutions, and interpret cultural phenomena through the framework of her late-Victorian training in missionary and newspaper work. There are, however, several telling differences between Edith's enterprise and that of Western ethnographers. Most obviously, Edith had no formal training and was neither male nor white. Though among her contemporaries there were several self-taught female ethnographers, such as Mary Austin and Alice Fletcher, anthropology was still a predominantly male domain. Moreover, Edith moved not from the West to the Third World but from a British dominion to a colony. Most important, Edith's audience was in Jamaica, not in the metropolis, a fact that, as I demonstrate below, greatly complicated her ethnographic practice.

Jamaica had a British governor at the time, eleven appointed members of the legislative council who were either Englishmen or local planters, and eleven elected members, the majority of whom were men of color. Technically, black male Caribbeans had been eligible to vote since 1838, but legislative assemblies had found ways of substantially limiting the franchise. All power rested with the governor and his appointed members; the elected members could bring motions before the legislature, but they had no effective power.[11]

According to the historian Bridget Brereton, "[T]he white community remained to a significant degree socially aloof from the colored middle stratum and the masses until the postwar [World War I] years" (93). She also pointed out that while whites preserved their property rights through endogamy, "no formal system of apartheid existed and intimate relationships between whites, coloreds, and blacks, including sexual ones, continued to be formed" (95). Beside the three social classes enumerated here, Jamaica had a substantial Asian underclass. Between 1838 and 1917, 39,000 Indians and Chinese were brought to the island on an indenture system subsidized by the British and local governments to remedy the labor shortage and keep free blacks in check (Rogozinski 193).

Gall's Daily News Letter, the second largest of four Kingston papers, was the closest Jamaica had to an oppositional press, though the editor, William Morrison, shared many of the dominant elite's social and economic views. As a result of Morrison's overt criticism of Governor Henry Blake, the Crown government clipped the *News Letter*'s wings by effectively subsidizing its competitor, the *Gleaner.* To stay afloat, the *News Letter* had to court the remaining power groups on the island: the hoteliers, store owners, small manufacturers, and elected council members. Most of the paper's subscribers belonged to the white elite or Jamaica's mixed-race planter-manufacturer class. The staff was down to two writers: Morrison himself and a succession of Canadian women reporters, who could be paid less than men.[12] Morrison reserved for himself the writing of political commentary under various bylines. His reporter covered the "soft" side of local life: social events, fashion, various forms of overt and covert advertising, as well as the tedious shorthand reporting on legislative council proceedings. Advertisements and material culled from the London *News Letter* filled the remaining space.

Whereas most of Morrison's editorials were written in an impersonal, authoritative voice, Edith was evidently required to write in the first person. She duly developed a cheerful, sententious but pleasantly chatty persona named "Fire Fly," who advised the women readers on the best places to buy ham, cheese, ribbon, and lace.[13] Gradually, though, she began taking over from Morrison such highly charged topics as education reform and discrimination in the hiring of civil servants. On several occasions, her texts even made the front page. Aside from the fashion column, she wrote cutting social satire, began systematic reports on welfare institutions, tackled the absence of health care for the poor, and started a children's column.

My purpose, however, is to not to survey Edith's *News Letter* writings that appeared between December 13, 1896, and May 29, 1897. Instead, I want to ask what happens to a writer's sense of self when the power dynamics between the self and other are, for a brief time, reversed? That is, what happens when the amateur ethnographer used to representing an exotic Chinese minority to white Montrealers with whom she is culturally aligned must earn her living by representing the (exotic) Jamaican middle and upper classes to themselves?[14] How does she reposition herself in relation to the dominant group? What ethnographic strategies come into play? On what does she base her journalistic—and ethnographic—authority? As I try to work through Edith's shifting and often contradictory positionings, I argue that initially she emphasized the cultural distance that divided her from all Jamaicans, white and black. Over time, she came to align herself with the *News Letter* readership but would frequently defamiliarize that group's cultural practices by positioning herself as an outsider. I propose that unlike the tourists who were also strangers to the island but came with independent means, Edith was dependent on the local elite for subsistence; she thus started out in a position subordinate to the dominant social group. In addition, the rigid racial stratification in Jamaica made her deeply conscious of her racial identity, which, if revealed, would compromise her efforts at self-definition.

Before I discuss passages in which Edith reflects on her own predicament, it is important to point out that the well-to-do white and "colored" Jamaicans for whom she wrote knew themselves to be exotic in the sense of being located on the imperial periphery. Though the colonial elite subscribed to many of the same values and fashion magazines as did their Western counterparts, Jamaicans knowingly practiced mimicry with a difference. Following the collapse of the slave plantation system in 1838, which brought sugar exports down by two-thirds, the elite came to regard tourism as a panacea and was anxious to understand how Jamaica might be perceived by foreigners, the better to style it into a vacation resort (Taylor 101–3). Assisted by the Crown government, local businesspeople in the early 1890s invested a great deal to upgrade the hotel infrastructure, but the returns were disappointing. "Metropolitan interest waned perceptibly," wrote Brereton, "and the Caribbean colonies gradually became forgotten backwaters, familiar but uninteresting corners of the expanding British and French colonial empire" (86). Edith, despite her initial ignorance of local affairs, was valuable to the *News Letter* as someone who could reassure readers that Jamaica did indeed possess that elusive aura of the exotic.

Some of the first columns Edith wrote for the *News Letter* were entitled "As Others See Us." She was evidently encouraged by Morrison to draw attention to her status of recent arrival from Canada, which under other circumstances might have disadvantaged her as a reporter. "You know, I come from the land of ice and snow and the demonstrations I have been witnessing are a novelty to me," she wrote in her article "The Woman about Town" (December 14, 1896). A few days later, reporting on the island's greatest sporting event in an article entitled "The Races as Seen by Fire Fly," she confessed, "Even a stranger cannot resist the contagion of enthusiasm which seems to inspire everyone during race week" (December 16, 1896). In the Christmas Eve issue, Edith was given a whole page to sketch a portrait of her Canadian self. As late as February, she used the byline "A Canadian Fire Fly" under a commentary on race discrimination in the legal system, possibly to call up the authority of an independent Western observer.

Cast as an emissary from the West, Edith was also required to solicit other visitors' opinions of Jamaica. Like her predecessors on the staff, she was boarded at the elegant Myrtle Bank Hotel so that she might have access to foreigners. A typical interview Edith wrote up for the *News Letter* began, "As I entered the inviting reading room of the Myrtle Bank Hotel yesterday afternoon, I saw seated in an armchair and having a quiet chat with somebody else, a fine-featured old gentleman with white hair. I . . . was informed that they were Colonel Plant of tourist fame, and his son. Whereupon I walked in and intruded myself on them. I was in search of information" (February 5, 1897). The aggressive stance Edith adopted to secure such interviews indicates that reflections on the exoticism of Jamaica and news of any investment plans that foreign visitors might have for the island were at a high premium.

Though not as good as a cash crop, exotic difference could be commodified, but local inhabitants sought the opinion of strangers in the matter. As the designated stranger, then, Edith occasionally slipped thumbnail descriptions of Jamaica into her society column and made cross-cultural comparisons. "Jamaica is old-fashioned and romantic and lovely, and when I was a little girl I used to dream about its coral reefs and coconut palms and monkeys and parrots," she wrote on December 19, 1896. Defamiliarizing the familiar was her favorite strategy in those early days, as in the following passage: "I don't suppose I can tell you anything quite fresh, for you have all been there before, but to me the streets lined in gay attire, carrying all sorts of comestibles and oddities were indeed a novel sight, and sent my imagination spinning. You know, or perhaps you don't know that this is a very romantic atmosphere for a person who carries romance with her" (December 29, 1896). As much for herself as for the readers, she seemed to be trying to define the cultural differences she observed. "I became more than ever convinced," she wrote after seeing the races, "that Jamaicans are on the whole what is called a sporting people. We have sporting people where I come from, you know, but I'd never think of classing the whole country under that head as I do the people of this Island" (December 19, 1896). Elsewhere she rhapsodized:

> Jamaica is a musical country. Nearly everybody sings and nearly everybody can play some musical instrument. I think it is the beauty of the country which impresses itself unconsciously upon the people, forcing them to give expression to the harmony which surrounds them. . . . I can tell you, the loveliness of the scenery around the Harbour made a never-to-be-effaced impression upon the impressionable mind of the wanderer from the land of ice and snow. It was something unlike anything that can be seen in America. (January 11, 1897)

People and place collapse into one in this vignette, in the middle of which is the indispensable "wanderer"—someone who is in a position to hold a flattering mirror up to the Jamaicans.

Perhaps because writing in the first person made her self-conscious and because her foreignness was an asset, Edith shared with her readers some insightful reflections on the nature of ethnography. Had she been writing for a home audience, these brief self-reflections would probably not have been revealed. But Edith's position was unusual in that she was trying to articulate the nature of cross-cultural observation for the very people she observed. "You know in a crowd we can be very much alone—much more than we are sometimes in our own little room when the only bodily presence is our own small self, and so as I sat in that crowd, it seemed to me as if I were separated from it by many miles, and so being separated I began to study the people and criticize them in a way I would scarcely have dared to do had I felt them near," she wrote. Expressing cultural distance in spatial terms was as common in the nineteenth century as it is today, so it is not surprising that Edith understood her position in those terms. What is interesting is that while she admitted to having critical thoughts because of this sense of distance, she kept them to herself and instead scanned the horizon for cultural commonalities. Watching the races, she concluded that "whatever changes may happen—one thing is certain—that men and women will never cease to admire strength and courage." She did not know the names of the horses or their owners, but she "came very near to clapping and shouting like the rest of 'em—just out of pure sympathy" ("The Races as Seen by Fire Fly," December 16, 1896). Whatever jarring differences she observed on that day were suppressed as she worked to establish good relations with her readers. This would change over the course of her stay, but writing for her ethnographic subjects occasionally meant privileging sameness over difference.

When difference is her subject, it has to be exciting and positive—the kind of difference "to catch the fancy of the ennuied eye." Though she confessed the inability to "distinguish between what is wild and what is cultivated" and ignorance of the names of most "native wares" in the marketplace, she relished telling about the exotic. Writing about turkeys and chickens, she explained, is "not of sufficient interest to me. . . . It is what is curious and native to the place which attracts the stranger" (December 29, 1896). Though obvious, this is not a statement a fieldworker writing for a metropolitan audience would ordinarily make. Readers must assume that the ethnographic text is a well-balanced representation: why draw attention to the fact that one was skewing the image? Edith, however, knew that *her* readers would compare her depiction of the marketplace with what they had just seen there.

Perhaps the clearest indication that Edith had moments of anxiety when writing for Jamaicans is in the opening lines of her full-page Christmas medley: "I am a little puzzled about what I shall write for Christmas. I wish to amuse, but at the same time you must acknowledge it is rather hard trying to amuse those to whom you are a stranger." Loosely organized around the holiday theme, this autobiographical essay could be interpreted as Edith's attempt to exoticize herself and Canada for the benefit of those she had thus far been exoticizing: "Canadians enjoy reading about Christmas in the West Indies because it is so different from their own, and for the same reason you may like to hear about the festive Canucks" (December 24, 1896). There is a nice reciprocity in Edith's gesture and a willingness to look at Canadians as eccentric for the benefit of breaking the ice between her and her readers.

But such reminiscences are rare in Edith's newspaper work. During the first five or six weeks on the *News Letter,* her main occupation was what ethnographers call "studying up," in other words, studying groups higher in the social hierarchy than one's own. She was to report on what the middle- and upper-class Jamaicans were wearing, where they spent their leisure hours, and where they shopped. This she did by asserting "Fire Fly's" license to hover on the outer edges of Kingston society, "peeping" and making notes.

Although written in a racially diverse country, her Jamaican articles contain remarkably few references to race. Occasionally—and in this Edith followed the *News Letter*'s standard practice—race is coded as class. Jamaican readers were probably accustomed to decoding race from place names, family names, and other clues in the text. For weeks on end, the only representations of black people in the paper were in an advertisement for a local restaurant: a close-up drawing of a place setting, with little spear-wielding savages running among the silverware. Small and supposedly tame, they furnish a good illustration for the argument that at the turn of the century observing "primitive" Jamaicans in their habitat was promoted as one of the tourist attractions (Taylor 116–19).

Big holiday events, such as balls and horse races, gave Edith a panoramic view of Jamaica's stratified society that at other times of the year was far more compartmentalized. She would meticulously note the spatial relations between people on such occasions: who stood or sat to her left and right, above and below her. It becomes apparent when reading her texts that where she, the observer, actually stood in relation to the observed and where she subjectively positioned herself were not necessarily one and the same. To see this, we may compare two accounts Edith wrote of the same event. Early in January, the *News Letter* carried the story of a picnic organized by the planter Mr. Burke for his black workers. "It was jolly for Mr. Burke's employees to dance and feast and sing as they did yesterday and it was pleasant for Mr. Burke and his friends to watch them from the piazzas of his commodious residence, from which also the writer observed a splendid view of the surrounding country, a large expanse of which belongs to Mr. Burke" (January 2, 1897). This conventional representation of carefree blacks dancing on the plantation lawn seems to have left Edith dissatisfied, for two days later she rewrote it—as a sermon on the responsibilities of the wealthy:

> I was very pleased to have a peep at Mr. Burke's big picnic crowd. I like to see employers thinking of the happiness of those who work for them. It is to be hoped that the close of the holiday season will find many who have enjoyed its festivities with tender hearts and an earnest desire to help and sympathize with those who are wearing out the best of their minds and bodies in a battle for existence, and for the sake of others' happiness, for it is a fact that the many toil and suffer that the few may enjoy and be glad. Remember this all of you who find it easy and have reason to smile serenely when you come across those who have grown miserable and dull through "the grinding of the mill of the Gods." Some of those who toil and suffer in Kingston are little children and women. Think of the outlook for these women—old before their time, and in the midst of temptations to do wrong. When one looks at the lives of the very poor, one wonders not so much at the amount of vice amongst them, but at the number of good and true men and women who spring from such surroundings. (January 4, 1897)

Here Edith's Presbyterian upbringing comes to the fore as she figuratively steps down from Mr. Burke's veranda and takes a closer look at the faces in the dancing crowd. This is Edith's first attempt at serious moral commentary in Jamaica, as well as a return to her genteel but committed activism, a penchant for which she had developed in Montreal. Starting in February, she would write one reportage after another that would explicitly or implicitly argue that structural discrimination rather than any racial predisposition was "the cause of the cause" of what white Jamaicans called the "laziness of the labouring class" (February 8, 1897).

One explanation for such a turn in her reporting could have been a personal one. There is no question that white Jamaicans were a close-knit caste: as late as February 14, 1897, Edith wrote about going to church with a friend one Sunday and being hounded from pew to pew three times by hostile and proprietary parishioners. It may have been around this time that Edith's racial identity became publicly known. Although in her memoir "Leaves" Edith wrote very little about Jamaica and nothing on how the disclosure came about, she did dwell on the humiliation of being eroticized by white men who perceived her as colored: "When it begins to be whispered about the place that I am not all white, some of the 'sporty' people seek my acquaintance. . . . One evening a card is brought to my room. It bears the name of some naval officer. I go down to my visitor, thinking he is probably someone who, having been told I am a reporter for the local paper, has brought me an item of news." Instead, she encountered a young man several years her junior who proposed going for a sail in the moonlight so that he could tell her "all about the sweet little Chinese girls I met when we were in Hong Kong" (226).

Timing might also have had something to do with Edith's shift of interest from the broad theme of colorful, flamboyant Jamaica to the systematic investigation of "how the other half lives." The holiday season was drawing to a close, and the newcomer's self-consciousness was wearing off, as was the island's exoticism in her eyes. By February, she was making fewer cross-cultural comparisons and had settled into the life of the small town where everyone knew everyone else. When she no longer felt surrounded by a generalized difference and when the people she met on her rounds became old familiars, Edith made time between her regular duties to find difference in such institutions as the prison, poorhouse, orphanage, and industrial school. How much her new role of *exploratrice sociale* was self-motivated and how much it had to do with the editor's local politics is difficult to say.[15] Certainly in the eighteen months before her arrival, the paper showed little interest in the affairs of the poor, limiting its coverage to petty court cases involving the working class. That Edith restricted her interest to institutional sites traditionally visited by *exploratrices sociales* places her squarely within that tradition; there is no indication that she ventured out of town into the black farming communities. If she had informal conversations with black, Indian, or Chinese laborers, they did not appear in print.

Her brief reports from the government-run prison and poorhouse insist on bringing before the readers the people society removes from sight: criminals, the elderly poor, and the physically disabled. Her studies of the charity schools and orphanages are long, detailed, immensely sympathetic to both the children and their supervisors, and driven by Edith's belief in the transformative power of these institutions. Two questions absorbed Edith on these field trips: whether education could transform the children of Jamaica's abject, unruly poor into productive citizens with solid Christian moral values and what role unmarried middle-class women might play in the process. Today's readers may be unconvinced by Edith's breathless praise for the charity institutions she visited and her representation of them as havens run by motherly nuns and fatherly clerics on supremely rational principles. But if the Caribbean was the forgotten backwater of Europe's empire and if the Crown government was so negligent of social welfare that as late as 1921 only 50 percent of Jamaicans were literate and most had no access to medical care until the 1960s, then Edith's excitement at seeing these remarkable social experiments was justified (Brereton 86–103; Rogozinski 197).

Edith's praise for the aptitude of the children of color—who include one "Coolie" (Indian or Chinese) child—was directly proportionate to the racial prejudice she registered around her. Had she not known that her readers doubted the intellectual and moral capacity of other races, there would have been no reason to detail the accomplishments of the children at Alpha Cottage and the Industrial Farm School.

> The very little children in the Elementary School took my fancy wonderfully; black eyed, round-headed chickabiddies. One little Coolie girl of three or four years of age gave us a recitation in a pretty baby voice in a manner which would have reflected credit on a child of seven.[16] The penmanship in all the classes showed not only careful teaching on the part of the teachers and attention on the part of the pupils, but an aptitude for forming letters which I could not but remark upon. As to the behavior of the pupils, I must say I have never seen a better and more docile appearing lot of youngsters. (February 2, 1897)

In both schools, Edith was received as a guest of honor; the Industrial School children even got half a day off to show her around their banana plantation and perform for her in their "fife and drum band." What the children were right then, she insisted, was but a shadow of what they would become under the nurturing care of their teachers. The reclaiming of these children is paralleled in the text by the children's successful reclaiming of "what was but fourteen months ago a wilderness": "I thoroughly enjoyed watching the streams of water flow over the land, and I think the little fellows enjoyed it too, for they laboured with hearty good will to divert the courses of the streams to the thirsty banana roots. Some of the trees were already bearing fruit. . . . all the sixty-five boys on the farm are on their way to be men. Sixty-five boys saved to be useful is something for the country" (February 16, 1897). *Succor, save, rescue, restore,* and *reclaim* are the verbs Edith used to describe the educators' mission. That they did so independent of the government was the mission's greatest merit. Here, as in many other pieces from this period, Edith sought exemplary grass-roots initiatives "carried on without Government aid"—aid that she surely realized would not be forthcoming.

In urging individual readers to take responsibility for restoring abandoned waifs "to the wicked world" (February 2, 1897), Edith echoed the creed of missionaries she had worked with among the Montreal Chinese. Unlike nineteenth-century racial determinists, missionary ethnographers did not see race as a fundamental problem; instead they focused on culture as a finite set of learned beliefs and behaviors. They studied other cultures to more effectively eradicate paganism and replace it with Christianity (see chapter 1 for a discussion of the missionary ethic). Here Edith suggested that the problem with Jamaican rural poor was also one of "doing," not "being." And ways of "doing" things could be altered through human intervention, as she argued in another article: "Now these people, in order to become an intelligent working class should be made to see the dignity of labour, and the only way to attain this end is by educating them to labour. Free born, educated men regard work as a blessing. Slavish and ignorant people regard it as degrading and something to be shunned whenever it is possible. I do feel sorry when I hear people declaring that education destroys the children of the labouring class" (February 8, 1897). In line with Booker T. Washington's widely accepted theory of uplift through industrial education, this argument may seem shortsighted and of limited value. The language of compulsion ("should be made to see") has an authoritarian ring to it. However, when we remember that Edith herself was taken out of school at the age of twelve to earn her living at lacemaking and street vending, it becomes apparent that her argument was not intended to patronize Jamaican blacks. Edith made it plain that her support for the industrial education scheme was motivated by a lack of alternatives, not by the belief that black children were incapable of benefiting from a liberal education: "The Industrial School boys are taught gardening, carpentering and painting, the girls everything that will make them good domestic servants. They will never set the world on fire, but they will be able to work and get enough to eat, and what more can a boy or girl sigh for. If they lived in America or even in the old country, it might be worthwhile to have some ambition, but in Jamaica the wise ones are those who hope for little" (February 2, 1897). Rather than read these reports as Edith's endorsement of industrial education for Jamaica's people of color, we should see them as an early plea for public elementary education, which would not be available for decades to come. To promote the schools and help the educators raise funds, Edith advertised them as near-idyllic havens, but she was certainly aware of their limitations.

Edith's perception of herself in relation to her journalistic/ethnographic subjects seems to have evolved during the course of her stay in Jamaica from a sense of estrangement from an undifferentiated otherness (white and black) to a constant shifting between a tentative alignment with the dominant group as she "studied down" and an equally tentative identification with the disempowered blacks, women, and children as she "studied up." Empowered by her professional license to roam where other women could not, "Fire Fly" kept writing across race and class lines and where neither her predecessor, "Kodak," nor her replacement, "La Petite," cared to tread. A parallel change seems to have occurred in Edith's attitude toward government institutions and the press as tools of reform. Though she was swept up by an electoral campaign on her arrival, she must soon have realized that Jamaica's representative government was a fiction and that the British and local ruling elites combined would effectively block social and political change. As the long hours of note taking at the courthouse, legislature, and city hall stripped her of respect for the Crown government, she was increasingly drawn to people who worked around, or in spite of, the administration. Edith's last contributions to the *News Letter* were three short stories for children on May 29, 1897. Soon afterward, she left the island exhausted and sick with malaria. For about a year, she remained in Montreal and then moved to the West Coast of the United States.

Edith did not establish the rapport with black Jamaicans that she had had with the Chinese in Montreal. Strict conventions circumscribed interracial contacts on the island, and there was no equivalent of the Chinese missionary society to mediate the racial boundary. But Edith did arrive at a clearer understanding of the systemic discrimination used to subordinate people of color in the island colony. She demonstrated this in her articles on the lack of educational and job opportunities for people of color and on the unequal treatment of blacks and whites by the justice system.[17] Fifteen years later, she would write in her memoir, "Occasionally an Englishman will warn me against the 'brown boys' of the island, little dreaming that I too am of the 'brown people' of the earth" ("Leaves" 225). Rather than an expression of Edith's consciousness in 1897, this statement may well reflect a thought process that took many years to complete. But if the younger Edith came to recognize that the possibility of being racialized made her somehow like the "brown people" of Jamaica, she could not have articulated that affinity or questioned the racial status quo without incurring a high cost: her acceptance as a journalist depended on her being perceived as white.

Edith's texts written in Montreal in the mid-1890s and in Jamaica in 1896–97 show a radicalization of her thinking about race and a growing sensitivity to the material consequences—both for herself and for her subjects—of talking about people of color. Her exposure to the problems of the ghettoized Chinese Canadian minority was mediated by missionary discourses and thus exacted from her a long-term commitment to those I have been calling the "deserving heathen" (see chapter 1). In Jamaica, her moral, political, and ethnographic focus necessarily became fragmented. Each day brought new social problems to investigate: the elderly in the poorhouse, the criminals in jail, the black boys in the orphanage, even the typists in law offices. It may well have been the frustration of having to spread herself too thin that led Edith to write a review of Kate Douglas Wiggin's just published novel *Marm Lisa*. The review foregrounds a minor character, Mrs. Grubb, a social activist whose fatal flaw is lack of focus and consistency. Mrs. Grubb dabbles in "Delsarte, Physical Culture, Dress-Reform, the Blue Glass Cure, Scientific Physiognomy, Phrenology, Astrology, Vegetarianism, Single Tax, Evolution, Christian Science Spiritualism, Theosophy, and Hypnotism" (*Gall's Daily News Letter*, February 9, 1897). The review makes no mention of the fact that Mrs. Grubb's antithesis in the novel is a single-minded progressive young educator (styled on the author herself) who runs a kindergarten for San Francisco's urban poor. The kindergarten is located on the edge of Chinatown. Two white kindergartners wander into the infamous quarter, lose their way, and are looked after by kind Chinese strangers before being returned home in the morning. Within a year of her departure from Jamaica, Edith herself would be living on the edge of San Francisco's Chinatown and, no less single-mindedly than Wiggin's protagonist, pursuing one—Chinese—cause.

3. Subjects of the Gaze

WHO IS ENTITLED to look at and represent whom is a charged question in a racially stratified society. As the Vietnamese American critic and filmmaker Trinh T. Minh-ha pointed out, "We have been herded as people of color to mind only our own cultures. Hence, Asians will continue to make films on Asians, Africans on Africa, and Euro-Americans . . . on the world" (*Framer Framed* 164). The publishing establishment has traditionally steered Asian American writers toward ethnography or autoethnography, genres that are, as a rule, optimistic about the United States and sell well because they give mainstream readers a sense of being open-minded and tolerant of difference. Biracial individuals have often been cast in the role of cultural go-betweens. As one commentator wrote of Onoto Watanna, being "a daughter of a native mother and of an English father . . . makes her perhaps the best interpreter of Japan and the Japanese who is writing today."[1] Ambitious to write, both Edith and Winnifred Eaton made the most of this common assumption, despite the limitations and vulnerabilities that came with the role. In this chapter, I consider the ways in which such factors as local and international politics affected Edith Eaton's publishing opportunities, as well as the form and content of her writing. I first look at Edith's entanglement in California race and class politics in 1898–1903, a period during which she wrote ethnographic fiction on the West Coast Chinese for Charles Lummis, editor of the *Land of Sunshine*. The account then follows Edith from the West Coast to the East, where in the years 1909–12, in a very different political climate, she published some of her longer and more complex fiction and essays on race relations. In a close reading of two stories, "Mrs. Spring Fragrance" and "The Inferior Woman," I suggest that by reversing the conventional positions of the observer and the observed, Edith began to probe the politics of ethnography.

Parables for Progressives in the *Land of Sunshine*

> Allegory prompts us to say of any cultural description not "this represents, or symbolizes, that" but rather, "this is a (morally charged) story about that."
> —James Clifford, "On Ethnographic Allegory"

In December 1905, the *Chautauquan* devoted an entire issue to China as part of a series on the "Orient" that started with Japan. Included in the issue were articles entitled "China, the Sphinx of the Twentieth Century," "The Teachings of Confucius," "A Reading Journey through China," and one piece of fiction: "Aluteh" by Sui Sin Far. A biographical note on the author published in the same journal six months later explained her biracial heritage. What is puzzling about "Aluteh" is not that the *Chautauquan* editors chose to publish Edith Eaton's tale as a piece of Chinese literature ("Aluteh" is, after all, set in China, in an unspecified time, and reads like a folktale). It is, however, surprising that having volunteered since 1895 as a teacher in Canadian and American Chinatowns, where the most pressing concerns were exploitation, lack of legal protection, and job and housing discrimination, Edith continued for so long to produce morally charged romantic "Chinese" tales much like her *Land of Sunshine* work.

Edith not only had done a good deal of Chinatown fieldwork since those early days but also had spent half a year as a politically engaged journalist in Jamaica. Judging by her journalism from this period, reporting had heightened her awareness of institutionalized race and class inequalities and authorized her to speak her mind on public affairs. In retrospect, she would write that the cultural contrasts she encountered made her feel as if she were "born again" ("Leaves" 225). Certainly the first story she sent to the *Land of Sunshine* after returning to Montreal, the semi-autobiographical "Sweet Sin" (1898), suggests that she was ready to take on racism and the meaning of race. "Sweet Sin" recounts a series of traumatic incidents from the childhood and adolescence of a biracial Chinese American that lead her to reject a marriage proposal from a white man and choose suicide rather than "return" to a China she does not know. The text resonates strongly with the opening chapters of Winnifred's novel *Marion* (1916), also an attempt to deal with the traumas of growing up biracial in Montreal. Edith's story is an early effort to describe the process through which a child is racialized by the gaze and language of white children and adults. "It's just because I'm half-Chinese and a sort of curiosity [that Mrs. Goodwin] likes to have me there. When I'm in her parlor, she whispers to the other people and they try to make me talk and examine me from head to toe as if I were a wild animal—I'd rather be killed than be a show." Racial identity, then, is understood as something imposed on the subject by the dominant culture—something to be resisted rather than performed. While Sweet Sin protests being racialized,[2] at the same time she begins to express her subjective experience of race as essence, in terms dictated by dominant discourse: "My Chinese half is good and patient, like all the Chinese people we know, but it is my American half that feels insulted for the Chinese half and wants to fight. Oh, mother, mother, you don't know what it is to be half one thing and half another, like I am! I feel all torn to pieces" (224). The story is an important first attempt to thematize race. Yet after a series of disturbingly realistic vignettes that would become the core of "Leaves from the Mental Portfolio of an Eurasian" (1909), the narrative takes a melodramatic turn, ending with the protagonist's suicide and the scattering of her ashes in the middle of the Pacific.

Edith neither abandoned the melodramatic mode after moving to the West Coast nor laid aside the Reverend Justus Doolittle's missionary ethnography, *The Social Life of the Chinese,* discussed in chapter 1. Doolittle's descriptions of Chinese rites and rituals continue to appear in Edith's stories, such as "The Horoscope" (1903), and Chinatown articles written for the *Los Angeles Express* in 1903. How, then, can we explain the fact that, notwithstanding better opportunities for "participant observation," for the next six or seven years Edith would continue to write stylized tales with little bearing on the living conditions and practical concerns of turn-of the-century Chinese in California? And if she was "born again," where should we seek the change? To answer these questions, I examine two aspects of Edith's literary association with Charles Lummis, editor of the *Land of Sunshine:* the role Edith played in his magazine and the role the *Land of Sunshine* played in her career.[3]

To understand these reciprocal functions, we need to look at not only the magazine text in which Edith's stories appeared but also the extra-textual context of California's intersecting class and race relations that is programmatically ignored in the pages of *Land of Sunshine.* In discussing the magazine's context, I refer to the three types of texts it carried most consistently: articles promoting settlement and investment in California; ethnographic studies of Native Americans as well as Spanish and Mexican settlers; and elite regional literature—fiction and nonfiction written primarily by recent migrants from New England. I argue that whereas Edith believed she was writing literature, Lummis published her pieces as fictionalized "native ethnography," that is, the study of an ethnic group by a native informant. This, I suggest, had serious consequences for the form and content of Edith's writings.

That Lummis, generally a stickler for "authenticity," was willing to pass off Edith's first four contributions postmarked in Montreal as stories about California Chinese suggests that he had a stake in representing this group in the *Land of Sunshine.* At first glance, every racial and ethnic group in California gets some representation in the magazine. Yet the token presence of the Chinese in the *Land of Sunshine* is offset by the erasure of the white working class from its written and visual text. The land of sunshine boasts row upon row of orange trees that need no pruning, gardens that need no tilling, and magnificent structures that need no builders.[4]

Looking at this peaceful glossy landscape, one can easily forget that at the turn of the century California was racked by some of the worst class and race antagonisms ever. According to the historian Alexander Saxton, beginning in the 1860s and 1870s, white labor unity in California was built around the question of Chinese exclusion. The interests of the white labor alliance conflicted with those of the moneyed class that relied on a Chinese labor pool and worked to stall exclusion legislation. It was largely the California entrepreneurs who subsidized the *Land of Sunshine* and middle-class progressives in and outside the state who subscribed to it. Among the progressives were intellectuals and churchgoers who rejected the wage-earners' view of the Chinese.[5] Having a regular "Chinese" contributor may have helped the progressives associated with the *Land of Sunshine* to see themselves as a tolerant and enlightened class defined against the Chinese-hating "sandlot hoodlums" and unionists.[6] Edith's sex and genteel aesthetic would have made her a particularly suitable spokesperson for the Chinese.

By no means do I want to argue that these circumstances were wholly responsible for the fact that Edith's stories continued to appear in the *Land of Sunshine* for eight years. That Edith maintained a cordial correspondence with Lummis nine years after he had published her last story indicates there was an affinity between the author and the editor. Edith found in Loomis an editor passionately interested in race, who combined his interest in anthropology with his literary interests.[7] Like his mentor Adolf Bandelier—an anthropologist and the author of a novel of ancient Pueblo life, *The Delight Makers* (1890)—Lummis believed in the importance of popularizing ethnographic knowledge. He himself contributed over 250 ethnographic pieces, editorials, fiction, and verse to the magazine (Bingham 82), and he pursued his own vision of racial justice, even to the point of taking on the calling of "My Brother's Keeper."[8] He appears to have appreciated the moral seriousness with which Edith invested her Chinatown work. Though he rarely published more than one of Edith's "sketches" per year, other editors consistently rejected her work; her letters to Lummis show that she appreciated this steady outlet.

Since the *Land of Sunshine* was mostly Lummis's brainchild, subordinated to his own and his sponsors' interests, it is worth looking at some of Lummis's exploits before he took on the magazine's editorship in 1895. Son of a Methodist seminary professor and itinerant minister, Lummis shared his father's moralistic turn if not his religious convictions. After dropping out of Harvard on the eve of his graduation, Lummis mapped out his own itinerary in 1882: a walking trip from Ohio to California. What began as a commission from the *Los Angeles Times* for articles written on the road turned into a position as city editor of the *Times*. While Lummis's itinerancy completely redirected his career, the historian Edwin Bingham pointed out that it had another, equally important, formative outcome: "The Southwest had made an impact on Lummis in many respects as potent as a religious conversion, with the result that he became a self-appointed and zealous missionary in its name" (108). Under Bandelier, he spent four years doing archaeological and folklore studies in the Southwest, Peru, and Bolivia, before settling into the editorship of the *Land of Sunshine*. In this capacity, Lummis played a key role in transforming the physical and cultural landscape of Southern California between 1895 and 1909.[9]

His periodical sought to define the meaning of California for both insiders and outsiders and to create a regional identity for the wealthier newcomers from the East. In subscribing to the moral values and aesthetic of high culture, as well as the ideology of regionalism, the *Land of Sunshine* had much in common with such East Coast magazines as the *Atlantic Monthly* and *New England Magazine*. Its regionalism served primarily the cultured elite, functioning, to use Richard Brodhead's words, as "an exclusion mechanism or social eraser, an agency for purging the world of [working class] immigrants to restore homogeneous community" (136). Like the quality East Coast magazines to which Brodhead is referring, the *Land of Sunshine* "produced the foreign only to master it in imaginary terms," while excluding "the ethnic groups associated with contemporaneous industrialization" (136–37). In his editorials, Lummis always represented the *Land of Sunshine* as an ambitious, self-made journal. In fact, despite a steady circulation of 9,000 to 12,000 in the years 1895–1904, it was never profitable and, relying on corporate sponsorship, it retained its promotional character (Bingham 57–62). As the real estate boom began in the 1890s, Lummis refashioned the *Land of Sunshine* into a regional literary journal and turned his Pasadena home into a regional salon (Davis 24–27). Grace Ellery Channing was a frequent contributor as well as coeditor in 1898–99. William E. Smythe, Charlotte Perkins Stetson (Gilman), Mary Austin, and others textualized the land, extolled its climate, and commemorated its native peoples. The magazine also spearheaded a campaign against the takeover of Indian lands and the federal policy of inducting Indian children into segregated schools.

On reading any issue of the *Land of Sunshine,* an inherent contradiction becomes apparent between Lummis's secular mission to preserve Indian lifeways and lands and the aggressive "selling" of the region to potential white settlers from the East and Midwest. Lummis's informal training in ethnography was, arguably, what enabled him to work around that contradiction. George Stocking, James Clifford, and others have claimed that ethnography at the turn of the nineteenth century served as the "conscience" of Western imperialism, claiming to "salvage" the worlds that were fast "disappearing" before the inevitable march of modernity. Clifford pointed out that "the very activity of ethnographic *writing*—seen as inscription or textualization— enacts a redemptive Western allegory" ("On Ethnographic Allegory" 99). One of many believers in the redemptive power of ethnography, Lummis also, in Clifford's words, "assumed that the other society is weak and 'needs' to be represented by an outsider (and what matters in its life is its past, not present or future)" (113). His magazine not only enshrined living Native Americans but also served its readers as a much needed conduct manual on relations with people of color.

Alongside his efforts to popularize regional ethnography through the *Land of Sunshine,* Lummis pursued his interests through the Southwest Museum, which he founded. According to the historian Curtis Hinsley, anthropological museums evolved as a postbellum cultural phenomenon that dehistoricized and commodified American Indians by "encasing [them] in time and space" (170). Under Lummis, the museum and magazine worked in tandem. In an article appropriately entitled "Catching Our Archaeology Alive," Lummis demonstrated how his team at the Southwest Museum recorded the words and music of Mexican and Indian folk songs and stories. "The speech is unwritten, and our civilized government is permitting the monuments and ruins to be pillaged infamously to the six winds. . . . We have killed off our schoolmasters without bothering to record the lesson!" he declared (36). Ten accompanying photographs of old Indian men and women drove home the fact that the "schoolmasters" were indeed dead or dying. For whom, then, was the record? Lummis made it amply clear: "We must not think of these songs as worthy of *salvation* only that scientists may dissect them for ponderous monographs. They are distinctly human in their value. We need them in our *pleasure.* If ever there is to be a real American music, these are the rock upon which it must be founded" (38, emphasis added). The music and oral literature of tribes in the decline, once recorded, could be appropriated by the rising white Western culture.[10] The ideology of ethnography thus allowed Lummis to solder together the otherwise incompatible elements of the magazine—selling the region, saving its native inhabitants, and creating a new regional cultural identity for the white elite. Instead of seeing themselves as impostors who displaced native peoples from their lands, the enlightened newcomers could salvage what remained of the old culture and celebrate it by incorporating its elements into the new. This, I suggest, is one of the underlying allegories of the *Land of Sunshine,* one it rehearsed month after month.

The Chinese whom Edith represented in the *Land of Sunshine* tales (several of which I discussed in chapter 2) were, I believe, an integral element of that allegory. Unlike Native Americans, the Chinese were not indigenous and were ineligible for citizenship. Consequently, they did not have a moral claim to protection, nor was their culture perceived as assimilable in the way that elements of Native American art, music, and oral literature could be appropriated in an effort to revitalize Western culture. But Edith's Chinese added "color" and variety to the region's ethnography; they also constituted a disappearing race (albeit one whose disappearance was being engineered by means of exclusion laws). Eaton's stylized tales, which often end with the protagonist's suicide, intraracial murder, or voluntary return to China, may have enacted for Lummis the larger allegory of the races. Anthropologists had long argued that Chinese culture was either arrested in development or regressing on the evolutionary scale. Although the "Mongolian" race was not in danger of extinction, Chinese culture could not, scientists believed, withstand competition with the youthful, energetic Western civilization. As I argued in chapter 2, the tragic ending that Edith strategically used to elicit the reader's compassion and respect for the Chinese, may, in fact, have played into popular opinions about the destiny of the Chinese in America. In representing the passing of the Chinese, the *Land of Sunshine* thus reinforced white hegemony on the West Coast.[11]

Edith functioned in the *Land of Sunshine* as both fiction writer and native informant, a voice ambiguously positioned between the makers of high culture, such as Mary Austin and Grace Ellery Channing, and the occasional nameless or named Mexican and Native American informants who told their folktales to the white ethnographer or made impassioned pleas against civil rights violations.[12] As Minh-ha astutely pointed out, "being merely 'a writer' without doubt ensures one a status of far greater weight than being 'a woman of color who writes' ever does. Imputing race or sex to the creative act has long been a means by which the literary establishment cheapens and discredits the achievements of non-mainstream women writers" (*Woman, Native, Other* 6). Yet we must realize that it was because Lummis perceived Edith as "a woman of color who writes" that he published her stories at all, for his elite journal mostly solicited the work of recognized authors and the editor's personal friends.

A footnote in an 1899 issue described Edith as a "bright little Chinese woman" who wrote "simple" and "naïve" stories. It was four years after publishing her first story, "Ku Yum," that Lummis included a biographical note and photograph of Edith in his column, "In Western Letters." Though Lummis gave her parentage accurately, nowhere did he mention her English family name. The biographical note reveals what Lummis valued most about Edith. He began by saying that she was "the only Chinese woman in America who is writing fiction" and that she was a "discovery" of his magazine. Her race gave her a "unique" insight into Chinese life on the West Coast and "intimate comprehension" of "her people." The text is studded with terms derived from race theory, including "breeding," "our strenuous Saxon blood," "native perception," and "birthright." Edith's frailty, implicitly linked to her mixed blood, is precisely what makes her interesting.

As did Winnifred's reviewers, Lummis described Edith's work as "unstudied" and "simple"—bare story without "literary graces"—and made a virtue of the fact. Though she wrote to him about her work in Jamaica, Lummis omitted the crucial fact that Edith was an experienced journalist. There is, in fact, evidence that Lummis encouraged Edith to produce short tales about Chinese "types," allowing no room for character development or psychological depth. In a letter to Lummis on June 30, 1899, Edith wrote, "I suppose you exchange with the 'Overland.' They have a long story in their July number called 'A Chinese Ishmael,' which I would like you to read. It is almost four times as long as any that I have written for the *Land of Sunshine,* but your magazine wants quality, not quantity."[13] Elsewhere, she thanked Lummis for his "skillful editing" of another story; we can only guess at what was edited out in the process.[14] Evidently Edith trusted Lummis's authority to discern literary quality, and if she questioned the limits he placed on the length of her stories, she did so obliquely.

It is tempting to assume that Edith's poor health and lack of leisure—she supported herself as a stenographer throughout her life—prevented her from writing longer, more developed pieces. Yet when given the chance, she did produce somewhat longer fiction in the same years. In an October 8, 1900, letter to Lummis she even mentioned having written a play that she had compressed "so that it was no longer a play but a story of 10,000 words" and that it still failed to meet publishers' requirements, being "too long for an ordinary magazine short story—and yet not long enough for a serial." I would argue that to publish at all, Edith continued to accommodate Lummis's predilection for short romantic tales of Chinese love and death.

What little work she managed to place in other magazines adheres to the romantic convention, but, with more strongly defined political themes, it reads better by contemporary aesthetic standards. "A Chinese Ishmael," published in July 1899 in the *Overland Monthly,* for instance, though it leans toward sensationalism, does describe at length how the Six Companies functioned as the economic and legal backbone of the San Francisco Chinatown. "A Chinese Boy-Girl," published in April 1904 in *Century Magazine,* explores a conflict between a white missionary and the Chinese community that entrusts its children to her care. "The Coat of Many Colors," published two years earlier in *Youth's Companion,* reveals the inconsistencies of the ideology of American individualism, which was used to brand the more community- and family-oriented Chinese culture as backward and alien. The story is a serious discussion of Chinese immigration in which Eaton foregrounded the racist attitudes that imposed "sojourner" status on Chinese laborers, precluding permanent settlement. Several stories in *Land of Sunshine* also tentatively probe the meaning of race, but the aesthetic of the short romantic tale does not allow for more than a hint of the larger historical context.

Though Edith may not have realized it, Lummis had no special interest in the Chinese as an ethnic group, nor did he believe they could or should become American citizens.[15] Commenting on the war in South Africa in his editorial column, "In the Lion's Den," in December 1899, Lummis, a staunch anti-imperialist, wrote that "economically [the British] occupy precisely the same relation to the Transvaal that the Chinese do to California. They are aliens, here to make money and take it home. Do we let the Chinese vote?" (50). Even more tellingly, he linked California's Chinese with the potential threat of mass immigration from the Philippines in his column in February 1900: "We cannot keep out nor fine the products of our new 'possessions' [the Philippines] which raise the same things as California does. We cannot shut subjects of the United States out of the United States, as we can—and have been obliged to—the alien Chinese" (193). Lummis shared these opinions with the progressive farmers and manufacturers, whose limited tolerance for the Chinese was linked to the fact that they relied on Chinese labor either directly or as a potential strikebreaking force (Saxton 232). But as Saxton explained, when the Geary Act of 1892 excluding Chinese labor immigration for ten years came up for renewal, anti-Chinese rhetoric and harassment became pervasive, subsuming the counterarguments of wealthy progressivists. Pressure to permanently exclude Chinese climaxed in 1901—

the year Edith disappeared from the *Land of Sunshine*. Though she wrote Lummis at least twice in 1901 and sent him at least one story with "more in it—both work and thought—than in any other story that I have written" (letter of January 8, 1901), her foothold in the magazine had evidently given way. Well after Chinese exclusion had been secured, after the Sinophobic frenzy had subsided, and before the new anti-Japanese frenzy erupted, Lummis did publish one more story by Edith, "The Horoscope," in November 1903.

Annette White-Parks discussed "The Horoscope" as a romance of star-crossed lovers that ends happily ever after through the agency of the unconventional female protagonist (121–22). It can also be profitably read as an allegory of the artist's tenuous position in society and a thinly disguised story of Edith's three-year publishing hiatus. The protagonist, a fortune-teller who takes his profession very seriously, loses his entire clientele when he refuses to tell a patron what the patron wants to hear. When he loses his clientele, he also loses his authority and the chance to marry the woman he loves. "Men are easy to please, so long as one seeks but to please; but when one tries to act in accordance with the truth, then they are difficult indeed to serve," he muses. After a reconciliation with the testy patron, the other regular customers also return, once again investing the fortune-teller with authority. "It takes little to make or mar a fortune-teller's fortune," concludes the narrator (24). As it happened, the story expressed wishful thinking, not fact: Edith did not manage to secure the favor of her most reliable patron. Neither were other editors forthcoming.

If the severing of ties with the *Land of Sunshine* released Edith to try her hand at other kinds of writing, one could equally well argue that for years afterward she tried to replicate the formula that brought her the recognition of the man of letters who was making a major impact on Southern California as a political activist, ethnographer, and historian. That Lummis's fictionalized ethnography and transcriptions of Indian folklore had become for her a measure of quality and a model is apparent in the following excerpt from a September 16, 1900, letter to Lummis: "There are quite a number of your books in the Seattle library—more than I found in Frisco. I suppose that is because the people in the former place are more interested in Indians. I'm not specially interested in these people (Indians). I'm interested in the books." An unusual apprenticeship is in evidence here: a Chinese-English-Canadian writer learning to think ethnographically from Charles Lummis, who, in turn, had apprenticed himself to the anthropologist Bandelier, who studied directly under the founder of American ethnography, Lewis Henry Morgan.[16] But whereas Morgan, Bandelier, and Lummis collected oral history and data on cultures they believed to be passing away, Edith had a stake in representing a Chinese American culture with a future, not just a past. Zora Neale Hurston, who trained under Franz Boas in the late 1920s, experienced a similar conflict when she began to study black communities in rural Florida through the "spy-glass of Anthropology."[17] In Edith's earliest stories, most of the Chinese protagonists either die in America or leave, but over time Eaton began to assert more forcefully the possibility of survival and settlement. Such is the case in "The Story of Tin-A" (1899), "The Horoscope" (1903), "A Chinese Boy-Girl" (1904), and several others. When she solicited oral history from her informants—many of her stories are structured as interviews with immigrant men and women—her interest in the past was different from that of professional anthropologists. The anthropologists sought clues of the origin and migrations of the races as encoded in folklore and human physiology, or they recorded the history of disappearing tribes for academic and popular consumption. To Edith, oral history was useful because it individualized the "heathen Chinee" for the white reader, revealed qualities of mind and spirit that went against the stereotype, explained diverse motives for coming to America, and showed the Chinese to be full participants in the American ethos.

"The Story of Tin-A" exemplifies the way Edith negotiated a compromise between editorial demands and the desire to present the case of the Chinese to California's white middle-class. The story can be read as a well-crafted tale posing as an ethnographic account or else as a piece of fictionalized fieldwork. The external narrator, a person of unspecified race and gender, provides a frame by recounting a chance visit to a Chinese farmer's home somewhere in rural California. At the center of the story is a moving narrative of women's friendship and adventure told by an elderly Chinese woman. The traveler represents him/herself as a skillful observer: he/she reads not only the Chinese characters above the door but also the faces of the hosts, the food on the table, and the lush flower garden outside. Yet the text implies that without the initiative to ask tactful questions and listen attentively to the answers, the traveler might have left with little more than a pleasant impression of a "stalwart Chinaman in a blue blouse" (100) and a glimpse of an aged and unbeautiful Chinese woman's face among the geraniums.

Intrigued by the Chinese woman—city merchants, scholars, and diplomats but not farm laborers could legally bring wives to America—the narrator asks the farmer about her. When the farmer suggests that his companion should speak for herself, the narrator does not immediately ask the questions that are on his/her mind, "Who was she? Why was she living there?" as a detached investigator might. Instead, the narrator chooses to observe the conventions that govern the meetings of social equals. The narrator invites the woman to share the meal and begins talking about the flowers outside. The exchange turns out to be more than small talk, for the Chinese woman's "knowledge of the life of plants amazed me." From botany they move on to the subject of America, and again, the interlocutor makes "original remarks." Only then does the narrator say, "I drew her out to talk of herself, and here give her story as she related it" (101).

The summary of Tin-A's story sounds fanciful: to avoid becoming the second wife of the man to whom her best friend is already married, Tin-A runs away from home with a company of actors. She crosses the ocean with them and sells her jewelry for a piece of California land, where she settles with the stage manager and his wife. On the surface, the story dwells on the cultural differences that vexed Christian missionaries. Tin-A's father has several wives and presses her to become the second wife of a man who is already married to her best friend. The friend is about to become a "discarded wife" because she has not given her husband a son. In response to Tin-A's pleading against the marriage, her father puts down his patriarchal foot and says, "Foolish girl, if you do not go to Ah Kim, he will choose some other" (102).

If we read the story carefully, however, it becomes apparent that instead of condemning polygamy, the author attempts a balanced representation. First, that Tin-A's father had secondary wives turned out to be a blessing when Tin-A's own mother died: "my father's secondary wives were always very kind and treated me like a young and favorite sister" (102). Because of the support of this extended clan, Tin-A has happy memories of her childhood. Second, the traditional patriarchal family is not the only model available in China: the marriage of the older couple whom Tin-A joins is evidently built on mutual respect and partnership. Third, traditional Chinese literature (such as the play Tin-A watches in her father's home) transmits through the generations alternatives to absolute filial obedience. Admittedly, the only recourse Tin-A has is drastic, since it involves severing family ties. Nonetheless, she needs no prompt from outside of Chinese culture to assert her subjectivity. But perhaps the most interesting twist in the story is that upon reaching America, Tin-A settles contentedly into a ménage à trois. The stage manager, his wife, and Tin-A reconstitute the Chinese family as best they can; Tin-A points out that it was her own choice not to marry in America. And as the narrator notes when entering their home, inscribed above the door are the words, "Here is Peace" (101).

The story is a good one. Having elicited it, a detached investigator might have closed the interview and gone on his or her way. But not Edith's narrator. As he/she is about to leave, a wistful look on Tin-A's face prompts a question about her emotional well-being. "'Am I happy?' she repeated. 'How can

I be happy when the greatest of all sins is to sin against one's parents? Ah, no. Heaven will surely punish me for my unfilial conduct. And yet—I am not altogether without gladness, for I know that I saved Ah-Ho much pain'" (103). Thus the story's last paragraph denies the reader access to easy interpretations of all that went before. After all, what we have read is more than an exotic adventure story; it is the story of a troubled, dislocated life. Tin-A now comes across as an intensely self-aware woman who understands the moral complexity of her decision.

To ask whether the story of Tin-A is "true" seems less to the point than whether it does something creative to change the way Americans perceived Chinese women at the turn of the century. The figure of Tin-A may be a composite of several individuals or altogether fictional. But the author uses specific details to make the portrayal credible, such as the fact that Tin-A was born in Formosa and so is not Cantonese like most Chinese in America. We even learn that Tin-A likes to munch lumps of sugar and has teeth "like two rows of fresh sweet-corn" (101). While the romantic story line makes for an exciting read, Tin-A, because of her age, experience, intelligence, and ungainly features, is not a typical romantic heroine. Perhaps the most remarkable element of the account is the deep respect with which the interviewer approaches the subject.

Furthermore, the Chinese in the story appear to be settled for good. They make a good living off their *own* land in California and have no intention of returning to China. Since the three are independent producers, they do not appear to be competing with white settlers and definitely do not fit the category of "cheap Chinese labor." If anything, they possess the "rugged individualism" that Americans claim to be part of the national character. As for adaptability—here are a professionally trained actor, his wife, and a wealthy tea-planter's daughter growing flowers and vegetables.

In a footnote to "The Story of Tin-A," Lummis explained that the author had written "several simple, naïve, human stories of California Chinese" (101). In the light of the above discussion, the irony of Lummis's comment should be apparent. Edith's strength as a writer was not that she knew a good story when she heard one or that she used her familiarity with the Chinese to solicit such stories and retell them for the enjoyment of the white readership. It is easy to forget that Edith's biracial status did not necessarily give her privileged access to ethnographic material. Neither did she produce straightforward transcriptions of oral narratives.

Reading her work today, we need to recognize that she made nuanced choices about how to represent people of color. This is perhaps best seen if we compare "The Story of Tin-A" with a thematically related story by Mary

Austin, "The Basket Maker" (1903). In Austin's account, Seyavi, an elderly American Indian woman whom the narrator recognizes and celebrates as an artist, does not tell her own story. Instead, the omniscient narrator tells it for her, proposing that "every Indian woman is an artist—sees, feels, creates, but does not philosophize about her process." Seyavi, then, is at once herself and an Indian everywoman. Her relation to the land is almost mythical: "The weaver and the warp lived next to the earth and were saturated with the same elements" (94). But being so close to nature, Seyavi cannot appreciate the true significance of her art. It takes a speaker from "our kind of society" to wrest her "golden russet cooking bowls" from the wear and tear of everyday use, "coveting them for my own collection." The narrator claims authority to tell Seyavi's tale on the grounds of having "been there": "To understand the fashion of any life, one must know the land it is lived in and the procession of the year" (99). The beautifully crafted descriptions of nature and the Indian village prove that the narrator does indeed know and understand. When Seyavi opens her lips during the course of the story, it is to utter the riddles of folk wisdom so the need for a professional interpretation goes without question. It is through the agency of the white narrator that folk wisdom is transformed into Art. In sum, while both "The Story of Tin-A" and "The Basket Maker" are based on (real or imaginary) encounters with older women of color, the narrators' position in relation to the subject determines who gets to speak and who interprets the moral of the story.

Although "The Story of Tin-A" is an interesting case in point, Edith used omniscient narration as often as Austin did, and her writing is certainly not free from patronizing gestures toward the Chinese. We must therefore be prepared to deal with the fact that often in an attempt to write "ethnographically" and at the same time to rewrite mainstream definitions of Chineseness, Edith *did* make choices that in retrospect seem problematic. The tight publishing market for nonmainstream fiction would have made it tempting to play up the exotic potential of the Chinese subject matter. Part of the problem lies in the very nature of ethnography, which assumes that there is a cultural difference that needs to be explained to a Western audience. What the ethnographer must therefore do is identify the peculiar and unintelligible aspects of the non-Western culture and, using his or her authoritative knowledge, render the unfamiliar in familiar terms. Not all peculiarities will do—only those that are attributable to a whole culture or subculture. The emphasis, then, is on the typical, the recurrent, the representative, to the exclusion of the peculiar in the sense of "unique." Such assumptions guiding cross-cultural studies had definite consequences for the settings, central events, and character constructions in Edith's stories.

In a sense, all of Edith's characters were representative types by virtue of being among the few available media portrayals of the Chinese. The characters were also representatives of certain classes or occupations: sing-song woman, gold prospector, sailor, seamstress, slave girl, market gardener, laundryman, merchant, fortune-teller, and so forth. But Edith was less interested in the jobs her subjects performed than in the circumstances that made them laundrymen or slave girls and the dreams that sustained them. For instance, having identified the protagonist of "A Coat of Many Colors" as a laundryman, Edith made no further reference to his work, for she consistently maintained that the Chinese take up certain occupations in America out of economic exigency, not as something to which they are essentially predisposed. This was a remarkable claim at a time when women's periodicals informed their readers that Chinese men made good servants; left-wing activists cast Chinese laborers as servile and therefore at odds with the American independent producer ethic; and the press represented Chinese women as both hypersexed and submissive. When sing-song girls and laundrymen appear in Edith's prose, they have usually been something else in China (scholars, merchants, ambitious younger sons, or daughters of impoverished families), and they treat menial work solely as a means to an end—as did the author.

If I am correct in arguing that Edith was perceived by Lummis as a native informant/ethnographer rather than a woman of letters, it is easier to understand why in her *Land of Sunshine* days she rarely overstepped the boundaries of her narrowly defined "field." Though Mary Austin and Charles Lummis practiced amateur ethnography in the Southwest and acted as self-appointed spokespersons for native peoples, they wrote with equal authority about westerners of all races. Austin, for instance, placed as much emphasis on the white settlers' experience as on the Native Americans'. Having started out as a naturalist, she also developed a short story genre in which the region functioned as a fragile ecosystem; here the land, flora, fauna, and human inhabitants, Indian and white, were leveled.

Once typecast as a "Chinese" ethnographer, however, Edith did not have the same license as Austin and Lummis to choose her subjects. It is apparent from a January 30, 1897, letter to Lummis written in Jamaica that she had internalized not only the assumption that her racial background predestined her for Chinatown "fieldwork" ("It was my ambition to have made a little name writing Chinese sketches") but also the dominant definition of her "field" as minor.[18] Although in the same letter she announced her intent to "write some West Indian stories—some day," she must have encountered a lack of editorial interest in a "Chinese" writer's observations of the West

Indies. It was not until 1911, when editing her collected works, that she included a single story set in Jamaica.

Arguably, then, using a Chinese byline and specializing in Chinatown ethnography undermined Edith's authority to textualize other people of color. Despite her deep interest in interracial relations, in seven of the ten *Land of Sunshine* stories, Edith represents Chinatown as virtually homogeneous, with barely a hint of the society at large. Interracial conflict is displaced in these stories by intraethnic friction caused by traditional patriarchal institutions. Those stories that do not fit the mold—"Sweet Sin," "The Smuggling of Tie Co," and "The Coat of Many Colors"—indicate that Edith did see Chinatown culture as evolving partly in response to Western incursions into Asia, white racism, and the exclusion laws. Nonetheless, she continued to write ethnographic tales because they were in demand.

Below, I consider several later stories in which Edith did turn the ethnographic gaze on white Americans and begin to articulate her own ideas on epistemology. Her role in the *Land of Sunshine* precluded reflections on the politics of ethnography: to have claimed a space in the magazine was an achievement in itself. Extolling California's many advantages over the East Coast, Lummis maintained that here "man has elbow-room and nature is not jostled off the earth" ("In the Lion's Den" January 1900). There *was* no elbow-room in California for Native Americans and Chinese, something Lummis knew full well. Along with most of his white contemporaries, rich or poor, Lummis believed both these groups would eventually disappear from California's landscape. His primary concern as ethnographer and local activist was that they not disappear without a written trace and that their passing not be effected by inhumane means.

My intention here has been to show some of the circumstances in which Edith's vocation to represent the Chinese minority in the American press took shape. It is ironic and at the same time revealing of the politics of ethnography that her work should have been absorbed into Lummis's project. If we read the collected volumes of the *Land of Sunshine* as a scripture that reinvents California's past and present for its new cultural elite, Edith's Chinese tales function as parables within it rather than as attempts at realistic representation.

For one determined to write on things Chinese, there was no ready literary tradition in English besides the missionary writings.[19] The stories of the Old and New Testament—stories Edith taught in Chinese Sunday school—were arguably her single most important model, their short format and moral seriousness being well suited to both her didactic bent and the word limits dictated by magazine editors. If Edith described her experience in Jamaica as one that made her feel as if she had been "born again," as a Christian she used these words knowingly. The "parable" form she adopted was an expression of her missionary bent. Having started out in Montreal as a missionary to the Chinese, Edith retained the zeal and sense of responsibility to the Chinese but applied them to converting the white American mainstream to a gospel of interracial harmony.

Reversing the Ethnographic Gaze in *Mrs. Spring Fragrance*

> And then he stared at me with all his might.
> —Edith Eaton, "Sweet Sin"

> After the negritude movement's reversal of the European gaze, after anthropology's crise de conscience with respect to its liberal status within the imperial order, and now that the West can no longer present itself as the unique purveyor of anthropological knowledge about others, it has become necessary to imagine a world of generalized ethnography.
> —James Clifford, *The Predicament of Culture*

By the end of the nineteenth century, many formalized ways had emerged in which the white American public could observe people of color. Racial difference was staged for mass consumption in ethnographic museums, world's fairs, Chinatown tours, and freak shows.[20] As one journalist remarked after a New Year's visit to the San Francisco Chinatown, "The Chinese are not the only ones to 'make hay while the sun shines.' White men have fake museums in the quarter, showing vividly colored daubs of mermaids, headless beings, human snakes, and other impossible oddities. They even hire cheap Chinese bands to play inside, and the banging of cymbals and rolling of drums attract crowds" (W. Wood 16). Newspapers and magazines supplied readers with firsthand reports on the Igorots of the Philippines and the Siberian Chukchee, while for those with more leisure and resources there was tourism. Most of these ways of knowing non-Western cultures privileged the gaze. Verbal communication between the observer and the observed was understood to be impractical in view of language barriers and time constraints. Observation became central to the new academic anthropology. When face-to-face communication came into play, it generally served to solicit myths and legends rather than knowledge about the subjects' present-day condition. The rise of ethnographic cinema after 1895, Fatimah Tobing Rony has suggested, was contingent on the belief that the bodies and movements of people of color captured on film "could serve as an unimpeachable index of race" (4) and as a record of vanishing lifeways that could be stored in a drawer (48). Whether in professional or amateur ethnography, the roles of the observer and the observed were assumed to be fixed: the white male or female subject looked at and interpreted the person of color. What passed between them was a unidirectional, objective, knowledgeable gaze. The fiction of that unidirectional gaze supported the belief in white Western superiority—a sense of superiority that was available to professional and amateur observers alike.

Having early been placed in the position of the scrutinized racial other—all the more curious and rare because her hybrid features blurred the pure racial categories that her observers were anxious to keep intact—Edith Eaton went on to forge for herself a professional writing career based on the study of the Chinese in America. On the one hand, the role of cultural mediator and writer of ethnographic fiction enabled her to define herself as a middle-class professional woman in spite of the stigma of race. On the other, her ambivalent racial status sensitized her to the politics of ethnographic investigation, so that unlike contemporary white ethnographers, she did not leave unproblematized her own position and authority as purveyor of knowledge about the Chinese. In a close reading of two stories, "Mrs. Spring Fragrance" (1910) and "The Inferior Woman" (1910), I demonstrate that Edith anticipated the turning of the ethnographic gaze that would occur in the wake of decolonization, when more people of color began to enter literature and academic anthropology—fields that I suggest here have considerable overlap. These and other stories Edith wrote toward the end of her career introduce the idea that the observer can also be the object of the curious or bemused gaze and that ethnographic interest may be mutual.

Besides the obvious fact that Edith wrote about a minority group for a mainstream audience, there are a number of telling similarities as well as some startling differences between her practice and that of academic ethnographers. Edith's writing career roughly overlaps with the formative years of modern ethnography in America. As she began to venture among her "own mother's people" in Montreal in the 1890s and subsequently into Chinatowns across the United States, anthropologists were also responding to, as well as generating, an interest in non-Western cultures. Previously they had relied on fragmentary data channeled to the Western metropolis through commercial, colonial-administrative, and missionary networks, but with Frank Hamilton Cushing's pioneering work in Zuni Pueblo (1879–84) and Franz Boas's sojourn on Baffin Island (1883–84), new standards were set for the practice of ethnography. In the 1910s and 1920s, "intensive fieldwork, pursued by university-trained specialists, emerged as a privileged, sanctioned source of data about exotic peoples" (Clifford, *The Predicament of Culture* 24). As outlined by George Stocking, fieldwork by participant observation requires the investigator to enter as a stranger into a "small and culturally alien community [and become] for a time and in a way a part of its system of face-to-face relationships" (*Observers Observed* 7). Since this specifies neither the length of stay nor the degree of involvement in the community, it is broad enough to accommodate a Chinatown English teacher and writer like Edith.

Parallels between Edith's self-positioning and that of white ethnographers become apparent when we look at questions of social status afforded by studying and writing about the Chinese, the writers' community of reference, and their language proficiency. New evidence throws light on Edith's self-perception: an anonymous article, "The Persecution and Oppression of Me," published by the *Independent* in August 1911. I attribute the article to Edith based on a combination of stylistic, thematic, and biographical details that link it with her "Leaves from the Mental Portfolio of an Eurasian."[21]

Because, as far as we know, Edith devoted her free time to teaching and writing about the North American Chinese, Annette White-Parks and other critics have tended to see her as strongly identified with the Chinatown communities for which she worked. Yet as she explained in the 1911 article, while she was proud to claim Chinese "blood," Chinatown remained for her a culturally alien ground: "Tho my left half is Chinese, yet I have been brought up among Europeans, and for many years my circle of friends and relations embraced no Chinese save one parent" ("Persecution" 426). That Edith's most intense and rewarding contacts—those that yielded the bulk of her story material—were with Chinese merchants and their wives is probably related to her own sense of class status. When they were offended that she preferred the company of whites, she admitted, "[I]t is hard for me to explain that there are class distinctions as well as race, and that it would be quite beneath my dignity, and certainly of little benefit to them, for me to tramp around with them to 10-cent shows and Chinese banquets, as do these women who have nothing better to do" (426). This statement is a far cry from the confessions of contempt for his subjects made by the ethnographer Bronislaw Malinowski in a diary that dismayed the anthropological community when it was published in 1967.[22] Nonetheless, Edith's anonymous disclosure of sentiments she must have felt was a call to rethink the dynamics that develop between the ethnographer and his/her subjects or between the Chinatown Sunday school teacher and her students.

Edith was far too invested in dismantling the binary of "racial superiority" and "inferiority" to set herself above the Chinese on racial grounds. In fact, when her white landlady suggested Edith might be "brighter than the ordinary Chinese" because she was half-white, Edith snapped back that she hadn't "the slightest doubt [she] is superior to a great many *whites* because [she] had *Chinese* blood in [her] veins" (424). In this article, she did, however, claim a class-based ethnographic authority. In an interesting rhetorical move, she had a Chinese voice invest her with it. As Chinese people told her, "You know more about the Chinese than the Chinese do themselves. But you live with the white people and you must love them best" (426).

The paradox of Edith's predicament is that although she lived with the white people, she clearly could not "love them best." For even as she identified culturally with the "respectable middle class," she complained bitterly that it was "the class which is the most antagonistic of all to the 'different'" (421). The article is constructed as an indictment of white middle-class racism. It piles incident after chilling incident of the narrator's encounters with bigotry and discrimination whenever she disclosed her racial identity. In contrast to the self-righteous but ill-bred whites whom she had seen "eat fish with a knife (and not silver either)" (423), she defined herself as a genteel woman of letters. Thus when reading Edith's work as an ethnographic record, we should not lose sight of the material and emotional price she paid as an openly biracial woman and spokesperson for the Chinese, nor should we elide the fact that her hard-won professional status was built on practicing ethnography from a distinctly middle-class perspective.

One other barrier that would have made it difficult for Edith to relate to the majority of Chinese immigrants was language. Though Edith maintained contacts with Chinese immigrants for over eighteen years, she spoke with them mostly in English. In this, she differed little from professional ethnographers, who seldom learned more than the rudiments of their subjects' language, using the services of native interpreters whenever possible. In an earlier essay, she wrote that "save for a few phrases, I am unacquainted with my mother tongue. How, then, can I expect these people to accept me as their own?" ("Leaves" 227). Only upon settling in Boston around 1911 did she find the leisure to systematically study Cantonese and was "in the habit of giving about half an hour to a Chinese manual every morning" ("Persecution" 422).

Yet as she became a more sophisticated fieldworker and established closer ties with her Chinese informants, Edith's early stance of a scout venturing into little-known territory on behalf of the white reader (discussed in chapter 2) gave way to an alignment with the Chinese she represented. Also belying the assurance of one who knows "more about the Chinese than the Chinese do themselves" is her growing awareness of the limitations of ethnography as a method for studying non-Western cultures. Symptomatic of this change is a series of texts that work against the assumption of a unidi-

rectional ethnographic gaze. To illustrate what I mean by the "unidirectional" gaze, I briefly examine two contemporary descriptions of American Chinatowns: one by a male academic, the other by a female tourist.

As I mention in chapter 1, China and Chinese expatriate communities were
of marginal interest to American anthropologists, who, having assigned to
Asians a relatively high position on the evolutionary scale, focused their attention on "primitive" cultures. Stewart Culin, author of several articles
published by the *American Anthropologist* in the 1890s, was a notable exception. In the opening of his article "Social Organization of the Chinese in
America," Culin claimed the Philadelphia and New York Chinatowns as "the
field of my observations" and stated, "I have seen the founding and development of several Chinese colonies, and watched their growth" for over ten
years (347). During this time, he established a working relationship with the
Lees of Philadelphia, a clan of laundrymen and merchants. Although in writing the article Culin had presumably questioned his Chinese informants
about clans, wages, and the Chinatown justice system, the passage that au-
thenticates the collected information is a description of the author's method of observation in the Lee pharmacy: "The mild-featured shopkeeper
would put on his great rimmed glasses and pore over a book, while I, a privileged person, would recline on the mat behind the peephole, in the little
apartment back of the shop, and watch all that happened" (349). Here Culin
emphasized the exclusivity of his gaze—its privileged status—for it is that
which transforms a jumble of facts into academic knowledge. The ability to
look without being seen, to follow the goings on in the store with an intensely
curious but supposedly detached gaze, also afforded Culin a good deal of
pleasure: "I can well remember the delight I had in the little store" (349).
Nonetheless, for contemporary readers, both lay and professional, his stance
at the peephole served as a guarantee of objectivity.

Culin did not dwell on Ah Lee's drug prescriptions or collect Chinese superstitions. Despite its disturbing power dynamics, his article comes across
as relatively free of sensationalism, in contrast with the bulk of Chinatown
tourist accounts in popular magazines of the day.[23] Not so Olive Percival's
"An Afternoon in Chinatown," published in the *Land of Sunshine* in 1899—
a striking example of observation-based Chinatown reporting. What is particularly interesting about this text is that it makes the reader the subject of
the gaze: "Gliding silently along the streets, or posing about the gloomy doorways, you see brightly-clad creatures, whom you have previously met only
on tea chests and fans. . . . You pass the Chinese theater . . . If you carry a
camera, you may be favored with a few little smiles" (50). In Chinatown, we
are entitled to peer into private doorways and take snapshots of the "crea-

tures" who stand about "posing." As we look through Percival's eyes at the exotic Chinese who are always already known, she initiates us into the camera-toting tourist ethic.

But had Percival stopped at describing that which was accessible to the eye of a white pedestrian, there would have been no story to tell. She brought in the expected exotica by detailing what we *do not* see: "This dame . . . did not come from the foot-binding section of China and so her feet are of natural size. She is a fine lady and does not whiten her face with rice powder, nor redden her lips" (51). A second way to exoticize what would otherwise be a commonplace street scene is to supplement the ordinary with extraordinary conjectures. She did just that: "That wonderful personage standing there in the shadow box of his own doorway is a wise and great doctor, skilled in the healing virtue of dragon's blood, bodies of lizards and snakes, dried blood and teeth of the tiger" (50). While the descriptions are so stereotyped as to be almost tongue-in-cheek and the reader is taking only a hypothetical Chinatown tour, the ethnographic "information" supplied by the narrator need not be taken as hypothetical.

Guiding us through Chinatown streets, Percival mentioned that we may be "inspected with interest" (50) by Chinese children. Only once, though, did she reveal the discomfort felt by an outsider aware of being the subject of an intelligent, resentful gaze: "That stupid, uninteresting coolie standing there on the edge of the unswept pavement (apparently unaware of your appearance) may suddenly turn and in very plain English hurl the old fact at you that his nation was civilized before the advent of Abraham, Isaac or Jacob" (51). Yet none of the Chinese the narrator paraded before us spoke, though she admitted that they might. We must ask no questions, and they must not speak, for if they did, Chinatown would be stripped of its mystique.

However influenced Edith may have been by such orientalist writings— and even her biographer conceded that Edith subscribed to a "benign Orientalism" (White-Parks 200)—she spent a good deal more than an afternoon in Chinatown, having made the study of the Chinese in America her vocation. If we choose to think of Edith's *Mrs. Spring Fragrance* (1912) as an ethnography—a book that brings the daily lives, customs, rituals, and lore of one ethnic group before the scrutiny of another—then the texts that open the book, like any self-respecting scholarly introduction, should provide a lens through which to view what follows. Interestingly, whereas conventional introductions try to establish the ethnographer's authority and the reliability of his or her research methods, the first two stories in *Mrs. Spring Fragrance* play with the limitations of ethnography. But the most remarkable aspect of the two opening stories, "Mrs. Spring Fragrance" and "The Inferior Woman," is that in turning the ethnographic gaze on white Americans and in parodying fieldwork, they foreshadow the self-reflexive current in contemporary ethnographic thought.

The two stories first appeared in *Hampton's* in 1910. Published around the time Edith moved to Boston, they were probably written before she left Seattle, where she had lived since the late 1890s. Both stories are set in the same middle-class Seattle neighborhood, where the "Americanized" Mr. and Mrs. Spring Fragrance live next door to the Chin Yuens, a traditional Chinese family, on one side and the Anglo-American Carmans on the other. Although I discuss the stories as ethnographic, the configuration of the three homes is probably allegorical rather than factual. It allowed Edith to explore on the basis of a simple model the negotiations that go on in what Mary Louise Pratt in *Imperial Eyes* called the "contact zone"—between the Chinese and American culture. The symmetry of this model integrated quarters is reflected in the neighborly interactions through which all three families are busy learning from each other, contrary to the American belief that minorities must assimilate to the dominant culture.

The first story, "Mrs. Spring Fragrance," reverses the reader's expectation about who is a fit object of study for whom. It is the Chinese immigrant, Mr. Spring Fragrance, a young, successful curio merchant, who conducts an informal investigation into the meaning of love in American culture—an issue in which he has a stake, for he suspects that his "Americanized" wife has formed a romantic attachment to another man. Eavesdropping, both accidental and intentional, is one method by which Mr. Spring Fragrance gathers information—a comic rendition of the fieldworker's ideal of seeing/hearing without being seen/heard. The value of this method is called into question right from the start, when Mr. Spring Fragrance tries to make sense of a fragment of poetry he overhears his wife reciting. Addressing her young friend Laura Chin Yuen, Mrs. Spring Fragrance explains that the two lines come from "a beautiful American poem by a noble American named Tennyson":[24] "'Tis better to have loved and lost / Than never to have loved at all" (18). The fragment is doubly decontextualized, since Mr. Spring Fragrance overhears it detached from the rest of poem and then interprets it without reference to the conversation in which his wife happened to cite it. The couplet becomes the crux of a series of cultural misunderstandings that nearly wreck the Spring Fragrances' marriage. What the reader knows but Mr. Spring Fragrance does not is that Mrs. Spring Fragrance has never loved anyone but her husband and that she quoted Tennyson to console the younger woman who was to give up her sweetheart and marry a man chosen by her parents.

Much as the fieldworker would consult a "native informant," Mr. Spring

Fragrance leans over the garden fence and has Will Carman, his white neighbor, explicate the Tennyson couplet. The two exchanges between Will Carman and Mr. Spring Fragrance share an unusual dynamic. Mr. Spring Fragrance asks most of the questions (eight in all). He decides when to change the subject, makes several pointed remarks about racial discrimination, and cuts the discussion short on both occasions, leaving without ceremony. Since the Chinese were known for their deference to whites, Mr. Spring Fragrance's controlling manner sets him apart from the stereotype.

Edith was determined to have fun at the expense of Carman, "a star student at the University of Washington [who] had not the slightest doubt that he could explain the meaning of all things in the universe." Posturing as an authority on the subject of romantic love, Carman offers nothing but clichés, while "more than a dozen young maidens 'loved and lost' were passing before his mind's eye" (19). That his idea of love is far from representative of most Americans' raises questions about the reliability of "native informants."

But the informant is not, Edith implied, the main reason for the failure of Mr. Spring Fragrance's investigation. Rather, his flawed assumptions and critical apparatus are at fault. Like his white scholarly counterparts, Mr. Spring Fragrance assumes that romantic love is essentially un-Chinese and comes as part and parcel of "Americanization." Now that his wife has been in the United States for five years, Mr. Spring Fragrance considers her to have undergone the full transformation: "There are no more American words for her learning," he says proudly (17). On the "Americanness" scale, whose existence he assumes, he scores below his wife but above his neighbors, the Chin Yuens. Consequently, while he spends his time plying Will Carman with questions across the fence, he never once considers Laura or her sweetheart, Kai Tzu, as authorities on the subject of love.

Another dimension in this ironic commentary on ethnographic investigation is provided by Will Carman, who is planning to exploit his contacts with the Seattle Chinese "to get in a scoop." An amateur reporter for the *Gleaner*, he is "delighted" when Mr. Spring Fragrance invites him to a Chinese party and even envisions a catchy headline: "A High-Class Chinese Stag Party." Significantly, he pleads with Mr. Spring Fragrance not to "invite any other white fellows" (23). As suggested by Culin's "exclusive" scoop on the Philadelphia Chinese, ethnography sells best when there is a scarcity of information about the exotic community to which the investigator has privileged access.

If the first readers of *Mrs. Spring Fragrance* expected a narrative of strange goings-on in Chinatown, perhaps something a Will Carman might have penned, they probably found the first two stories disconcerting. The most

Chinese thing anyone does here is to fold a fan. The Spring Fragrances lead well-regulated, respectable lives. They read the paper, celebrate a wedding anniversary, and take walks in the park. The matchmaking in which Mrs. Spring Fragrance dabbles actually goes against Chinese tradition, for the matchmaker conspires to break up one match so that four star-crossed lovers might marry people of their own choosing. While in San Francisco, she visits friends who have new babies, is taken by a white friend to hear a lecture on "America, the Protector of China," and makes fudge. Only the flowery prose of her letters home, presumably translated into English, creates a comic effect and prevents the narrative from becoming too ordinary.

By denying that there is an essential difference between Chinese and Americans, the text conflates cultural differences in an idealized diverse but integrated middle-class culture. "In China it is different!" (24) asserts Mr. Spring Fragrance, frustrated in his efforts to understand the American concept of love. But having read the story, we know better than to trust his authority. Whom, then, can we trust as an authority of things Chinese? And who may authoritatively write about America? How does one establish the authority to write? For whom does one write? The difficulty of claiming the authority to write, of establishing one's agency in a male-dominated society is the theme of "The Inferior Woman," the second story in the volume. As Mrs. Spring Fragrance sets out to study the "interesting and mysterious" Americans, the story reverses Edith's practice of studying the Chinese. "Many American women wrote books. Why should not a Chinese? She would write a book for her Chinese women friends. The American people were so interesting and mysterious. Something of pride and pleasure crept into Mrs. Spring Fragrance's heart as she pictured Fei and Sie and Mai Gwi Far listening to Lae-Choo reading her illuminating paragraphs" (28). Her ambition to write is presumptuous, yet she modestly limits her future audience to the women she knows. The suggestion, then, is that the book is intended to help immigrant women get their bearings in the larger culture in which they now live. Mrs. Spring Fragrance's guiding principle is "Be not concerned that men do not know you; be only concerned that you do not know them" (34). There is power in knowing others, she implies.

However, not everyone has what she calls "the divine right of learning," that is, the authority to write an "immortal book." As Trinh T. Minh-ha aptly put it several generations later, "For a laywo/man to enter the priesthood—the sacred world of writers—s/he must fulfill a number of unwritten conditions. S/he must undergo a series of rituals, be baptized and ordained" (*Woman, Native, Other* 8). Though Mrs. Spring Fragrance is resolved to go ahead with the project, she first applies for male validation. "Is not the authority of the scholar, the student, almost divine?" she questions her husband (33). Mrs. Spring Fragrance proposes to focus her investigation on the idea of the "Inferior Woman"—an expression she has heard her white friends use. She has been observing the progress of Will Carman's love affair with a young woman, who, in the eyes of his mother, Mrs. Carman, is just such a woman. Either ingenuously or to flatter her husband, she asks for advice on method. He suggests, "It is the way in America, when a person is to be illustrated, for the illustrator to interview the person's friends. Perhaps, my dear, you had better confer with the Superior Woman" (34). With such advice and endorsement, Mrs. Spring Fragrance sets to work without further delay.

Edith borrowed from and parodied such scientific modes of investigation as observation and interview. The controlling metaphor for what Mrs. Spring Fragrance does in this story is bird-watching. Sighting Will Carman and the Inferior Woman, Alice Winthrop, in a local park, Mrs. Spring Fragrance "retreated behind a syringa bush, which completely screened her from view" (29). That same day, the Spring Fragrances tackle Carman on the subject of marriage, and Mr. Spring Fragrance pointedly quotes some flat-footed verses on the subject of birds. Some days later, the Chinese couple, sitting together on the verandah, espy a dejected Will Carman returning home. "Will Carman has failed to snare his bird," comments Mr. Spring Fragrance astutely (33). In the epilogue, Mr. and Mrs. Spring Fragrance are bird-watching once more. "I am so glad," she says, "that Will Carman's bird is in his nest" (41).

Like the true scientist who aims to be nonintrusive, Mrs. Spring Fragrance contrives to listen without being heard. Although she intends to interview her "native informants," the college-educated Superior Woman and her mother, she first takes the opportunity to eavesdrop on their conversation through an open window. Caught in the act, she is quite unabashed, for her investigation is, of course, scientific.

> "I'm sorry that we did not hear you ring, Mrs. Spring Fragrance." . . .
> "I did not expect you to hear a ring which rang not. I failed to pull the bell."
> "You forgot, I suppose," suggested Ethel Evebrook. . . .
> "I have an ambition to accomplish an immortal book about the Americans, and the conversation I heard through the window was so interesting to me that I thought I would take some of it down for my book before I intruded myself."
> (37–38)

With her notebook and pink parasol, Mrs. Spring Fragrance comes across as a comical version of the cultural anthropologist in the field.

At this point, however, the investigation takes an unexpected turn, as the protagonist improvises her own set of procedures quite unlike those of the scientist who gathers data in the field to later process and publish in the metropolis. Hers involve partnership, exchange, and the participation of the "native informant" in the production of the ethnographic text. At the end of a very satisfactory interview with Ethel and Mrs. Evebrook, Mrs. Spring Fragrance says:

> "With your kind permission I will translate for your correction."
> "I shall be delighted—honored," said Miss Evebrook, her cheeks glowing and her laugh rippling, "if you promise that you will also translate for our friend, Mrs. Carman."
> "Ah, yes, poor Mrs. Carman. My heart is so sad for her," murmured the little Chinese woman. (38)

Unlike the anthropologists of her era, Edith admitted the possibility that ethnography, which entails an invasion into the space of another community, leaves a mark on the observed. The Chinese woman's comic project to understand the meaning of the binary opposites "Inferior" and "Superior Woman" in American culture succeeds in collapsing the two terms not only in the her own glossary but also for her white friends (and possibly the reader). When Mrs. Spring Fragrance reads her account out loud to Mrs. Carman and asks, "Why then do you not admire the Inferior Woman who is a woman who has made herself?" Mrs. Carman slowly replies, "I think I do" (39).

Mrs. Spring Fragrance set out to write her book for an audience of four friends—not for publication. It might be interesting to ask how her project would have differed had she intended to publish her "immortal book" in China, for, in the words of the literary critic King-Kok Cheung, "ethnography is precisely *not* writing for one's personal friends" (personal conversation). Would Mrs. Spring Fragrance have downplayed cultural differences and highlighted the commonalities had she set out to captivate and entertain a wide Chinese audience rather than four immigrant women? Would she have chosen an in-depth study of a single problem (such as "The Inferior Woman"), or would a broad, panoramic view of America have seemed more appropriate as an introduction to an exotic culture? Would she have read her notes back to the Evebrooks and Mrs. Carman had they not been her neighbors?

Where Edith differs most from turn-of-the-century ethnographers, both lay and academic, is in her preference for participant observation and the interview, as opposed to "pure" observation borrowed from the natural sciences. Her Chinese characters are participant observers in American culture: they do not stop at "birdwatching" but tirelessly "question," "inquire," "interview," and "confer" with Anglo-Americans (19–39). Mrs. Spring Fragrance articulates her ambition to "write an immortal book" only after living in Seattle for five years, when she speaks fluent English. The suggestion that studying another culture is a lengthy process would not have seemed as patent to Edith's contemporaries as it does to a present-day audience. Western anthropologists possessed of "the divine right of learning" usually made do with considerably less time than did Mrs. Spring Fragrance.

No other stories in *Mrs. Spring Fragrance* thematize cross-cultural investigation to the extent that "Mrs. Spring Fragrance" and "The Inferior Woman" do, but several are concerned with related issues. Aside from method of investigation, Edith emphasized the ethic of responsible reporting in "'Its Wavering Image'" and the dangers of blocking cross-cultural communication within the "contact zone" in "The Wisdom of the New."[25] The latter is perhaps the most disturbing of her stories, ending with a Chinese immigrant woman's killing her young son to save him from what she perceives as the perversions of American culture. What at first might appear to be an account of one woman's paranoia may also be read as an indictment of both the American and Chinese cultural chauvinism that prevents the two sides from communicating.

"The Wisdom of the New" endorses neither ethnic segregation nor the newly formulated national policy to enculturate immigrants into the American way of life. Without denigrating the "old" wisdom to which the Chinese female protagonist clings or idealizing the "new," the story deplores the parochialism that hampers cross-cultural contacts. In the West, studying other peoples is, Trinh Minh-ha has proposed, "better defined as 'gossip' (we speak together about others) than as 'conversation' (we discuss a question). . . . Scientific gossip takes place under relatively intimate conditions and mostly without witnesses; hence the gossipers need to act in solidarity, leaning on and referring to each other for more credibility" (68). Academic anthropology—the target of Minh-ha's critique—has merely formalized what nonacademics do when faced with difference. Significantly, the events of "The Wisdom of the New" are driven by gossip. Gossip draws the male protagonist from China to the United States. Gossip is what his two white women friends, "secure in the difference of race," do among themselves as they try to fathom his relations with his Chinese wife (51). And gossip about the meaning of America circulates among the Chinese immigrant women, who live isolated from the world at large. Assuming that he alone can understand both Chinese and American ways, the assimilated Chinese man in the middle blocks contacts between the two groups of women. "The Wisdom of the New" is a deeply ambivalent story that cannot be reduced to one reading, but the fundamental problem it raises is that the two cultural groups are limited or limit themselves to just looking at each other. This leads to the reification of cultural difference and, subsequently, to a struggle for dominance fought over the body of a child.

With the exception of "The Wisdom of the New," all the articles and stories I refer to were first published in major American magazines at the peak of Edith's career. By 1910, the market seems to have opened up to the kind of serious work she was interested in doing. Whether because she had more leisure time, more confidence in her own writing, or more elbow room than Charles Lummis had allowed her, Edith's stories grew considerably longer, and her characters acquired new depth. Though she continued to write romantic tales, she also experimented with the realistic mode and an outspoken first-person voice. Between January 1909 and August 1911, the *Independent* published some of her most overtly political fiction, as well as two pieces of personal criticism.[26] Giving Edith unprecedented license to speak her mind, the editors positioned her shoulder to shoulder with such prominent figures of the day as Upton Sinclair, Booker T. Washington, and W. E. B. Du Bois.

That her stunted literary career finally took off just four years before her death in 1914 may be explained by a combination of factors. Her literary style had definitely become more modern and readable since she abandoned what I have called the "parable" form. No less important, Edith had moved to Boston, closer to the nation's major publishing industry. But as I suggest throughout this study, because the Eaton sisters wrote ethnographic fiction about Asians, their popularity was contingent on the see-sawing public sentiments toward China and Japan. What jump-started Edith's career was likely a change in the political climate.

At home, Chinese immigration had been virtually cut off by the renewal of the Geary Act in 1902; meanwhile, Japanese immigration was on the rise, and anti-Japanese slogans replaced the Sinophobic ones on the banners and placards of previous years. In international relations, since the end of the Russo-Japanese War, Japan increasingly had come to be perceived as America's competitor in China and as a potential military aggressor (Iriye 83–91). With aspirations to sovereignty and republicanism stirring in China, the historian Marius B. Jansen observed that at least for a time, "China's image [shifted] from one of superannuation and ineffectiveness to one of idealism and youth, while Japan's image changed from promising youth to threatening bully" (258). Now that Japan could no longer be envisioned as America's "little protégé," U.S. foreign policy began to assume a protective stance toward China (Jansen 257). Even the title character of "Mrs. Spring Fragrance" wryly comments on this development in a letter to her husband after hearing a public lecture entitled "America, the Protector of China" (21). But no matter how infuriating the Chinese found America's "protectorship," it was reflective of a new era of goodwill toward China and a growing commercial interest in that country.

Most significant, the unrest that culminated in the revolution of 1911 began to alter the perception of China as the "sleeping giant," an expression commonly used by the media. "In Asia," declared an *Independent* editorial writer in 1909, "great peoples are awakening to political consciousness: Persia and China will follow closely upon Japan . . . third world countries will not be dominated indefinitely by western armies, navies or civilization" ("Editorial" 108). Less than two years later, this prediction would be confirmed by another writer: "China is awake! China is awake! CHINA IS AWAKE!" ("The Awakening World" 906). Between 1910 and 1911, the number of texts attempting to interpret the political and economic changes in China and to reassess the Chinese "civilization" rose sharply in the *Independent* and other magazines. According to Jansen:

> In contrast to Taft's "realistic" dollar diplomacy, [the newly elected] Woodrow Wilson showed a more idealistic and even visionary approach that was informed by his missionary friends. . . . The missionary opinion . . . was overwhelmingly enthusiastic, indeed euphoric, about the Revolution of 1911 [which] seemed to augur well for the evangelization of China. Missionaries reported [in private correspondence with Woodrow Wilson] that the United States was immensely popular in China, that revolutionary leadership was in the hands of the young and Western-educated, and that political events indicated not only political unrest but also a moral awakening when new ideas triumphed over the old. (259)

It would be misleading to contend that Edith's modest and belated success as interpreter of the Chinese to the American public was the result of these historical developments. What we can safely say, however, is the same political climate that made it possible for Wilson to implement his new policy toward China and spurred a wave of writings on China and the Chinese in the American press also made editors and the reading public more receptive to Edith's vision of the Chinese.

That vision was, as I have argued, of Christian missionary origin, though informed by Edith's experience of race. Having long maintained loose ties with home missionary societies, Edith remained ambivalent about Christianization, but she certainly endorsed the missionary ethic of responsibility toward people of all races, as well as the belief that the Chinese were capable of change and participation in modernity on par with any nation. Her writings on the Chinese that had been out of sync with the public sentiment on the West Coast resonated with progressive intellectuals on the East Coast, where even the official political discourse about China acquired religious overtones.

In an autobiographical piece printed in the *Boston Globe* in 1912, Edith, looking back on a life of austerity and hard work, presented herself as an unconventional woman with a mission: "If there was nothing but bread to eat and water to drink, absorbed in my work I was immune to material things—for a while. . . . I am not rich and I have my work to do" (*Mrs. Spring Fragrance and Other Writings* 295). What she understood her work to be is subject to speculation. Studying the Chinese in America to represent them sympathetically to a white audience was certainly one aspect of it. To judge by the handful of available reviews, this was the work her first readers appreciated most. All of them expressed fascination with Chinese customs and ways of thinking to which Edith supposedly had privileged access. Although the ways of European Americans are a major theme of *Mrs. Spring Fragrance*, the reviews made no mention of them. Yet to bring before the scrutiny of European Americans images of themselves offset by those of Chinese Americans was an important part of Edith's work.

While it is tempting to see Edith's writing as ethnographic fieldwork by an "insider," we should neither lose sight of her strong cultural identification with the white middle class nor fail to explore the consequences of her "outsider" status in Chinatown. A good deal of Edith's "fieldwork" was, as in Winnifred's case, "home work" based on reading but inspired by personal contacts with the Chinese. Edith's ethnography can also be troped as "home work" in that writing allowed her to work at home (usually a room in a boardinghouse). To a woman who spent her life doing clerical work in newspaper, railroad, and law offices but subscribed to the ideal of domesticity, "home work" was the preferred way to earn a living. Much that was going on in Chinatown consequently did not meet Edith's ethnographic eye. Some of her decisions about what to include or exclude may have been strategic; others were the result of her class bias or limited access to certain people and spaces.

What this discussion demonstrates is that Edith was not as close to Chinatown communities as once supposed and that even a sympathetic observer can feel a sense of detachment from or superiority toward the observed. Yet Edith's sense of accountability to the Chinese set her apart from such contemporary lay and academic ethnographers as Adolf Bandelier, Charles Lummis, Mary Austin, Stewart Culin, and Olive Percival. Engaging in both "salvage ethnography" and efforts to improve the living conditions of American Indians, some of these men and women were no less socially committed than Edith. However, none of them envisioned people of color as a readers and critics of their work. They also assumed non-Western cultures were transparent to the trained ethnographic gaze. Edith's position between conflicting racial groups, social classes, and cultural and religious systems denied her the comfort of assuming the knowability of other cultures and privileging the gaze.

PART 2

Winnifred Eaton

4. Strategies of Authentication

This novel is written, we are told, by a young Anglo-Japanese girl whose opportunities for observing her countrywomen have been exceptional. . . . It has thus an interest apart from its literary merit. . . . One expects an amount of ethnological truth which is difficult to get from the descriptions, however convincing, of the outsider, and this expectation is certainly not disappointed.

—Review of Onoto Watanna's *A Japanese Nightingale, New York Times Book Review*

Authenticity cannot be determined simply by retailing the objective material attributes of the artifact. It has to do not only with genuineness and the reliability of face value, but with the interpretation of genuineness and our desire for it.

—Brian Spooner, "Weavers and Dealers: The Authenticity of an Oriental Carpet"

"I CAN SPEAK about the subject with authority because I have been there" is the conventional claim nineteenth-century orientalist travelers made to assert discursive authority. Having "been there" remains the ethnographer's most powerful claim to representing other people and places.[1] When in 1982 Florinda Donner, the author of the ethnographic novel *Shabono*,[2] failed to produce evidence of having "been there" (in the Venezuelan jungle), the novel came close to being discredited not only as a scientific document—which it never purported to be—but also, through insinuations of plagiarism, as a work of fiction. The critic Mary Louise Pratt interpreted the heated debate over *Shabono* as an instance of academic anthropology's anxiety about its own disciplinary boundaries, its unwillingness to face "the anguished and messy tangle of contradictions surrounding the interrelations of personal experience, personal narrative, scientism, and professionalism in ethnographic writing" ("Fieldwork in Common Places" 29).

Interestingly, the initial denunciation of Donner came from "there." The anthropologist who challenged Donner in the *American Anthropologist* is undersigned as "Rebecca B. DeHolmes, Caracas, Venezuela." Speaking from "there," DeHolmes detailed Donner's borrowings from existing ethnographic materials but left her most damning evidence for last: no anthropologist and no Indian commissioner in Venezuela had ever heard of Donner or of any young female anthropologist who could claim experiences similar to Donner's. She simply was not there (667). Given the hubbub generated around *Shabono* by DeHolmes's 1983 article and sustained by Pratt's 1986 inquiry, it is surprising that we still do not know who Florinda Donner is. The novel's publisher, Delacorte Press, is not about to give away the identity of the author, either. Pratt's insightful placement of the novel in the contested ground between scientific practice and fiction has won for *Shabono* a place on reading lists for academic anthropology courses. Apparently, the thicker the aura of ambiguity around the novel, the better it will sell.

Discussions about epistemology and authenticity like those surrounding Donner would have sunk Winnifred Eaton as a writer in her lifetime. Though some reviewers doubted the genuineness of Onoto Watanna, most assumed she either was Japanese or had experienced Japan firsthand. Those who did not, like one *Independent* reviewer who pointed out glaring historical, geographic, and cultural inaccuracies in Winnifred's 1904 novel *The Daughters of Nijo* ("Novels Japanese and Japanned"), were outnumbered by those who did. Fortunately for Winnifred, the doubters had neither time nor opportunity to investigate her past. She kept it veiled at all times, allowing the curious public an occasional glimpse in authorized and partly fictional biographical notes. Meanwhile, the publishers—Rand McNally, Harper's, Dodd, and Doubleday—stood firmly by their investment.

One way to understand the ease with which Winnifred established herself as an authority on things Japanese is to rethink the meaning we assign to *authenticity*. As the anthropologist Brian Spooner pointed out in the epigraph, authenticity has as much to do with the objective attributes of an artifact (or person) as with our "interpretation of genuineness and our desire for it" (200). To redefine *authenticity*, Spooner used the intriguing case of oriental carpets in Western culture. Since the time such carpets began arriving in the West as a rare commodity several hundred years ago, their quality, availability, and provenance have radically changed—without affecting their price range and symbolic value. The authenticity of imported carpets, Spooner argued, is constructed on the basis of incidental lore that each dealer in a chain of dealers acquires with his wares. Connoisseurs have always been aware that they do not control their sources of information, yet they settle for unverifiable lore because of the desire to maintain the value of carpets as status symbols in Western culture (198–200).

A similar mechanism operated on the novels of Onoto Watanna as commodities. Her public persona was as much a figment of her imagination as a product of her white mainstream readers' desire for the exotic, for a new yet intelligible aesthetic, and for an insight into Japan's leap from the "feudal" era directly into modernity. At the price of a dollar or two, the American reader could purchase a little piece of Japan in a decorative binding—a romance that doubled as a lesson in Japanese customs, morals, and manners. Like oriental carpets, Onoto Watanna's novels arrived on the market divorced from their social context. The publishing industry, which had an investment in the authenticity of the novels, sought to reconstruct that context for the reader in the form of photographs and biographical notes on the author. Such "trade lore" helped authenticate Onoto Watanna's wares and maintain her ethnographic authority. Her youth and gender made her a perfect synecdoche for the New Japan; her biracial status seemed to destine her for the role of cultural interpreter. The Japanese persona became inseparable from the commodities Winnifred produced. It not only authorized her to produce ethnographic texts but also became a commodity in itself, subject to the rigors and constraints of the marketplace.

Authorizing the Self

As a literary celebrity, Winnifred was the subject of countless biographical articles, interviews, and reviews. All these she scrupulously collected and pasted into scrapbooks. In one scrapbook covering the early years of her career (1897–1900), fragments of printed stories and typescripts are interspersed with biographical notes and reviews. Scrawled next to the reviews are the names of cities in which they appeared. To read these names—St. Louis, Boston, Chicago, New York, Detroit, Philadelphia, Omaha, New Orleans, Indianapolis, Los Angeles, Houston, Brooklyn—is to see that Winnifred's work was marketed and read across the continent before she turned twenty-five. Yet these clippings are only a foretaste of the publicity she received after 1900. Every local paper between New York and San Francisco seemed eager to acknowledge Onoto Watanna—however briefly. No less eager, the author pasted the reviews onto the map of her conquest. To explain her phenomenal success, I attempt to answer the following questions: What made passing for Japanese a thinkable career move for Winnifred in the late 1800s? What popular assumptions about race and culture enabled her to become an authority on things Japanese? How did she understand her own strategy of self-authorization? And finally, what issues does her writing raise about contemporary academic standards of literary authenticity?

Winnifred could not have afforded to "be there"—in Japan—before she won recognition as a writer. But it is not certain whether she would have gone out into "the field" in search of Japanese material had she been in a position to do so. Even after her Japanese novels had made her famous, she did not visit Japan. We do know that her independent life began with a voyage to the Caribbean—a firsthand experience that might have provided ample ethnographic material had Winnifred been looking for it. Her 1915 fictionalized account of the sojourn in Jamaica begins, like the classic island ethnographies of Louis de Bougainville, Raymond Firth, and Bronislaw Malinowski, with a reconstruction of an arrival scene dominated by reaction to people of color:

> A crowd seemed to be swarming on the wharves, awaiting our boat. As we came nearer, I was amazed to find that this crowd was made up almost entirely of negroes. We have very few negroes in Canada, and I had only seen one in all my life. I remember an older sister had shown him to me in church—he was pure black—and told me he was the "Bogy man," and that he'd probably come around to see me that night. . . . It was, therefore, with a genuine thrill of excitement and fear that I looked down upon that vast sea of upturned black and brown faces. (*Me* 19–20)

Many have suggested that there can never be an unmediated encounter with the other. For instance, Greg Denning noted in his discussion of "first encounters" that "the other is rarely met in a present divorced from all the meetings that have gone before" (464). Nora's seems to have been thoroughly overdetermined. Her position on board ship, high above the "sea of upturned black and brown faces," above the nakedness and gaudiness, becomes reified during the course of her stay, as prejudices brought from home are reinforced by the white Jamaicans' undisguised racism. Before her fear of the vast, undifferentiated blackness has time to wear off, the young journalist flees the island, physically sickened by the marriage proposal and kiss of a black member of Parliament.

On reaching the United States, the narrator sets out to become a professional fiction writer, yet she does not reach for the Jamaican experience. Instead, she immerses herself in a fantasy world she calls "my mother's land" (*Me* 178). The story of Winnifred's real voyage and cross-cultural encounter would have to wait almost twenty years to be told. Presumably when she started writing fiction, the story of a biracial woman's encounter with blackness in Jamaica and her rejection of a wealthy black suitor would have appeared as lacking in literary potential. But an account of a white woman's voyage to Japan and her tragic love affair with a Japanese nobleman was another matter. A book with just such a plot, entitled *Miss Numè of Japan: A Japanese-American Romance,* did launch Winnifred as a novelist in 1899. And the claim on which she built her career was, "I can speak about Japanese culture with authority because I am the daughter of a Japanese woman."

Winnifred constructed her "Japanese" persona in reaction to both the "Chinaman" stereotype and to Chineseness as represented by her sister. Edith had found an alternative discourse of Chineseness in missionary circles and through those circles had claimed a limited authority to study and represent the Chinese in print. As I demonstrated in chapter 1, nineteenth-century China missionaries had evolved a powerful evangelical discourse that called for responsibility and compassion for those in need of the gospel. They resisted scientific theories that conflated race and culture, arguing instead for the shared humanity of the races and the possibility of replacing pernicious, backward cultural practices with Christian values and norms of conduct. However, the "positive" meaning of Chineseness offered by the missionaries came at a high price. When Edith selectively embraced that ideology, she also committed herself to an unpopular social cause—that of Chinese immigrants—and in so doing had to curb the desire for commercial success as a writer.

To Winnifred, the material and psychological cost of claiming Chinese descent must have seemed prohibitive. Admitting that one was half-Chinese boded social ostracism: obstacles to finding employment, accommodation, and a spouse. (Edith's 1911 article "The Persecution and Oppression of Me" recounted the day-to-day abuse a person of Chinese descent could expect to face.) Passing for Japanese was a logical career move for Winnifred at the turn of the century. As Amy Ling pointed out, Winnifred had "a keen marketing instinct and sense of timing" ("Creating One's Own Self" 310). Neither fifteen years earlier nor fifteen years later would embracing a Japanese identity have made as much political or economic sense. In the 1870s and 1880s, Japan was still an insignificant player in the international arena. Its name connoted little of the glamour that it would acquire in subsequent years. However, in the year preceding Winnifred's arrival in the United States, the Sino-Japanese War, which had long been making headlines in the Western press, ended with Japan's victory and unofficial annexation of Korea. China's defeat and the deprecation of things Chinese, then, was directly correlated in the North American media with the valorization of Japan and Japonica. Yet the fascination with Japan would prove short-lived: first the Californians and then most Americans began to perceive Japan's military prowess as menacing, while the Japanese immigrants, whose numbers increased from 24,326 in 1900 to 111,010 in 1920, began to draw the wrath of nativists in the first decade of the century (Daniels 1). The turn of the century was a perfect moment to become a "Japanese" novelist.[3]

According to the art historians Julia Meech and Gabriel Weisberg, *Japonis-*

me reached a high point in America in the 1890s. European and American art dealers worked aggressively to educate mainstream Americans in the new aesthetic and promote the artifacts that entered the United States in ever-increasing quantities. Japan itself took advantage of the favorable climate by sending lavish art and architecture exhibits to American world's fairs (N. Harris 24–54; Meech and Weisberg 26–34). In literature, Japanese influences resonated as strongly as in art. Even if Winnifred had not read the orientalist writings of Pierre Loti, Lafcadio Hearn, and Edwin Arnold (see chapter 1) while living at home, she could scarcely have ignored their ubiquitous presence in Chicago and New York. Indeed, we know from one of her first articles, "The Half Caste," published in November 1898, that she knew the work of Arnold and Hearn and was particularly interested in them as westerners who had married Japanese women. For the young apprentice writer, then, a thirty-year-old tradition already existed into which she could step. It was an orientalist tradition, strongly dominated by the male traveler's perspective. To insert herself into it, Winnifred found it necessary to take on the role of the exotic woman of color.

Whether she made this move after grave deliberation or on a wild impulse, she could not have chosen better. On a personal level, her strategy of passing accomplished what Teresa Kay Williams described as a shift "from one 'minority' status to the 'more acceptable minority' status—in order to raise [one's] prestige and advance [one's] chances for a qualitatively improved life" (62). Winnifred's ambiguous phenotype would thus no longer be a risk factor, which it was in passing for white. By passing for Japanese, she shifted her status from undesirable to desirable immigrant at a time when West Coast lobbyists were stepping up the pressure on Congress to contain Chinese immigration. In 1902, the year the Geary Act was renewed and Chinese exclusion was secured, we read, "Miss Watanna's striking success in this country ought to encourage other Japanese novelists to learn English and come to this country" (*Buffalo Commercial,* September 24, 1902).[4]

Professionally, being half-Japanese catapulted Winnifred onto another plane, where her work was no longer held up to Western literary standards. The naïveté and lack of literary technique that would have disadvantaged her as a white writer suddenly became part of what reviewers recognized as the "peculiar charm" of her untutored style. For some, the "childlike simplicity" of the texts (*Chicago Tribune,* January 6, 1904) guaranteed their authenticity, an assumption that reflected mainstream conceptions of race and evolutionary progress. The reading public fascinated by Japan's rise to power clamored for ethnographic knowledge that would explain the phenomenon.

On an economic level, passing for Japanese afforded her a degree of exceptionality she would not have had as a white woman. While passing for white when she first began to seek employment in the Midwest removed the disadvantage of race in the job marketplace, her sex and class limited Winnifred's opportunities to the lowest-paying and most tedious clerical positions. (It takes the white protagonist of her autobiographical novel *Me* several weeks to find a job with the Chicago meatpacking industry, and even then her pay is so low that she dates men in exchange for a free dinner.) By becoming Onoto Watanna, Winnifred enacted mainstream orientalist fantasies, exploiting the discourse that feminized and aestheticized Japan. Her gender became a major selling point in the publishing marketplace. By the time she started writing, the subject of Japan had long been occupied by white travelers, yet there was ample room, particularly in the women's magazines, for a "half-blood Japanese who . . . is a clever writer of stories [and] speaks and writes English fluently" (*Boston Transcript*, December 1898).

Erving Goffman in his discussion on the management of public and personal identity argued that passing is a strategy available to people who possess what is designated within their society as a stigma yet whose stigma is not immediately apparent. Stigmatized individuals may partition their world into what he called "forbidden, civil, and back places" (81) and manage information about their stigma accordingly. In some spaces, the stigma remains concealed; in others, it may be revealed to a circle of the "wise" (73–104). Winnifred certainly engaged in various levels and strategies of passing—passing of a peculiar kind, for she embraced a stigma and turned it into an asset. Besides her parents and siblings, it is likely that her husband, Bertrand Babcock, and close friends, such as Jean Webster, were among the "wise"; to her New York neighbors, publishers, and readers, she was simply Onoto Watanna or Mrs. Babcock; in public places where she was unknown, she probably passed for white.

Though she frequently made minor alterations to her persona, for the most part, her passing was quite serious and consistent. Nagasaki, Japan, figures as her birthplace even on her children's birth certificates and as late as 1914 in an obituary for Edith Eaton (attributed to Winnifred) that stated the deceased was the daughter of a "Japanese noblewoman" (White-Parks 50). In seeing Winnifred's passing as serious, I differ with Yuko Matsukawa, who argued that "like the archetypal trickster, in exposing the slippage between what she is supposed to be (a Japanese woman writer) and what she appears to be (a biracial woman mimicking a Japanese woman writer), Winnifred Eaton playfully questions our assumptions on how we construct anyone's identity" (112). Matsukawa confused the meaning Winnifred and her writings have for contemporary critics interested in the constructedness of identity with the serious business of passing in order to make a living at the turn of the century. Although there was a good deal of slippage in Winnifred's passing act, I believe the slippage was unintended—evidence of the difficulty of managing personal information rather than an expression of playfulness.

Passing for Japanese was not a single act but a process of sustaining and adjusting the public persona. To evaluate her assets and fine-tune her persona, Winnifred had to see herself reflected in the public eye. Through the book reviews, readers had direct input into the making of Onoto Watanna. Winifred's self-representations are discussed in the next section. Here I look only at the way the representations were received to understand how readers came to invest her with ethnographic authority.

Winnifred's fiction was read for "pleasure, for the titillation of the sensibilities," as one reviewer put it (*Republican,* December 6, 1902). But the pleasures of reading an "ethnic" text were distinct from those afforded by an all-American novel. The general consensus among those who enjoyed the work of Onoto Watanna was that its charm "does not lie in the plot but in the telling, in the strange method of expression, in the delightful descriptions of Japanese habits of life and thought, and in the somewhat mysterious success with which the author gives the reader the Japanese point of view" (*Seattle Times,* July 10, 1904). An Australian reviewer would go so far as to say that Onoto Watanna's work "gives a deeper insight into Japanese life than exhaustive tomes of erudite scholars" (*Sydney Herald,* July 30, 1904). In the same year, an American commentator would assure readers that "Onoto Watanna is, after the late Lafcadio Hearn, the best foreign delineator of Japanese life. She possesses a thorough knowledge of the people and country" (*Baltimore Sun,* December 21, 1904). What all these statements seem to express is a desire for authentic inside knowledge about Japan as well as a preference for simple narrative over erudite prose.

Since Winnifred's authority did not originate in her actual knowledge or seniority "in the field," it seems appropriate to ask what made her a credible and sought-after source of information on Japan in the eyes of her readers. Aside from good timing and a rare ability to anticipate expectations, there must have been other reasons. First, nineteenth-century scientific theories of race had succeeded in conflating race and culture in the popular imagination, so the Japanese half of Onoto Watanna's heredity was understood to carry an essential Japaneseness—a form of cultural knowledge, not just the visible markers of race. Second, although world's fairs, curio shops, reproductions, and photographs had exposed westerners to Japanese artifacts, few readers had any sense of Japanese literary conventions; the naïveté of Winnifred's prose was therefore recognized as expressive of the Japanese aesthetic.

Third, Winnifred's narratives resonated well with the widely accepted ethnographic narratives of the "first encounter" with and "salvage" of exotic cultures facing modernization. In effect, readers were willing to either enjoy or turn a blind eye to Onoto Watanna's stylistic crudities because they read her work primarily as fictionalized native ethnography or a record of a passing civilization.

At the turn of the century, Franz Boas had barely begun his lifelong project of cleaving the concept of "culture" from that of "race." Cultural patterns were understood to be at least partly hereditary. Little wonder, then, that in the popular imagination "blood" conferred ethnographic authority on a writer in much the same way that documented presence "in the field" does today. The discourse of biological determinism was so pervasive that Winnifred, who had an avid interest in race theory, probably deceived herself as much as anyone else. This is how she presented her position through her fictional counterpart, Nora, in *Me:*

> I told him of the stories I was writing about my mother's land, and he said:
> "But you've never been there, child."
> "I know," I said, "but, then, I have an instinctive feeling about that country. A blind man can find his way over paths that he intuitively feels. And so with me. I feel as if I knew everything about that land, and when I sit down to write— why, things just come pouring to me, and I can write *anything* then." (176)

Although Winnifred, like her character Nora, concealed the hours of library research that must have gone into the making of her stories, she was not being entirely disingenuous. In the many interviews she gave, she did invoke an Asian heritage but never claimed to have lived in Japan beyond her early childhood. That she was raised in the West as an Englishman's daughter was public knowledge. Yet, odd as it may seem, for Winnifred's early readers her "being Japanese" was a more important credential than her having "been there." In the eyes of many, her racial hybridity, coupled with a Western education, made her an ideal go-between. As one reviewer put it, "Onoto Watanna's stories of Japanese life have in them just that touch of Western civilization to make them thoroughly comprehensible to Western readers, but not so much as to spoil the delicate fragrance of the spirit of old Japan" (*Post Intelligencer,* July 10, 1904).

Since the Japanese aesthetic was a recent import, the majority of Winnifred's reviewers were uncertain what criteria to use in critiquing her romances. They scrambled for popular anthropological explanations of the "primitive," invoked the discourse of the "eternal feminine," and were generally willing to give Winnifred the benefit of the doubt. "Needless to say," wrote one bewildered critic, "this type is new, the ethical quality is foreign, and the artistic form a thing by itself. There is beauty and a spirit of fine breeding in this curious love story, as well as in the pictures which are Japanese in detail and delicacy of line" (*Critic*, August 1904). The winds of modernism, fanned by, among others, Winnifred's contemporaries Yone Noguchi[5] and Sadakichi Hartmann,[6] wreaked a pleasurable havoc in the aesthetic sensibilities of mainstream audiences.

That westerners were delighted as well as baffled by *Japonisme* is not surprising when we consider the seductive language used by such critics as Hartmann to challenge realism with a new aesthetic. Although the passage quoted below comes from his essay on the visual arts, Hartmann, who was also a writer and propagator of the haiku, symbolist poetry, and drama, defined new trends in literature in similar terms:

> We do not want representations of facts, but of appearances, or merely the blurred suggestion of appearances. The swift reflections and subtle quivering light do not permit exact copyism. . . . Peculiarities of style like these may easily deteriorate into trickery and mannerisms, but even then they are preferable to pure mimicry. . . . The art connoisseur of today wants to see subjects bathed in light and air, and wants an actual atmosphere to be interposed between his eyes and the representation of figures, flowers, fields, trees, etc. (Hartmann 151–52)

Winnifred excelled at creating appearances and atmosphere. Though mimicry *was* her basic literary strategy, she mimicked not "life" but existing textual representations of Japan and imbued them with the mystique of an "authentic" Japanese sensibility. As one enthusiast attested, "[H]er language is the flower talk of the flower land. It is musical, and when one reads her book he seems to be enveloped in an atmosphere sweet with the mellow, fruity, lulling odor of opium. And like the smoker of the drug, he must have more" (*American Illustrator*, May 1903).

A reviewer of her first novel, *Miss Numè*, made much of the fact that "the author herself is a Japanese, writes English remarkably well for a foreigner and moreover she regards American life with a remarkably clear vision" (*Union Advertiser*, May 6, 1899). Another admired *Miss Numè* "notwithstanding a certain crudeness of style, due probably to the author writing in a tongue not her own" (*Chicago Chronicle*, n.d. [1899]). This would remain a common refrain for years to come. Lack of polish was no obstacle to publication when the narrative was "redolent with the atmosphere of Japan [and] could not have been written except by someone who understands the people and enters intimately into their lives" (*Pittsburgh Times*, October 29, 1904). Next to a story manuscript in her scrapbook, Winnifred scrawled a commentary that sheds light on her early relations with magazine editors: "I wrote this story inside of an hour one morning, took it to the editor of the American Home Journal, waited while he read it, and it was accepted on the spot—cheque being handed me at once—quick work—and profitable! However, the story is trite—poor." Whether Winnifred dressed the part and put on a foreign accent to deliver the story (her interviewers occasionally mention a faint accent), she found a rapt audience.

Literary critics and ordinary readers alike succumbed to *Japonisme.* It is worth remembering that Henry James was an admirer of Pierre Loti's *Madame Chrysanthème* and *Madame Prune,* while William Dean Howells in an article entitled "A Psychological Counter-Current in Recent Fiction" found Winnifred's *Japanese Nightingale* (1901) "irresistible" (878). Given Howells's insistence on writing from experience, his wholehearted endorsement of Onoto Watanna is nicely ironic. He commended Onoto Watanna on her "very choice English" and praised the "indescribable freshness in the art of this pretty novelette . . . which is like no other art except in the simplicity which is native to the best art everywhere. . . . It has its little defects, but its directness, and sincerity, and its felicity through the sparing touch make me unwilling to note them. In fact I have forgotten them" (873). Howells and most of his contemporaries responded to a repertoire of icons—chrysanthemum, bamboo, spray of almond blossoms, geisha, and samisen—popularized by travel writers. By naming any one of these not-yet-hackneyed icons, Winnifred could conjure up associations "redolent" of the spirit of old Japan.

But I would suggest that what readers responded to in Winnifred's work was not just her Japaneseness and the ability to suffuse her narratives with a poetic atmosphere. The ethnographic narratives that underlie many of her plots were also an important source of interest and pleasure for her readers. Ethnography emerged as a subdiscipline of anthropology toward the end of the nineteenth century as a methodology for studying exotic cultures at the moment of their first encounter with modernity or before the native lifeways were irrevocably tainted and displaced by Western ones. Japan, though it was understood to have an advanced rather than "primitive" culture, was an unusual case in point, having long isolated itself from contact with the Western world. The memory of the "first encounter" in 1855 was very strong, and remote islands and out-of-the-way settlements continued to provide Western travelers with opportunities to relive that thrill of encountering "Old Japan." Winnifred was quick to see the usefulness of this ethnographic paradigm for her fiction. A *Globe Democrat* critic admired *The Wooing of Wistaria* (1902) for the "delicate touch" of its rendition of "Japanese life in the days before the entering of the wedge of civilization" (October 5, 1902). *The Daughters of Nijo* garnered praise for its treatment of "the period of transition, by no means gradual and natural evolution, when Japan elected to cast off her ancient civilization, and hastily adopt, with magazine rifles and torpedo boats, the often incongruous habits of the West" (*Winnipeg Telegram,* May 14, 1904). Those who relished the drama of "salvage" treated the romantic conventions of Onoto Watanna's prose as transparent and unproblematic. As one critic argued, "[R]omance permits a view of the conflict . . . between the old and the new social customs, and shows Japan in its evolutionary stage of becoming a member of the family of nations" (*Washington Star,* May 7, 1904).

A substantial number of clippings—perhaps a third of the post-1902 reviews preserved at the University of Calgary—attest to the fact that not everyone was taken in by the Japanese persona. A doubting voice from the West Coast commented, "This little lady who is pleased to write under a Japanese name and who has done some very pretty stories of Nippon, has yielded, it is to be feared, to that bane of all authors, popularity, and now she is simply retilling the field that brought her first success" (*San Francisco Call,* October 30, 1904). Another astute reader noted that Onoto Watanna painted with "all the delicate combinations of color that America ascribes to Japan," suggesting that *The Love of Azalea* (1904) was written from an American perspective, though daintily dressed in a "mauve binding sprinkled with tinted azalea blossoms" (*Louisville Courier,* December 3, 1904). A Londoner seeking ethnographic knowledge came away frustrated: "The Japanese have yet to be explained, to be accounted for, and Mr. [sic] Watanna's pleasant work does no more to this end than did [Pierre Loti's] "Madame Chrysanthème" (*Illustrated London News,* July 2, 1904).

The doubters were many, and the further into Winnifred's career, the more skeptical the reviewers became (though apparently not the general readers, for her novels continued to sell well into the 1910s). Even among the doubters, though, there was a general willingness to suspend disbelief in order to become immersed in the exotic, be it authentic or not. There was the Londoner who suspected *The Daughters of Nijo* was "the work of a shrewd artificer who knows the market for local color," yet the reviewer found value in the book, "for the tale is excellent and we should scarcely enjoy it the less for knowing that the theme and treatment were merely pseudo-indigenous. It brings Japan a little nearer to us . . . and in itself it has the stimulating freshness of unfamiliar ways" (*London Pall Mall Gazette,* May 21, 1904). Pseudonyms abounded in the turn-of-the-century press, readers were used to literary games, and yet the magnetism of things Japanese persisted. Whether the readers saw Winnifred's work as autoethnographic, as ethnographic, or as fairy tales "after the most charming pattern of Western day dreams" (*New York Times,* April 30, 1904), her novels got an extraordinary response—a response she heeded.

Since her position as an ethnographic authority depended on sustaining the fiction of Japanese descent, Winnifred did not indulge in much public introspection or attempt to theorize her work. There are, however, stories in which she obliquely approached the problem of wresting the authority to write from those privileged by gender, race, and class. Two of her stories are particularly useful for understanding her social positioning and offer a rare insight into Winnifred's understanding of authorship. "Eyes That Saw Not" (1902), cowritten with Bertrand Babcock, and "A Neighbor's Garden, My Own, and a Dream One" (1908), thematize the notions of authenticity, authorship, and originality. They demonstrate the workings of such contestatory mechanisms as mimicry, appropriation, and autoexoticization. Both stories contest and at the same time reinscribe the structures of power that marginalize women and people of color.

"A Neighbor's Garden, My Own, and a Dream One" is really a meditation on a plot of land, with minimal plotting. The Japanese narrator, who presents herself as a writer and mother of "three fat babies" (349), has recently moved to a modest house on a "frowsy acre" (348) on Long Island. She hints that she herself is a "child of the slums" (347), which is why she yearns after a flower garden. A society matron from the neighborhood offers a few gardening tips and sets a good example, and an Englishman from across the fence gives the narrator a basketful of roots for planting. Encouraged, she sets out to turn the "frowsy acre" into the garden of her dreams. But because of her ignorance, poor planning, lack of stamina, and shortage of funds, her gardening comes to naught. To console herself, she dreams up an idyllic Japanese-style garden, complete with a lily pond, a pagoda, and a trellis bedecked with wistaria.

The story appeared in *Good Housekeeping* in two issues, the April installment getting front-page placement. Lavishly illustrated by Alden Peirson, the Japanesque drawings took up as much space as the printed text. With its competent discussion of various styles of garden design and strong emphasis on the aesthetic, the story was appropriate for a woman's magazine. Also the topic was timely, since April was the start of the gardening season in many parts of the country. Yet if we look through the screen of plum, cherry, and wistaria blossoms, it becomes apparent that Winnifred was using gardens as a way to comment on creativity, authority, and class; she was also asserting what the anthropologist Dorinne Kondo called "a marketable difference" (184).

For a "child of the slums," the nameless speaker has done very well: she lives in an affluent suburb and employs both an Irish nurse and a black domestic.

Yet she is very conscious of her own and other characters' race. Soon after moving into the white neighborhood, she tells the Irish woman Norah, "If the people don't call on me, I'll call on them, or rather their gardens, and if they snub me, Norah, I'll send you over to steal their flowers" (350). When the first white visitors do call, they catch the speaker about to do her own stealing. She disarms them with her frankness: "Why, I'll confess to you the truth. Ten minutes ago I was sitting on my back fence, coveting my neighbor's flowers, some of which, you see, Norah had already stolen for me" (351). Stealing buttercups is just a prank, but behind it is the fact that this working mother of three, with an absentee husband, has no flowers because she lives above her means. She cannot even afford to even keep the grass clipped and worries that the "neighbors will regard [her] with suspicion, convinced [that she] is an eccentric individual" (348). Gardening is thus presented not as a matter of choice but as a precondition of acceptance in the suburban community.[7]

The speaker understands the garden as something that needs to be taken in hand, as well as a space for creative work and the performance of individuality. Fenced in, the garden seems to be private, yet all the gardeners in the story invite spectatorship and crane their necks over other people's fences. They pass judgments, imitate one another, and at the same time define their gardening style against their neighbors'. Where the text is most insightful is in drawing attention to the fact that the physical space of the garden circumscribes free creativity. As the Japanese woman tries to assume control over her garden, she realizes that it is not a pristine space. It bears the traces of other plantings and previous efforts at landscaping:

> [M]y acre yielded only two large lilac trees, one wistaria, some Virginia creepers and two peony bushes. Such a bare acre with nothing set out save the great trees. Yet the fair actress from whom I purchased the place had smilingly informed me she spent five hundred dollars each summer on flowers. . . . The bed, boxes, and tubs, so far, had been empty since my advent. I cannot afford five hundred dollars to fill them with the desired annuals, and at this time I cannot make up my mind whether to plant a maple tree in the huge round bed or turn it into a great sand pile for fat babies and doggies to roll in. (349)

The empty, obtrusive tubs and boxes are a constant reminder of the actress, whose ephemeral career is troped by the costly "annuals" that have disappeared without a trace. All the newcomer can do is fill the demarcated spaces as cheaply as she can.

To claim authority over the plot, the narrator must learn the rudiments of gardening. Two mentors, Mrs. C and Mr. B, undertake her training. Mrs. C's "place is on the top of a hill. She has seventeen acres of rolling lands and lawns" (351), but she claims only the space behind the house as her very own, making it distinct from the formal gardens that are under her husband's supervision. An elaborate description of her garden follows, all of it, she claims, tended by her own hand. With the words, "Now you must meet my teacher and master in the art of gardening," Mrs. C introduces the narrator to her English neighbor, Mr. B (353). Over the lilac hedge, Mr. B authoritatively dispenses knowledge to the new apprentice. The Japanese woman listens politely and comes away with a basketful of roots, too embarrassed to ask what will grow out of them.

"If a woman the age of my neighbor (she was about fifty-five) could with her own hands set out and plant a garden, why could not I, young, healthy and ambitious, do likewise?" asks the narrator. Thus encouraged, she works until her back aches and she is grimy as a hired man (485). In time, Mr. B's gift turns out to have been a practical joke: a visitor points out that the rudbeckia roots in the veranda boxes are the common roadside golden glow.[8] Mrs. C has also been disingenuous, concealing the fact that she hires men to do her digging and weeding. To make matters worse, the narrator has weeded out her sprouting flowers to cultivate the weeds. She takes her defeat in good spirit, blaming no one but herself. The lesson learned is that to imitate her white neighbors who have the advantage of wealth and expertise is a poor strategy. Her response to failure is an escape into an oriental Eden of the mind. In the fantasy realm, the gardener has no rivals. Her Japanese descent gives her the license to interpret the Japanese aesthetic.

In the dream garden, all financial and physical constraints fall away: it has no fences, only a gate; its natural border is the forest; and it contains a profusion of wild and cultivated flowers. Curiously, though, even the dream garden cannot be imagined outside the social context that gives it meaning. There are hostile neighbors here, too, so the narrator inserts a serpent to guard the flowers in their fenceless state: "It shall be a great and beauteous creature whose fame shall be known to all the neighborhood, and I also shall share in its fame." The snake is the visible sign of the Japanese woman's sense of alienation from the neighborhood and a challenge to those who find her despicable. Yet the snake is a benevolent creature, a friend to those "who fear it not—or know the secret" (490).

While the fantasy removes material constraints on the speaker's creativity, social pressures, especially those of mainstream ideology, remain. Here and there the gardening discourse merges disturbingly with the discourses of race and war, suggesting that the "perfumed, lovely Eden" may be read as a racial allegory: "I know a long, narrow bed of yellow coreopsis. When the wind blows ever so faintly these small gorgeous flowers look like an Oriental army

marching with flying colors. Beside them, more brilliantly, more triumphant-
ly, move an army of brazen poppies of enormous size and beauty. But the
coreopsis sway with the wind, and every toss of their little heads makes me
feel they are a stronger, cleaner race, and more beautiful even than the opi-
um-freighted poppies" (489–90). There is threat of war in Eden between the
Orientals (coreopsis) and the Caucasians (poppies). Beautiful and brazen, the
poppies, like the British trading ships in the Orient, are freighted with opium. (To foist Indian opium on China, the British waged the Opium Wars of
1839–42). Neither race can be described without the other—comparison and
competition are built into the language of race. Though the text struggles to
recuperate the "oriental race" from charges of filth, degeneracy, and weak
moral fiber, it does so by reversing the binary, so that the Occidental is now
less clean and less strong. Coreopsis, poppies, and all the other "races" in the
garden are relegated to separate beds, where they can presumably toss their
heads and fly their colors without ever mixing or doing one another harm.
In attempting to escape the gardening, social, and literary conventions that
hem her in, the author becomes entangled in the discourses of war, invasion,
and racial superiority.

"A Neighbor's Garden" shares its central metaphor, as well as the rhetoric of struggle, with an influential essay by Thomas Huxley, "Evolution and
Ethics" (1894). Huxley was one of several writers the narrator of Winnifred's
autobiographical novel *Me* claims to have read aloud to her father (*Me* 26).
The garden model Huxley constructed to explain natural selection in human
society likely made a strong impression on Winnifred. Gardening, Huxley
claimed, is contrary to the natural principle of struggle for existence through
which the fittest members of the species survive and reproduce. By nurturing the weak as well as the strong and using artificial selection criteria, the
gardener disrupts the natural processes of variation and adaptation, weak-
ening the original stock. Such a garden, Edenic though it may look, inevitably has its own "serpent, and a very subtle beast too" (*Evolution and Ethics*
20). Raised in luxury, all the plant species will reproduce faster. Overpopu-
lation will, in turn, set off the natural life-and-death struggle or else force the
gardener to eliminate excess plants as "unfit." Huxley made it quite clear that
he favored the "natural" way, mistrusting the gardener's competence. Seam-
lessly, Huxley's garden merges with another trope, that of an island colony:

> The administrator might look to the establishment of an earthly paradise, a true
> garden of Eden, in which all things should work together towards the well-being
> of gardeners . . . and this ideal polity would have been brought about, not by
> gradually adjusting the men to the conditions around them, but by creating

artificial conditions for them; not by allowing free play of the struggle for existence, but by excluding that struggle; and by substituting selection directed towards the administrator's ideal for the selection it exercises. (*Evolution and Ethics* 20)

Winnifred's ideal garden is a compromise between artifice and nature, a half-wild imitation of nature along the lines of Japanese gardens. It is set "close to some densely wooded land," with the trees acting as "a sort of wild protection for the transplanted creatures from their heart" (489): ferns, wood violets, and lilies-of-the-valley. By segregating the plant species, Winnifred aimed to eliminate struggle and substitute it with harmonious coexistence. Winnifred's poppies and coreopsis march not against but *beside* each other; the wood violets thrive next to the thoroughbred pansies, as do "the lilies and Oriental exotics apart also" (490). Even the serpent in her garden takes on a positive meaning: it protects the garden from outside threats instead of wrecking the scheme from within. It is difficult today to see Winnifred's segregated flower beds as a progressive model for race relations. Nonetheless, in dreaming up a garden in which uncultivated nature is permitted to overflow freely into the garden and lends itself to cultivation, she overrode Huxley's rigid extremes: total regulation of natural processes versus total deregulation that forces each living organism to struggle for existence. A juxtaposition of the story with Huxley's social theory reveals that Winnifred was far from thoughtlessly absorbing racist paradigms, as some critics have suggested. Rather, she engaged the dominant discourses at every turn, questioning some and being seduced by the apparent inevitability or dramatic potential of others.

To dismiss "A Neighbor's Garden" because it reinscribes an orientalist fantasy and puts forward a coded social model that would explode in the 1960s is to miss the author's active engagement with the social theory of her day and to insist that a pure form of resistance can exist outside hegemonic discourse. Writing stories for mass reproduction is not unlike designing clothes for the fashion industry. In her discussion of the way Japanese clothing designers function within the Western hegemony that has long dictated fashion trends, Dorinne Kondo pointed out that to uncompromisingly contest fashion—or discourse—one would have to dismantle it altogether, whereas designers want to have careers in the fashion industry (131). She continued, "Even if new colors or fabrics or shapes or drafting techniques might appear, the game of fashion itself can never be fully called into question, for ultimately the new or subversive strategies are attempts by designers to distinguish themselves from others in order to succeed at that game" (144).

In the context of such a conservative magazine as *Good Housekeeping*, Winnifred's narrative does engage in a form of contestation, however narrow its scope. By the very act of moving her Japanese narrator into white suburbia and making her a landowner, Winnifred transgresses a racial boundary. By using a narrator who blatantly disregards fences, she invites questions about their function and meaning. In response to the rhetoric of Asian exclusion, she creates a realm where there is no exclusion—though there is segregation. Most important, Winnifred asserts narrative control not just over armies of poppies and coreopsis but also over the representations of white suburbanites whom she succeeds in satirizing.

If "A Neighbor's Garden" obliquely posits race and class as an impediment to claiming authority—in this case over a plot of land—"Eyes That Saw Not" goes further in questioning the ways in which gender problematizes the process of authorizing the self. Since the text published in *Harper's Monthly* was signed jointly by "Onoto Watanna and Bertrand W. Babcock," the reader is drawn into a game of detecting shifts in style and narrative point of view to attribute the authorship of certain ideas or passages to one or the other of the writers. The undecidability makes for an unusual reading dynamic and reflects back on the thematic content.

By making the central characters white and comfortably well off, the authors remove the problems of race and writing for a living from the already complicated discussion of authorship. At the age of fifteen, the recently orphaned protagonist, Elizabeth, becomes a ward of "Graytown's leading family," the Swinnertons. She and the young John Swinnerton fall in love, with the family's approval. John leaves home for college and then embarks on a journalistic career, which is disrupted after three years when he loses his sight in unexplained circumstances. When John comes home, he keeps up his spirits by making ambitious plans to become a fiction writer and so capitalize on his reporter's experience. John's mother volunteers Elizabeth as his assistant, a job the younger homebound woman takes up with utter devotion. She reads aloud from John's notebooks, and he narrates the stories behind the notes and then formally dictates them while she writes them down. Yet as John attempts to transform the raw stuff of experience into "literature," his flair for purple prose proves fatal. Publishers reject one manuscript after another. Elizabeth, whose literary talent has never had a chance to develop, takes matters in her own hands. Partly for her lover's sake and partly to give vent to her unfulfilled ambition, she begins rewriting John's stories and sending them out in his name. John Swinnerton soon becomes in his own words "an author whom the world recognizes" (34), and having thus proved his manhood, he asks Elizabeth to marry him. Elizabeth's deception comes to light when John's blindness is cured. Being a man who "despised dishonesty" (36), he spurns her. But after rereading his own prose and realizing it is inferior to hers, he recants.

"Eyes That Saw Not" raises a number of fundamental questions: What is a story? Who owns it? How does a story relate to field notes? Can a good storyteller do without participant observation? What if social conventions prevent the storyteller from doing her own fieldwork? These questions, the text implies, are related to the unequal treatment of young men and women in Middle America. Allusions to John's free-wheeling lifestyle—nights spent in a New York morgue, hair-raising adventures in the Tenderloin, visits to women's clubs "with orders from the city editor 'to write up a funny story about them'"—contrast with the absence of any information on Elizabeth's life in the same period, presumably because there is nothing to tell (31). Mrs. Swinnerton, whose life is confined to waiting outside closed doors with breakfast trays and straining to hear what transpires inside, is a good indication of what Elizabeth may expect to become. On one level, then, the text reinscribes the ideology that valorizes men's activities "out there," while it devalues the domestic. On another level, though, the domestic is recentered by the love plot. Since the entire drama takes place in the home, the references to John's prior adventures seem pale and juvenile in comparison.

Thus Elizabeth, who has no story, must wrest authority from John, who has many stories but tells them like an "ecclesiastic who enters the pulpit in cleric robes" (32). In principle, John owns the stories because he has "been there." To justify his decision to become a writer he argues, "I have had three years of living where life most abounds. I have plenty of incident and plenty of color." The fieldwork he has done among the urban poor, the criminal underclass, and even among New York's club women is the capital he banks on. Elizabeth, in contrast, has untapped literary talent and a prospective mother-in-law who, on hearing of her blind son's plans to "write," exclaims enthusiastically, "And Elizabeth and I will be your secretaries!" (31). The Swinnertons' conviction that Elizabeth will remain their son's subordinate is so strong that when she does decide to write, she does so covertly, late at night, scribbling "with a quick nervous pencil . . . on an old pad of John's," and then transfers the credit for her work to John. By day, "hour after hour she took his dictation. She thought of those prisoners condemned to work forever at machines that merely registered their efforts—a round of endless labor with nothing but a dial face to show what might have been accomplished." By night, she guiltily appropriates John's stories. On seeing them printed under his name, she thinks guiltily, "[W]ere they not as much John's as hers?" (33).

In contrast to her fictional character Elizabeth, Winnifred did not hesitate to sign her name to the finished product when she appropriated ethnographic material from travel narratives and fiction on Japan. The most direct parallel between her appropriations and Elizabeth's is the fact that, because of their gender and class, neither woman has the resources or freedom of mobility necessary to "be there"—in other words, to see for herself the places and people that mainstream readers pay to read about. A variety of restrictions, such as social taboos, gender-segregated spaces, and women's financial dependence on men, turned certain spaces into almost exclusively male preserves, which, in turn, raised their prestige or endowed them with the aura of adventure. Even if Elizabeth could have afforded to leave the shelter of the Swinnerton mansion, romping around the Bowery would have compromised her respectability. Similarly, Japan remained the travel destination of America's wealthiest and a handful of middle-class professionals: academics, teachers, journalists, and medical missionaries. The very inaccessibility of such places as the squalid Bowery or the glamorous Japan created a market demand for their literary representations. To write marketable stories, Elizabeth and her author had to get story material through alternate channels.

A "story," as the Babcocks demonstrated, has multiple layers and locations. It is John's immediate construction of what he observes. It resides in the notes and newspaper articles he wrote. It is in John's lively narrative of his "personal experience" prompted by the notes and shared with Elizabeth, which he then transforms through dictation back into the "time-chipped phrases of the daily newspaper." From Elizabeth's point of view, what matters is "'the story of the story' as told by the reporter," whom she sees as an active participant in the events he is reporting (32). The further into the narrative, the more blurred the line between copy and original. Right after John has regained his sight, "he arose and stumbled around the room, more helpless than when he was totally blind. He began feverishly gathering the scrap-books in which the printed stories cut out from the magazines were pasted. Then he groped his way across the room to a chest of drawers. He drew out the original manuscripts—'the copies' she had called them. These, at least, were his own" (38). Ultimately John accepts Elizabeth's interpretation of what a story is. Her storytelling talent is understood to legitimate the appropriation. What makes "Eyes That Saw Not" particularly interesting for my discussion of the role of ethnography in Winnifred's writing is the way in which the coauthors attempted to subordinate "fieldwork" to "literature" and split these activities between two subjects.[9] The story rationalizes Winnifred's literary practice that involved appropriating and transforming other people's Japanese "fieldwork." The fact that in "Eyes That Saw Not" a homebound woman empowers herself by wresting authority from a free-wheeling man suggests that Winnifred saw her own representations of Japanese subjects in similar terms. It was from such male figures as William Griffis, Edwin Arnold, John Luther Long, and Lafcadio Hearn that she saw herself taking the power to represent, not from the Japanese subjects she represented in her work.

"Eyes That Saw Not" also gives us an important insight into Winnifred's epistemology. Although the Babcocks suggest that there are many ways of telling a story, on an epistemological level they imply that each narration still reflects the same objective truth. John's narrative of a particular experience projects for Elizabeth as true an image of that experience as if she had witnessed it herself. The possibility that Elizabeth might have a different perspective on John's subjects—corpses, working-class women, club women—or that the *living* subjects, at least, might see themselves differently is absent from the text. Elizabeth's sole concern is to make the story "sufficiently attractive" (33) to be publishable. When she rewrites John's words, the truth of the experience supposedly remains intact—only the telling is better. "Being there" is not essential when it comes to writing ethnographically.

It is important to remember that Winnifred asserted her authority to write insofar as others—her publishers, readers, and her husband-manager—enabled her to pass. Once she stepped into the popular fiction marketplace, however, she was subject to what James Clifford described as "the action of multiple subjectivities and political constraints beyond the control of the author" (*The Predicament of Culture* 25); in response to these forces, she reached for available strategies of authority. Her sister Edith was more resistant to mainstream orientalist discourses partly because the Chinese identity that marginalized her as a writer also removed her from market forces. Troubling and contradictory, Winnifred's writings nonetheless provide a rare insight into the interplay of reinscription and contestation. Understanding what made for her success is no less important than understanding what kept Edith from achieving it in the same historical moment.

Performing Difference

> The non-white child nourished on stories of Tarzan cannot grow up forever identifying with the white explorer; what does one become when one sees that one is not fully recognized as Self by the wider society but cannot fully identify as Other?
> —Fatimah Tobing Rony, *The Third Eye*

Although the protagonist of *Me* claims that she spins tales of her mother's land out of an innate knowledge, we know that to perform this feat Winnifred needed to do extensive library research. Pierre Loti provided her with a master plot that would structure much of her early prose, even as she sought an oppositional stance within the orientalist race and gender economy. References in her writings to Matthew Arnold and Lafcadio Hearn suggest she was familiar with some of their work. The flyleaf of William Griffis's *Empire of the Mikado* (1877) lies among her papers in Calgary, while some of her scenes and characters may have been suggested by Alice Mabel Bacon's *Japanese Girls and Women* (1891) and *A Japanese Interior* (1893). What other sources Winnifred used in her armchair anthropology is difficult to determine because she borrowed eclectically and transformed the borrowings with lively storytelling.

What the travel narratives of Japan discussed in chapter 1 have in common is an idealizing, feminizing, and occasionally eroticizing vision of the Japanese. Contacts between travelers and "natives" rarely involved deep emotional ties or long-term commitment; they were dominated by the exchange of money for goods and services in hostelries and teahouses and on the road. In the first pages of their journals, most newcomers to the country marveled at the low prices and the extraordinary respect they themselves commanded. Often, however, the prosaic element of economic exchange was written out of the narrative; what remains are memories of being bowed to and fed dainty morsels, transported, and entertained mostly by women and working-class men. In effect, the narratives imply that behind the signs of respect paid to westerners lies a recognition of their racial or cultural superiority. Japanese of both sexes are feminized by their inferior social position. The traveler is there to observe and record the spectacle, whether it is the muscular body of the rickshaw man or the movements of a dancing geisha.

To see oneself reflected in the gaze of the Japanese is also part of the tourist experience, one often discussed with relish, as in this hotel scene from Albert Tracy's *Rambles through Japan without a Guide* (1892): "The maidservants seemed perfectly curious; I should almost think they had never before seen a foreigner. . . . There was a brief dispute who should break open the eggs and who should fan his eminence the traveler. Everything he did seemed to be regarded with a kind of wonder and awe, as if he were a celestial visitor who had touched the earth for a day, but would fly away tomorrow" (36). The self-consciousness of this "celestial visitor" is heightened by the switch from first to third person to describe this moment of seeing himself observed by two awe-struck teenagers. Like other travelers, he also has a keen awareness of being "here today, gone tomorrow," of being able to enjoy transient relationships with the Japanese without commitment (at the end of the quoted passage, the narrator presents each girl with a pin and sets out on the road again). Tracy's is an acute case of narcissism, but almost every travel-writer indulges in such reflections. The role of the Japanese is then twofold: to perform for the westerner's pleasure and to allow the westerner to see him- or herself as an emissary of the (more) civilized world.

When Winnifred became a "Japanese" writer, she stepped into an already scripted role: that of an exotic female entertainer. She not only produced orientalist spectacles for the mainstream reading public but also performed them as a public figure and literary celebrity. The terms of the orientalist discourse she adopted may seem restrictive and problematic today, yet she must have found some relief in its definition of Japanese women as beautiful and desirable, in contrast with Chinese women, who supposedly acquiesced to the sin of polygamy and whose subjection to a despotic patriarchy was made outwardly visible in their disfigured bound feet. Winnifred may not have attended the dancing class in Montreal during which one of the Eaton sisters "overheard a young man say to another that he would rather marry a pig than a girl with Chinese blood in her veins" (Edith Eaton, "Leaves" 223). She would have heard of this incident, though, and been involved in others like it. To a young woman of marriageable age, brought up on Victorian romantic literature, the possibility of exchanging a stigmatized identity for a sexually desirable one must have been a strong motive for passing.

As for opportunity, the physical distance from her family, Montreal neighbors, and others familiar with her private identity, as well as the relative lack of moral restraints in the furnished-room districts of Cincinnati and Chicago, created a space for Winnifred to perform a new identity. Writing about the ways in which the emergence of furnished-room districts in the 1890s altered sexuality and gender relations in the United States, Joanne Meyerowitz pointed out that on Chicago's North Side the "high turnover rate created an atmosphere of anonymity in which lodgers rarely knew their neighbors well. Community pressures to conform to conventional familial roles were weaker than in more settled neighborhoods. And parental authorities were absent. Many rooming-house keepers, eager to keep their tenants, refrained from criticizing or interfering with roomers' sexual behavior" (188). Onoto Watanna was probably conceived in just such a bohemian setting, where not only sexual but also racial taboos were broken with impunity. Autoexoticization may have initially meant an easier meal ticket for Winnifred the underpaid typist. For Winnifred the writer, it opened the doors to commercial presses.

Performing the role of a Japanese writer meant giving interviews and supplying material for biographical notes to the magazines that published her stories and advertised her novels. As a rule, these texts were accompanied by photographs. Family snapshots of Winnifred from the period show her wearing stylish Western clothing and a jaunty smile. By contrast, in many of the early publicity photos, she wore a kimono and a serene expression. Turn-of-the-century Americans assigned more meaning to clothing than we do today. The historians Henry Yu and Peggy Pascoe have interpreted clothing as a semiotic marker representing "not only the difference between the American and non-American, but also the distance between the two" (Yu 122). For instance, Donaldina Cameron, a Chinatown missionary in San Francisco, saw the switch her female charges made from traditional Chinese to Western clothing as a visible sign of their cultural—and possibly even religious—conversion. Yet when her mission was visited by white philanthropists, the Chinese women were asked to dress in traditional attire to emphasize their heathen, needy condition (Pascoe 114–17). Conversely, Robert Peery, a missionary to Japan, warned his colleagues against wearing kimonos or otherwise "going native," for "the missionary must not be orientalized, else he will be in danger of becoming heathenized" (Peery 213). In dressing the part, then, Winnifred reached for a powerful signifier. Since the rule of hypo-descent was very much a part of mainstream consciousness,[10] the biracial writer's kimonos were seen by those who wrote about her as somehow more expressive of her true racial identity than was Western dress.

The earliest fictitious biography we have of Winnifred, entitled "Onoto Watanna, the Japanese Woman Writer," appeared in *Current Literature* in 1898, the year her stories began appearing in national magazines. Presenting herself as simply Japanese, born in Yokohama, she withheld her English family name and gave "Kitishima Kata Hasche" as "the real or family name" behind Onoto Watanna. Being racially "pure" may have initially seemed preferable to the despised "mongrel" or "half-breed" designation. But probably because Winnifred did not look very Japanese and because "hybridity" in a cross-cultural interpreter could be an asset, she claimed biracial status in subsequent texts. What also made her exceptional according to the author of this biographical piece was her initiative and adventurous spirit: "she has seen more of life and experience than the average woman of twice her age." That age is given as twenty-one (Winnifred was actually twenty-three).

When we next meet her in late 1899 in a short piece entitled simply "Onoto Watanna" in *Frank Leslie's Popular Monthly,* she is still twenty-one. A passport-style photo shows a smiling girl in a cherry blossom kimono. To bolster her authenticity, Winnifred must have brazenly informed the editor that she also wrote for the Japanese press, which was interpreted as follows: "Even her fellow countrymen have so far overcome their prejudice against women writers as to read her contributions to the *Kokumin-no-Toni* and the *Hansei Zasshi,* two magazines published in Tokyo" (553). Setting the stage for the "exotic" young writer whom *Frank Leslie's* would publish for the next three years, the editor suggested that "her position in the literary world is unique," which indeed it was. Fiction and reality merged in this persona, for "in simplicity of manner and faith in human nature [she resembles] certain of the characters created by her pen" (554).

This likeness discovered by editors between Onoto Watanna and her young Japanese heroines, who in turn functioned as tropes for Japan in the popular imagination, made Onoto Watanna a fascinating object of contemplation in her own right and for many years prevented her from aging. She was still just twenty-three in 1903, and though subsequent biographies passed over her age, the age at which she was said to have published her first story kept receding. Rather than ascribe this to custom or vanity, I would suggest that readers weary of fin-de-siècle decadence and pessimism regarded youth in an author as a major asset. "Young" and "fresh" were the adjectives most frequently applied to Onoto Watanna and her heroines, even by such seasoned critics as William Dean Howells. In his glowing page-long review of *A Japanese Nightingale,* he found the heroine young, frank, sweet, pure, and endowed with indescribable freshness and irresistible charm. Like his contemporaries, Howells extended this aura to the writer herself ("A Psychological Counter-Current in Recent Fiction" 872–88).

Today, Onoto Watanna's performances may seem idiosyncratic or excessive. Yet the ability to demonstrate not only firsthand knowledge of Japan but also blood ties with the country was the ruse that moved her out of the drudgery of office work and into the privacy of a writer's study. While Winnifred undeniably had literary talent, in her readers' eyes it was not so much talent but the biological fact of being "a daughter of a native mother and of an English father" that made her "perhaps the best interpreter of Japan and the Japanese who is writing today" ("Onoto Watanna," *Frank Leslie's,* August 1902). Dressed in the fabric of her Japanese biography, Onoto Watanna became "one who to the hereditary poetic instinct of her native land has added what of taste the Occident could teach" (Review of Frank Putnam's *Love Lyrics*).

The West—or rather the Midwest—not only taught her a great deal but also readily appropriated her as a local product. One midwestern paper presented a smiling, kimono-clad Onoto Watanna as proof that "the great west is constantly producing clever writers, so fresh and vigorous as to be a never-ending source of surprise to the older part of the continent" ("A Japanese Novelist"). Several others stressed that she was a resident of Chicago. The *Detroit Free Press* went furthest in this direction in an article subtitled "Now Chicago Boasts of a Japanese Woman Writer Who Is Destined to Make a Hit": "Although not strictly a western product, Miss Watanna may justly be claimed by this portion of the country, as it is here that she has done most of the work that has brought her fame, and she says that this busy city, with its ceaseless energy and ambition, is her greatest inspiration" ("A Japanese Novelist"). Apparently the young midwestern publishing establishment saw in Onoto Watanna not only a model immigrant who was pulling herself up by her bootstraps but also a rising literary figure who had the virtue of not being from the culturally dominant East Coast. Chicago was a city of new-comers it drew from the surrounding rural areas, from the East and South, and increasingly from abroad. Winnifred thus performed the thoroughly westernized yet exotic immigrant.

But no sooner had the Midwest launched her than she moved east. To see how she adjusted her role for the New York literary stage, we may look into a 1902 biographical note, "General Gossip of Authors and Writers," in *Current Literature.* Her image featured on the first page of the magazine is very different from the smiling passport-style snapshots hitherto reproduced by syndicated papers across the country. The new Onoto Watanna is photo-graphed almost full length, in a kimono, against a Japanese screen. She stands turned away from the camera, looking down into a book, her face shaded by an upswept hairdo. The individual features are muted; all the elements of the photograph project her as a type: a subdued, genteel Japanese woman. The kimono and screen are emblematic of her invented Japanese origin, the book—of her profession as a writer. The new *Current Literature* persona is already a best-selling novelist and "in private Mrs. B. W. Babcock." Establish-ing a respectable middle-class background takes precedence here over the "self-made woman" image. For this reason, her parents' identity is fore-grounded, "her father being an Englishman in the consular service, and her mother a full-blooded Japanese." The new Onoto Watanna is "educated here and in England . . . and has studied at Columbia University." Being the Co-lumbia-educated daughter of a British diplomat was an asset for a woman entering society, but it was her liminal racial status, particularly the associa-tion with Japan, that sold books. Granted, the review praised the "strength and power and poetry" of *A Japanese Nightingale,* but it ended by hinting at "a vague analogy between it and her life, which the curious might care to draw [and which] gives it additional interest" (236).

By December 1903, *Harper's Weekly* was ready to announce that Onoto Watanna had arrived ("Onoto Watanna"). This article was occasioned by the opening of *A Japanese Nightingale,* the play, on Broadway. A reader prepared to do some quick calculations would find that Onoto Watanna is twenty-three (Winnifred was then twenty-eight). In a striking large-collared blouse of heavy lace, she looks us straight in the eye from a 6"x 7" portrait. Two other photographs in this issue show her reading in her library and "starting from her home in Fordham Heights, New York, for a spin in her automobile." These images strongly support the story of Onoto Watanna's literary and financial success: she is a modern American woman in full control of her life, whether in the seclusion of her private study or driving a car. Here for the first time the author's persona and her everyday self are permitted to diverge, the latter being glamorous enough in itself. Taking off the kimono at this stage in her career did not detract from Onoto Watanna's mystique; on the contrary, it emphasized the feat she had performed as a Japanese woman who had become fully assimilated into American society.

In September 1904, a *Century Magazine* editorial writer analyzed at length the sudden growth of "sympathy of the American People with the Japanese . . . an utterly alien race" (Editorial, "The American Sentiment concerning Russia and Japan" 815). A general admiration for Japan's "superior preparedness, unexpected expertness and prompt victories" (816) in the Russo-Japanese War was among the major factors, he argued. It was in such a climate that Winnifred found a ready market for ethnographic articles on the Japanese character, daily life, cultural practices, and attitudes toward the West. On February 12, 1904, she was approached by an journalist from the *Evening Telegraph* for a commentary on recent developments in the Russo-Japanese War ("Natural Fighters"). The result was a fascinating interview subtitled "Daughter of Japanese Mother Says Natives Are Natural Fighters as Descendants of Famous Samurai." On this occasion, Winnifred presented herself as descended from Samurai on her mother's side and the daughter of an English army officer. "Speak[ing] with just the suggestion of an accent," she insisted that "if I were not married and did not have a baby, nothing could keep me away from Japan." Samurai blood still ran in the family: what better proof than the fact that "her seven-months-old son, a cunning little Japanese American, has been heard to cheer in his baby language for Japan." During the course of this long conversation, Winnifred displayed a fair knowledge of Japanese history, the samurai tradition, the modern Japanese army, and current events. She answered all questions competently, to the interviewer's satisfaction.

Ensconced in her elaborate Japanese identity, Winnifred felt safe enough to mention that some of her relatives were Chinese and to claim a cosmopolitan identity: "I am not Oriental or Occidental either, but Eurasian. I must bleed for both my nations. I am Irish as well as English—Chinese as well as Japanese. Both my fatherland and motherland have been victims of injustice and oppression." This cosmopolitan identity—one of double oppression—reinforced Winnifred's position of cultural mediator. However, there may have been another reason for the insertion of Ireland, the birthplace of her paternal grandmother, into the genealogy. She may already have begun writing *The Diary of Delia,* a tale narrated by an Irish maid. This was the only time in her life when Winnifred drew attention to her distant Irish ancestry, which suggests that she may again have been playing on ideas of heredity to authorize herself. The novel was to appear under the name "Winnifred Mooney." By this time, however, the Japanese persona had a life of its own, and Doubleday refused to risk publishing *Delia* under a new pseudonym.

Fewer biographical articles are available from the later part of Winnifred's career. Reviewers continued to refer to *Who's Who* notes on Onoto Watanna, and she volunteered little new information. After her 1916 divorce from Bertrand Babcock and Winnifred remarried and went with her second husband, Frank Reeve, to Alberta, Canada, she tended to downplay her racial heritage in interviews. Than, working in Hollywood in the late 1920s and early 1930s, she occasionally referred to it again, finally dissociating herself entirely from Japan during World War II. In Naomi Lang's "Alberta Women Who Make News," Winnifred was quoted as saying, "I'm ashamed of having written about the Japanese, I hate them so." For the first time, she publicly presented herself as "partly Chinese on her mother's side and very proud of the fact." Publicity photos of the older Winnifred show a very ordinary white woman, usually dressed in a modest hat and fur collar.

Variations on the theme of performance are a staple of Winnifred's writings, starting from one of her earliest stories, "A Half Caste" (1899), through her last "Japanese" novel, *Sunny-San* (1922), to a number of her Hollywood screenplays. That the characters in these texts mimic their counterparts in Western orientalist texts is apparent. I suggest, however, that we pay close attention to how and why they mimic orientalist icons. "Mimicry repeats rather than re-presents," wrote Homi Bhabha (88). When complicated by colonial relations, homophobia, or prescribed gender roles, mimicry is rarely a straightforward reinscription of pernicious stereotypes. "Those inappropriate signifiers of colonial discourse—the difference between being English and being Anglicized; the identity between stereotypes which, through repetition, also become different; the discriminatory identities constructed across traditional cultural norms and classifications, the Simian Black, the Lying Asiatic—all these are metonymies of presence," he continued (89–90). If each repetition does in fact produce change, whether by inserting new elements or drawing attention to its own imperfect approximations, then Winnifred's "formulaic" characters and scenarios (to which I return in chapter 5) are an interesting case in point. Scholars are increasingly turning to orientalist texts in search of historically situated uses of mimicry. Emily Apter, for instance, found that "campy Orientalist scenarios have always been and continue to be good value within gay drama; their over-acted quality points to the way in which nonconformist sexual identity must perform its way into existence, more often than not through the transformation of originally conservative methods" (109). Neither overtly political nor necessarily subversive, Winnifred's own "campy scenarios" allowed her to cover some unconventional ground that would have probably been out-of-bounds in any other literary mode.

Along with the anthropologist Dorinne Kondo, I argue that orientalist discourse cannot be contested from an untainted place located safely outside it and that any contestation involves recirculating the terms of the dominant discourse. This, as Kondo pointed out, may lead to the situation of subaltern peoples' reproducing forms of their own domination (10). Ali Behdad expressed a similar view; discussing the travelogue of Anne Blunt, wife of a British explorer, Behdad noted that "even a marginalized female traveler . . . could not avoid the cultural authority and epistemology of Orientalism." Anne Blunt's complicity in the production of orientalist discourse "demonstrates the impossibility of occupying a position outside the orientalist formation" (111). Having acknowledged that reinscription and contestation are inseparable, Kondo and Behdad set out to find in texts that appear to merely reinscribe dominant discourse moments that disrupt the primary reader's desires and expectations and thus alter the discourse. The question to ask about Winnifred, then, is, What does her performance accomplish besides reproducing forms of her own oppression?

I begin by looking at *Marion: The Story of an Artist's Model* (1916), a novel that paradoxically has an all-white cast, although we know now that the title character was based on Winnifred's older sister Sarah. *Marion* followed on the heels of the much publicized autobiographical novel *Me* (1915) and was the product of a collaboration between the two sisters. That of a family of gifted and unconventional sisters Winnifred should have chosen Sarah, a painter, artist's model, and actress, as her lifelong confidante and the protagonist of a novel suggests that the two had much in common. Marion is perhaps the most psychologically complex character in Winnifred's fiction, as well as a reluctant performer of difference. The text sensitively traces the protagonist's growing consciousness of being positioned as an object of many men's gazes, her ambition to become an artist in order to exchange her object-status for that of subject of the gaze, and the cultural constraints that keep her "in her place." While race is not thematized in the novel, the "white" characters represent a full spectrum of color, from Marion, whom a painter likens to a half-caste Indian girl, through the Jewish Cohen family and the "small and dark" (32) Italian suitor named Benvenuto whom Marion rejects, to Paul Bonnat, who "looks like a young Viking" and wins her heart (261).

Marion opens with two scenes in which the eleven-year-old protagonist is stared at and reacts to the stares of men. Realizing that men consider her pretty in an exotic way, Marion resolves to give up her previous ambition to be a painter like her father and instead pursue an acting career. At eighteen, she tries her hand at amateur theatricals, but the first man she falls in love with—one who would rather "keep" her than marry her—forces her to give up what he considers a "dirty life" (54). To escape the degrading love affair and pursue a career in art, Marion tries to get a job as a painter's assistant in Boston but learns that she cannot sell her professional skills at all. The turn-of-the-century art scene is split along gender lines: men study art and own the studios, women pose.[11] During the academic year, she can barely earn enough for room and board by posing in costume, and the only way to make a living through the summer is in the nude. One prospective employer, who laughs when she presents herself as "an artist and the daughter of an artist," informs her:

> I don't doubt that you will get plenty of work. You are an exceedingly pretty girl. . . . I'll safely bet that you have just the figure we find hard to get. A perfect nude is not as easy as people seem to think—one whose figure is still young. Most models don't take care of themselves and it's the hardest thing to find a model with firm breasts. They all sag, the result of wearing corsets. So we are forced to use one model for the legs, another for the bust—and so on, before we get a perfect figure, and when we get through, as you may guess, it's a patchwork affair at best. Your figure, I can see, is young and—er—has life—esprit. Are you eighteen yet? (151)

This mental undressing of Marion, the dissection of the female anatomy by the hard, normative, "objective" male gaze sets off a recurrent pattern in the novel—one of visual assault and resistance, of objectification and repossession of the self. When Marion feels she is losing control, she runs. During the course of the novel, she makes four moves, each taking her farther away from home and out of the controlling gaze of others; each time she finds herself pressed into performing her femininity to sharp commands: "Pose! Pose please! . . . Stand a little to the left. . . . Rest! Rest! . . . Pose!" (218–19).

Before she is finally rescued from this life by a painter who gives her a home of her own and removes her from the public eye, Marion joins a theatrical group that does "living picture work," the popular tableaux vivants, in which human figures were used to reconstruct scenes from famous paintings. The entire episode is written off with the words, "We played every night in the theatre in Providence, and we made what theatrical people call 'a hit.' The whole town turned out to see us" (291–92). There seems little for the woman painter to say after being bodily pressed into a copy of someone else's painting.

By using her sister Sarah as a combination of "native informant" and "participant observer" in turn-of-the-century bohemian culture, Winnifred was able to defamiliarize gender and class relations as they intersected in the production of the aesthetic. She laid out the process of making art to highlight the material and psychological costs incurred by models who were at once the most and least visible members of the artistic milieu. Rather than idealize art, she assessed its price: the cost of room and board, the risk of sexual abuse models incurred when working one-on-one with an artist, the swollen feet, and the dirty wraps provided for walking to and from the platform. For a story about the making of art, *Marion* is a deliberately anti-aesthetic text. Hovering on the verge of pornography, it nonetheless resists the expectations set up by the genre. Not only does it show little nudity, but also it is aimed to make the voyeur uncomfortable as he or she strains to see beyond the text.

As I have already suggested, the many resonances between Winnifred's life and her sister Sarah's may partly explain why *Marion* is such a thematically focused, vivid, and psychologically motivated novel. Certainly the two sisters would have had a similar experience of becoming aware of race as a stigma—but so did Edith, whose life Winnifred never attempted to explore. What may have drawn Winnifred to Sarah is the fact the two had devised similar strategies in response to being marginalized because of their race and gender: both performed the exotic difference that mainstream society inscribed on their bodies, but they tried to maintain a distance between the role and their sense of self—a distance that allowed them to always keep in sight and occasionally parody the sexist/orientalist frame within which they posed.

Winnifred had been experimenting with the idea of race as performance long before 1916, in fact ever since she took up Japanese subject matter and started constructing her Japanese persona. Though her earliest pieces are the most derivative of Japanese travel narratives, they are also the most disruptive of orientalist discourse, perhaps because they were written before Winnifred had become accustomed to her role. To demonstrate what I mean by "disruptive" I look at a short story entitled "A Half Caste," which appeared in *Frank Leslie's Popular Monthly* in 1899.

Just like Pierre Loti's *Madame Chrysanthème* and John Long's *Madame Butterfly*, Winnifred's "Half Caste" opens with a conversation between two white male travelers on board a ship about to land in Yokohama. In each case, the men on board are sex-tourists considering the possibility of meeting and "marrying" Japanese women for the duration of their stay. All three narratives feature sensuous young women who speak heavily accented English. For the men, the experience follows the orientalist paradigm of "loving, leaving, and grieving" (Blanch 116). But the similarities between Winnifred's tale and those of her predecessors stop here. The male protagonist of "A Half Caste" resists being drawn into talk of "artless, jolly, pretty" Japanese women, not because he is a prude but because he is guiltily revisiting the site of his sexual exploits. For as Norman Hilton confesses to his colleague, "on a former voyage he had married a Japanese girl—in Japanese fashion—adding with an unconcealed grin of contempt for himself, that of course he had left her in American fashion." There was not only a wife but also a child. Finding himself middle-aged and alone, Hilton yields to one of his "unconquerable impulses" to recover the forgotten daughter (489). Readers familiar with the genre would have instantly recognized "A Half Caste" as a sequel to or a parody of its famous predecessors.

No sooner does Hilton land than his fascination for exotic women overwhelms him. One in particular, the geisha Kiku, arouses his latent desires. Seeing that Hilton has hardly left a particular teahouse in two weeks, his American friend begins "to scent real danger" and advises him to "marry [Kiku]—for a while, of course, as you did the other one," for, he says, "Japanese women are different" (494–95). Hilton first tries to stay away from the teahouse, but then "intoxicated with his hunger" for Kiku, he asks her to marry him and leave for America. It is then that the broken-hearted Kiku declares she is his daughter and has been playing out her private vendetta only to find that the game has gotten out of hand.

From a contemporary vantage point, all is not well in "A Half Caste." For one thing, Hilton finds Kiku so overwhelmingly attractive because she has "red cheeks, large eyes, and white skin" (490), the implication being that racially she is a more suitable partner for him than the other geishas, including her own mother. He is also fascinated by Kiku's outspokenness, which he finds un-Japanese. Kiku confirms the stereotype: "You nod fin' thad 'mong Japanese—only me! I different from aeverybody else" (492). By making Kiku exceptional, Winnifred foreclosed the chance to extend to all Japanese or even all Asian women the assertiveness and self-awareness with which she endows Kiku. Yet with all its flaws and crudities, the story is a good example of how Winnifred, a young woman of color, read and refashioned orientalist texts. This early story demonstrates a range of strategies Winnifred devised to recuperate the meaning of her racial heritage from orientalist discourse—strategies she would return to in all her "Japanese" novels.

Where Winnifred's narrative diverges decisively from Loti's and Long's is in the portrayal of the half-Japanese woman as a shrewd, self-aware individual. Kiku, as Hilton recognizes, is neither artless nor jolly unless the teahouse proprietor happens to be nearby. In fact, she so obviously disdains the role of entertainer that the proprietor is obliged to apologize for "the girl's unreasonable dislike for foreigners" (491). Kiku not only refuses to dance for Hilton but also makes it plain that she waits on him as a matter of duty. Surly and artificially courteous, Kiku does make conversation with Hilton but only to remind him that he is paying for it. "Worg" (Kiku's pronunciation of "work") comes up ten times during their short conversation and "pay" is used three times.

> "Now you look like a Japanese sunbeam," he told her, softly, looking unutterable things at her out of his deep gray eyes.
> "Tha's account I 'fraid gitting discharged," she told him calmly, still smiling. . . .
> "Ah, I see. Then you are only pretending to smile?"
> "Yes," she said indifferently. "Tha's worg' for geisha girl. Whad do you thing we goin' to git paid for? Account we frown?" (492)

The cadences of Kiku's speech and the mispronunciations are all Madame Butterfly's, but the tone is not. Neither is her insistence on talking about the vulgar economic motive for the services rendered to tourists. Winnifred thus supplied the element of economic exchange that was so often missing from the travel narratives. Kiku "worgs" not because the Japanese traditionally indenture their daughters to teahouse owners, as some westerners claimed,[12] but because the rise of tourism has created jobs in the service industry. Couched in a distracting accented English, this is nonetheless a serious indictment of Western attitudes that dehumanize Japanese women, as well as an effort to hold one fictional perpetrator accountable for the consequences of those attitudes. In exposing Norman Hilton and his colleague as racist, unprincipled, and hedonistic, the text breaks away from the tradition that set up the Western male as conquering hero. The story may parody well-known teahouse scenes, but it does not trivialize the interracial relations that unfold behind teahouse walls as Pierre Loti's novel does. It narrates the encounter between the Western traveler and the Japanese woman through to its tragic consequences, without letting the Western traveler off the hook, as does John Long's work. Loti and Long had shielded the white protagonist from moral responsibility by erecting a wall of racial and cultural difference between him and his Japanese lover that made true companionship unimaginable. Winnifred's Hilton has to admit that the (half-) Japanese woman is not essentially "different," as his companion would have it; on the contrary, she has self-respect and a moral code superior to his own. Read as a cautionary tale, "A Half Caste" shows that the sins of the fathers are visited upon the children.

"A Half Caste" is a story about nonperformance—a familiar scenario gone awry. A later story, "The Loves of Sakura Jiro and the Three-Headed Maid" (1903), rehearses the reverse response to racism: exuberant, unabashed performance of difference. Set in a New York freak show, "The Loves of Sakura Jiro" has an entire cast of performers fooling a gullible audience and occasionally even one another. As the grotesque title suggests, the tale is somewhat surreal, but its cultural observations are historically accurate. With a rare cynicism, Winnifred told the story of ethnicity gone to market.

The story's protagonist is a Japanese student who has come to the United States for two reasons: to avoid the draft—for he has the "soul of a poet, a dreamer, no swallower of blood"—and "to pursue his study of the 'barbarians,' who fascinated him." Eight months after his arrival, the remittances from home stop coming, whereupon he finds himself out in the street and hungry. A practical man, he first tries to get jobs with Japanese businessmen, but they offer only long hours, minimal pay, and tedious work. He gazes wistfully at an American office building but dares not enter. On East Fourteenth Street, the world of commercial entertainment thrusts itself on him "through the medium of a glaring poster" (755). Sakura Jiro joins a host of other "freaks" in a dime museum.

Jiro assumes the role of "racial freak" as defined by the critic Andrea Stulman Dennett, who divided turn-of-the-century side show attractions into four categories: natural freaks; performers such as snake charmers; racial or cultural freaks; and fake freaks. A freak was a commodity that the museum operators skillfully packaged as they ushered visitors from one platform to another and provided made-up biographies, assisting viewers in the consumption of freakery (317–26). Jiro and his companions straddle the standard categories. He and the Irishman Kelly (billed as "Ostero, the Spanish Juggler") double up as ethnographic exhibits and performers. The museum's manager is delighted to hire Jiro, whom he can fit into a ready discursive framework: "We'll put up a stand there by Ostero. It will be the East and the West, side by side, exploiting the best of their characteristic civilizations" (757). Next to Jiro is the female snake charmer Yido, whose ethnicity is left ambiguous. Farther still sits the blond all-American Three-Headed Maid Marva, Jiro's love interest. Finally, hovering in the wings is the indispensable press agent, who chronicles the latest attractions and writes the speeches that the manager recites on "his adjective-distributing trip" from one exhibit to another.

The museum functions on sound business principles. A sign above the entrance advertises "the wonders of every clime, assembled from millions of miles into one aggregation, offered to public gaze for the nominal sum of a dime" (756). Each performer deals in a different brand of tricks and must differentiate him- or herself from all the others. Jiro captivates the audience with a performance that is "subtle, weird, [and] delicate" in character, while Ostero belches balls of fire and stands on his head. Downsizing soon becomes a threat: the snake charmer warns Jiro that "the manager is thinking of getting rid of one juggler and paying the other more money." Forced to invent new tricks daily, Jiro gives "signs of breaking down under the strain of the competition" (758).

But the act that sells ten-cent tickets does not guarantee Jiro success in wooing the Three-Headed Maid. In her eyes, the tobacco-chewing Kelly is far superior. She will have none of Jiro, declaring his tricks effeminate, "just like any lady who happened to be born a Hindu could do; but there is nothin' manly and bold-like 'bout them." To stand a chance against Kelly, Jiro must try "something more in Kelly's line, but something better than he can do" (758). Desperate for love, Jiro attempts an elaborate "manly" trick that nearly kills him—and wins. Marva slips off her two false heads, vaults over the rail of her platform and onto Jiro's, and clutches the Japanese man to her chest.

The dime museum may be usefully interpreted as a trope for the popular publishing industry of which Winnifred was, by 1903, a seasoned worker. The two businesses have a similar social function and structure: a metropolitan location, a publisher/manager (also called "purveyor of amusement" in the story), a press agent, a stable of expendable writers/performers, and a broad, unsophisticated customer base. Dennett also pointed out that the freak show was just a lucrative venture for the owner; for the performers, many of whom would have faced discrimination in the regular job market, it was a source of substantial income (317). Working in the "amusement" industry certainly placed Winnifred in an income bracket far higher than her biracial siblings'.

Then again, a museum that claims to harbor the "wonders of every clime, assembled from millions of miles into one colossal aggregation" (756) begs to be read as a trope for the nation. To enter, Jiro is asked to present his credentials at the box office. Though he gets in by demonstrating his job skills (he stabs his hand with a dagger that leaves no wound), once inside, he is immediately framed into playing the Oriental to Ostero's Western act. The Janus-faced American woman is out of his reach; performing on a distant platform and encased in a cabinet, she seems triply desirable with "three mouths to kiss" (757). Yet Ostero, who stands higher than Jiro in the turn-of-the-century racial hierarchy, "had only to put a quid of tobacco in his mouth, with his Gaelic grin, and shoot balls of flame to move the triple-necked lady to admiration" (758). It is probably no coincidence that the primary source of tension in the story is the rivalry between the Japanese student and the working-class Irishman. Winnifred had little sense of ethnic identity, but she did have a strong interest in racial politics. She was aware that the two ethnic groups had been at loggerheads ever since the Irish-dominated labor unions secured Chinese exclusion and Japanese immigration became the new menace on the West Coast ("The Japanese in America" 100–104).

"The Loves of Sakura Jiro" is an awkward but intriguing tale, unlike anything else Winnifred wrote. Read as a parody of the entertainment business/ popular press, it announces that appearances are all that matters and that everyone must compete as best they can. The story pays close attention to the ways in which difference is produced and staged. To function as freaks, all the characters learn how to perform exaggerated versions of race, class, or gender: Marva becomes a superwoman by wearing two false heads; Yido is the oriental factotum, a snake charmer who can turn into a kimono-clad housemaid in a flash; Kelly makes a show of such masculine working-class attributes as muscle power and belching; and Jiro works hard to be subtle. The story thus raises a number of questions that drive contemporary discussions in literary and cultural studies: How and why do we construct difference? How does difference get displayed and in what designated spaces? The contributors to the 1996 anthology *Freakery: Cultural Spectacles of the Extraordinary Body*, edited by Rosemarie Garland Thomson, suggest that objects designated for display are not in themselves of visual interest but that interest is always deliberately generated. They undertake a critical examination of the ways in which such displays as nineteenth-century world's fairs and contemporary television talk shows constitute ethnic subjects.

Jiro, Kiku, and Marion allow Winnifred to preserve a critical distance from her own performance of difference. They are smart, versatile, ambitious, and do not easily acquiesce to the place assigned them in the social hierarchy. But while they demonstrate considerable ingenuity in manipulating social and cultural expectations, the author and her characters still do not feel they have the agency to overtly challenge oppressive institutions and ideologies. They either outwit those who marginalize them or else prevail on society to embrace them as exceptions. One thing all four share is the lack of any sense of larger community: Jiro because he is a self-exiled conscientious objector during the Russo-Japanese War; Kiku because she is a half-caste in a race-conscious Japan; Marion because she is a single woman working for strangers; and Winnifred because her Japanese connection is largely imaginary, unsustained by human contacts and emotional investments. Without a community that would provide them with models of how to be "Japanese" or "Chinese" or "respectable" and monitor their performance, Jiro, Kiku, Marion, and Winnifred are left to their own devices.

In his 1998 study, Jinqi Ling historicized the issue of authenticity that emerged in the mid-1970s as a "crucial site for the Asian American community's self-contestation about how it relates to mainstream culture and the majority society." He pointed out that when the editors of the 1974 anthology *Aiiieeeee!* dismissed certain Asian American literary works as inauthentic, they invoked "such binary views as historical truth versus appropriation, artistic freedom versus cultural censorship." As an alternative, Ling proposed defining ethnic authentication as the "process through which Asian American writers had to pass in their cultural struggles in order to gain oppositional—and ironic—consciousness about their being America's racial other" (147). If we judged Winnifred Eaton by the 1970s standard of authenticity, she would be the quintessential "fake" ethnic writer. Even if we embraced Ling's formulation of ethnic authentication, trying to bring the recalcitrant Winnifred into the fold of Asian American literature would be tricky. Few writers have had a stronger sense of being "America's racial other." But since Winnifred identified culturally with the white mainstream, not with any ethnic minority, she cultivated and thrived on exceptionalism instead of gaining an oppositional consciousness. Critics may well ask, Hers is an intriguing historical case, to be sure, but is her work really any different from that of white orientalists?

"A Neighbor's Garden, My Own, and a Dream One" is a good case in point. Undeniably, the story's value for contesting the ways in which Asians were perceived and treated in America is limited. It indicates no awareness of the material situation of Japanese immigrants, the majority of whom had entered the country after 1900 as laborers, lived on the West Coast, and were segregated, harassed by nativist groups, denied citizenship, and largely restricted to menial occupations. If they cultivated gardens, they did so to eke out a living. Even the few Japanese students and student-laborers on the East Coast, where racial tensions were not as high, faced their share of discrimination, according to the historian Yuji Ichioka. Yet if we insist on bringing the material conditions of Asian immigrants to bear on Winnifred's fiction, we should not lightly dismiss her own. In the ten years preceding the publication of "A Neighbor's Garden," she had produced eight novels that established her in the literary marketplace. She had become an American citizen through marriage, she had given birth to four children, and she was writing to support them and her husband. By this time, her imagined community consisted of her publishers, her readers, and her own Long Island neighbors. Membership in this community was contingent on her ability to accommodate to a racist ideology that made her racial identity a stigma.

In her literary garden, as in the Long Island one, Winnifred cultivated flowers—Wistarias, Azaleas, Hyacinths, and Delias—as an upstart female in a tradition dominated by Pierre Loti and John Long. Winnifred's contestations are less apparent to us now because the intervening years have changed the aesthetic and political expectations through which we read both her texts and her passing strategies. Some of Winnifred's resistances now seem ineffectual or contradictory (such as the fact that she rejected Chineseness as an essential and binding category but relied on essentialist meanings of race to claim authority as a Japanese writer). But as I go on to argue in the next chapter, while mimicking a male-authored genre, Winnifred shifted its thematic focus and used the fictional space it afforded to broach such subjects as interracial marriage and discrimination against biracial children before her more politically engaged sister Edith did so.

5. Decoupling Race and Culture

All improbabilities are sheltered behind Japanese witchery, for—
what may not happen in Japan?
—Review of *The Wooing of Wistaria* in the *Critic* (1902)

IN THE 1850s, an Austrian monk named Gregor Mendel conducted a series
of botanical experiments on pink and white sweet peas in a monastery garden. We remember him today as a scientist who was ignored by his contemporaries, but whose article on pea hybridization was simultaneously redis-
covered in 1900 by three far-seeing researchers, giving rise to modern genetics.
Yet recent studies have shown that scientists at the turn of the century would
not have responded as enthusiastically to Mendel had they not already been
invested in developing a theory of biological inheritance, a project that had
acquired great urgency in their lifetimes (Bowler 110–12; Darden 40). Before
the geopolitical upheavals of the late nineteenth century, before the colonial
race, before the mass movements of peoples between continents, and before
the tremendous class upheavals in the West caused by the Industrial Revolution, Mendel's sweet peas were just that: sweet peas in an agricultural experiment. The rhetoric of "dominance" versus "balance" of "dark and light
population types" did not acquire its special resonance for several decades.
By 1900, however, Mendel's sweet peas were found to hold the answer to the
genetic transmission of "unit characters": dominant and recessive traits that
determined not only the number of grains in an ear of corn but also, supposedly, the color of a child's skin, physical and intellectual "fitness," and even
criminal tendencies.[1]

In turn-of-the-century Western thought, "race" was understood to account for differences in behavior, cultural practices and beliefs, and technological advancement of different peoples. In other words, the terms *race* and
culture overlapped to a much greater extent than they do today. The word

culture was used in the singular, interchangeably with *civilization*, until Franz Boas introduced the plural usage around 1900. Boas also argued for the transforming influence of the environment on heredity, but decades would pass before this idea, popularized by his students, would gain wide acceptance.[2] In Winnifred Eaton's formative years, popular discourse was straining in the opposite direction. The volume of writings that invested race with meaning rapidly increased as the vernacular absorbed such scientific concepts as "hybridity," "natural" and "sexual selection," "superior" and "inferior races." Herbert Spencer and Thomas Huxley had given a new impetus to the "nature versus nurture" debate, but though popular sentiment at the turn of the century had tipped in favor of nature, the debate was far from settled, and Winnifred needed no encouragement to join it. Because of the social disadvantage imposed on her by the "half-caste" designation, Winnifred had reason to question racial determinism. She also had ample counterevidence gathered from personal experience and observations of her Chinese mother and biracial siblings—evidence she marshaled in the genre of ethnographic romance. In representing successful "couplings" across race and in showing culture to be a product of nurture rather than nature, Winnifred attempted to assuage the fears of "coupling" with nonwhites.

At the end of the nineteenth century, Winnifred began to conduct her own genetic experiments, using a fictional "Japan" as her field. Her complex racial, class, and gender positioning drove her to seek new perspectives that would account for her own biracial female subjectivity. Mendel-like, she created characters of different races, made their paths cross, monitored the environmental factors, introduced control groups, and kept records. Several of her early works discussed below suggest that race is something of a cipher and that culture is not genetically transmitted. Ten years into the new century, however, Winnifred came out with the novel *Tama,* which reinstates the position of race as essence. In the language of genetics, the biracial heroine's Caucasian "characters" are aligned with the traits that allow the "light population" to dominate the "dark." As the white half of Tama's genetic makeup dominates her looks, so must the white man—a scientist—subdue the hostile Japanese to win her. He does so as an individual, by overcoming an armed samurai with his bare hands, but also as a metonym for Western civilization, secure in the knowledge that he is "a citizen of a mightier country than this" (146).

Criticism of Winnifred Eaton's work does not account for this shift toward a more conservative mainstream view of race during the first decade of her career. Until recently, Winnifred's "Japanese" novels were discussed as formulaic romances set in exotic locales or as exercises in literary tricksterism by a writer resistant to racial categorization. Lately, critics have been reading Winnifred's work in new and productive ways to explore such themes as "cultural liminality" (Lape) and the bonding of women across racial lines (Najmi). I propose reading several of the novels through the trope of controlled field experiment. In this chapter, I argue that Winnifred combined "romance" and "Japan" into a fictional space where almost anything could happen, in order to work out racial and gender conflicts that she experienced in North America but would not bear discussion in the realistic mode and in American settings. While I agree with my predecessors that to a certain extent Winnifred succeeded in "decoupling" race from culture, I caution against reductionist efforts to claim Winnifred as the unrecognized practitioner of race theory as we know it today. By doing so, we may repeat the error of Mendel's rediscoverers who, as Peter Bowler argued, "read a great deal into his paper" to claim him as the precursor of their young discipline (103).

Yuko Matsukawa's 1994 essay "Cross-Dressing and Cross-Naming: Decoding Onoto Watanna" marked a change in the scholarly attitudes toward Winnifred from a guarded curiosity to an almost unqualified enthusiasm for her subversive strategies. Noreen Grover Lape set out to recuperate Winnifred from the status of Edith's errant younger sister by pointing to Winnifred's successful representations of the "fluidity of cultural identity" (252). For Carol Vivian Spaulding, Winnifred is an inspiring example of radical racial indeterminacy and a creator of characters who elude all efforts at racial categorization. Similarly, introducing her discussion of Winnifred's *Heart of Hyacinth*, Samina Najmi suggested that "Onoto Watanna is far ahead of her time in breaking free of the notion of biological race to show how a fluid identity can empower women" (129). Going furthest in vindicating Winnifred, Najmi claimed that "Watanna advances a concept that has only recently been termed [by Jonathan Okumura] 'situational ethnicity'" (144). Although my chapter title, "Decoupling Race and Culture," places me squarely in this camp, I want to complicate these recent interpretations of Winnifred's race theory by juxtaposing three of her earlier novels, *Miss Numè of Japan* (1899), *The Heart of Hyacinth* (1903), and *A Japanese Blossom* (1906), with *Tama*, the 1910 "Japanese" novel that ended a four-year hiatus. To get a clearer sense of Winnifred's ideas on race, we need to ask not only whether she saw culture as independent of race but also how her views evolved over time, who in her fiction had access to "cultural fluidity," and how her works reinscribed racial determinism.

Japan as a Field Experiment

In the first years of her career, from about 1898 to 1904, Winnifred wrote well-researched ethnographic articles on such topics as "New Year's Day in Japan" and "Every-Day Life in Japan." Judging by the contents of contemporary magazines, demand for such reading matter was high, and editors welcomed contributions from "native informants." Her first novel, *Miss Numè*, was brought out by Rand McNally, a publishing house that specialized in maps, guidebooks, and missionary tracts.[3] The first edition was illustrated with studio photographs of Japanese women, much like those in Edwin Arnold's *Seas and Lands* (discussed in chapter 1). Evidently the publishers felt *Miss Numè*'s ethnographic content would appeal to one or both of their target audiences: tourists and missionaries. Yet Winnifred was less of an ethnographer concerned with the particulars of Japanese culture than an armchair ethnologist trying to understand the nature of race—the source of her own exotic difference in the eyes of mainstream society. Using ethnographic information collected by travel writers, in one novel after another she probed the relation between race and culture and tested the possibility of interracial love.

Winnifred's first novel, written two years before she married, studies the role played by race in courtship or love, which social science had come to call "sexual selection." Marriage, the crowning moment of traditional romantic fiction, together with the process of selection leading up to it, acquired a new significance in the last decades of the nineteenth century, when evolutionary theory began to take hold of the popular imagination. In Gillian Beer's words, "Darwin . . . emphasized not only natural—that is unwilled—selection, but also sexual selection. Both the individual will and the internalized values of a community play their part in the process of sexual selection. . . . It began to be asked what emotions, values, and reflex actions help the individual and the race to survive" (210). To write about love and marriage in turn-of-the-century America was to engage such highly charged discourses, whether one was Edith Wharton observing the courtship rituals of high society or Winnifred Eaton contemplating the marriage options (or lack thereof) for a Eurasian working girl.[4] Such scholars as Xiao-Huang Yin and Noreen Grover Lape have looked closely at the theme of marriage in the fiction of the Eaton sisters, but they have done so with little reference to turn-of-the-century race theory and the stakes surrounding racial intermarriage in Winnifred's lifetime.[5] My interest lies in the ways in which Winnifred used the genre of ethnographic romance to express her ideas on race and culture.

The children of Grace and Edward Eaton surely did not doubt that interracial love existed: they were a product of it, and they experienced love for non-Eurasians. The question was not *whether* but *where* interracial love could exist. Place is therefore central to the "sexual selection" debate. Racial taboos regulating sexual selection posed problems for any literary treatment of miscegenation on American soil. Here white workers demanded the exclusion of Asians to protect what few privileges they had against "unfair competition," while eugenicists argued for the protection of middle- and upper-class whiteness from contamination through intermarriage with the "unfit"— those morally, physically, intellectually, and racially "inferior." Winnifred's sister Edith, who in 1909 would write, "I believe some day a great part of the world will be Eurasian" ("Leaves" 224), avoided the subject of miscegenation for the first fifteen years of her career. A single newspaper article, "Half-Chinese Children" (1895), and a short story, "Sweet Sin" (1898), are the sole exceptions. In both cases, the lives of the people concerned are deeply troubled, and "Sweet Sin" ends with the protagonist's suicide. Evidently neither the real America nor a fictional "America" offered an acceptable setting for interracial love and marriage.

Japan, by contrast, was outside the purview of American labor unionists, nativists, and eugenicists alike, and since miscegenational unions were not uncommon in the history of Western imperialism, the idea of interracial love in an exotic land was perfectly acceptable to late-Victorian readers. As Amy Ling wrote, "[T]hough laws against miscegenation were on the books in many states during this time, Onoto Watanna's interracial romances seemed acceptable as long as they took place in Japan" (*Between Worlds* 51). Cases such as those in Winnifred's fiction (including "A Half Caste") involved a handful of Western tourists abroad and were no cause for concern. By locating the action of her stories in "Japan," Winnifred removed her characters from the field of U.S. racial politics. She planted them in a society stratified by gender and class but not race, where she could either invert the value of whiteness and color or create situations where white people are so few and have entered "Japan" so recently that the meaning of their whiteness is still negotiable. Westerners enter communities that already have preconceived notions of whiteness, but they are given a chance to prove their individual worth. Upper-class Japanese are often portrayed as paradigms of tolerance and intellectual curiosity, while, middle- and working-class Japanese take on some of the characteristics of North American nativists.

Winnifred's "Japan" is constructed out of such easily recognizable iconic images as Mount Fuji, lily ponds, pleasure booths decked with wistaria, houses with shoji instead of windows, and streets with jinrikishas instead of carriages. Japanese words used sparingly, often with the English meanings given in parentheses, remind us that we are on foreign soil. Wherever white

characters are present and the dialogue is in English, the Japanese characters
are marked by what Richard Brodhead called "ethnically deformed speech"
(133), an important element of "local color." Otherwise the effect of foreignness is achieved through the use of an archaic, courtly English. For descriptions of Japanese landscapes Winnifred needed to go no further than to a
tourist guidebook or travelogue. When writing her first novel, she stayed close
to the insipid guidebook chatter:

> Kyoto is by far the most picturesque city in Japan. It is situated between two
> mountains, with a beautiful river flowing through it. It is connected with To-
> kyo by rail, but traveling accommodations are far from being as comfortable
> or commodious as in America; in fact, there are no sleeping cars whatsoever,
> so that it is often a matter of complaint among visitors that they are not as
> comfortable traveling by rail as they might be. . . . Most of the merchants of
> Tokyo, however, prefer to live in one of the charming villages a few hours' ride
> by train from Tokyo, on the shores of the Hayama, where there is a good view
> of Fuji-Yama, the peerless mountain. (*Miss Numè* 54)

This lengthy treatment of railway transportation is irrelevant to the plot; it
probably found its way into the passage together with Fuji-Yama, which *is*
meaningful to one of the central characters. But in future novels, Winnifred
covered her tracks more carefully, and the occasional descriptions of nature
are carefully crafted and poetic: "The great red sun had finished its day of
travel and had dropped into the waters far off in the gilded western sky. How
very still were the approaching shadows, how phantom-like they seemed to
creep, spreading though they scarcely stirred. The glow of the sun was still
upon the land, reflecting the light on the dew-dampened trees and the upturned faces of nameless flowers, which seemed to raise their heads, hungry,
as though loath to part with the light" (*The Heart of Hyacinth* 182). Aside from
the "great red sun," an unmistakable reference to the Japanese flag, this passage evokes images of a pastoral landscape suffused with a golden light, where
anthropomorphic flowers bloom unburdened by Latin names. Such "Japanned" descriptive passages provide an appropriately poetic, surreal setting
for stories of interracial love, a concept that many of Winnifred's readers
probably also found less than real.[6]

Amy Ling (*Between Worlds* 49) and others have argued that Winnifred's
"Japanese" fiction follows old formulas, and even the narrator of Winnifred's
autobiographical novel *Me* confesses, "My success was founded upon a cheap
and popular device" (153–54). There is, however, a startling novelty about her
miscegenational plots, for how conventional is the story of a young white
American woman who seduces a Japanese student on his way home from the

United States, while her fiancé woos and weds the Japanese student's betrothed (*Miss Numè*)? Where else do we encounter a formulaic tale of transcultura- tion in which a white female infant is left to the care of a Japanese woman and develops a fierce attachment to Japan, while her surrogate mother's half- English son is bred to become an Englishman (*The Heart of Hyacinth*)? Can we really categorize as formulaic a romance that begins with the marriage of a widowed Japanese businessman to a young American widow (*A Japanese Blossom*)?[7] Each of these plots is a skeleton straight out of the American clos- et. Each plays on age-old racist narratives: of white women despoiled by brown men, of white children snatched by gypsies, of the oriental despot who holds a white slave in his harem. What allowed Winnifred to bring these skeletons out of the closet was her willingness to accommodate some reader expecta- tions while defying others. The drapery around the skeletons *is* convention- al, as is the creaky machinery of "mistaken identity" and "changing places" she used so often. Yet the machinery that made Winnifred's novels stagy and therefore nonthreatening allowed her to sidestep the Asian equivalent of the "tragic mulatto" narrative: that of Madame Butterfly. Although this narrative evolved in times of slavery to reify the boundary between the proprietor class and human property, the racism that doomed white-Asian unions and their offspring was an extension of that which created the "tragic mulatto." Only with distant "Japan" as a setting was Winnifred able to conceive and publish stories of miscegenation with happy endings.

If we read Winnifred's "Japan" as a field experiment, her plotting is bet- ter understood as controlled rather than contrived. Plot and character dia- grams of *Miss Numè, The Heart of Hyacinth,* and *A Japanese Blossom* are deliberately symmetrical. In Mendelian experiments, the scientist plants a "dark" and a "light population" of the same flowers on opposites sides of a field, then manually cross-pollinates them, and in the following season as- sesses whether one color has come to "dominate" or the "population types" balance each other. Similarly, Winnifred's novels throw together two "pop- ulation types" and follow the outcome. The cross-pollination occurs on a cultural or biological level or simultaneously on both. Of course, because of the social/cultural dimension, the symmetry can never be perfect: the sto- ries are enacted on "Japanese" soil where whites are a minority; gender- specific conventions in Japan and in the West create another asymmetry; and the unequal power of Japan and the United States in the international arena further distorts the picture. Nonetheless, in such novels as *Miss Numè* and *Hyacinth,* Winnifred attempted to match every interracial encounter with one in which the race and gender are reversed. For every successful experiment in cultural assimilation, there is usually a control group of characters who for various reasons resist the influence of the other culture. Finally, since Winnifred's "Japan" functions like a photographic negative of North America, American racist assumptions have their Japanese equivalents.[8]

To produce *Miss Numè*, Winnifred rewrote an existing novel, John Long's *Miss Cherry-Blossom of Tokyo* (1895), partly redressing the race and gender imbalance of the earlier text and making alterations to disguise the borrowed elements. The borrowings have, as far as I know, gone undetected. Long is better known as the author of a collection of short stories that includes "Madame Butterfly" (1898), itself a rewrite of Pierre Loti's *Madame Chrysanthème* (1893). As I suggested in chapter 4, Winnifred had already once critically engaged Long in her short story "A Half Caste" (1899), which exposes the racist underpinning of the "Madame Butterfly" narrative. Interestingly, like Winnifred, Long never visited Japan; according to the *Dictionary of American Biography*, all his Japanese writings were "based on the observations of his sister, Mrs. Irwin Correll, wife of a missionary" (244). Winnifred's "Japan" is thus thrice removed from reality: observed by a missionary's wife and transformed into a fantasy by her brother. Drawing selectively on Long, Winnifred absorbed some of his racist stereotypes. Yet the changes she made were substantial enough to alter the meaning of the story, so a comparison of the two texts is in order.[9]

Long set *Miss Cherry-Blossom* in Tokyo's diplomatic milieu. His characters are a mix of Western consular staff, white men and women of leisure, and a handful of their Japanese counterparts. On the Japanese side, the central figure is Miss Cherry-Blossom, the American-educated daughter of a Japanese civil servant. On the American side, there is Dick Holly, secretary of the American legation, and Mrs. Haines, who secretly loves Holly. Since she cannot claim him herself, she engineers his betrothal to her younger sister. When this relationship fails, she introduces him to Miss Cherry-Blossom. Dick thus becomes the victim of both Mrs. Haines's scheming and Cherry-Blossom's artlessly seductive ways. He loses his good name and job in Japan. It is only by a stroke of luck that he and Cherry-Blossom are reunited in the last scenes and that tragedy is averted.

Winnifred maintained Long's cast of major and minor characters, including a Japanese girl and an American diplomat, a scheming married woman and an abandoned fiancée, but she inserted several figures that alter the balance of power in the story. The Japanese girl, Miss Numè (Plum Blossom) and the white diplomat, Arthur Sinclair, are both betrothed to other people. Arthur's fiancée, Cleo, and Numè's childhood sweetheart, Takashima, meet on shipboard on the way to Japan, and it is Cleo rather than Takashima who initiates their love affair. The text constructs the Japanese man as a desirable partner for Cleo (and several other white women on board), though one rendered "impossible" by the taboo against miscegenation. A sympathetically drawn busybody, Mrs. Davis introduces Arthur to her friend Numè to cure him of his prejudice against Japanese women. But when Arthur comes to like one Japanese woman too much for Mrs. Davis's liking, she does all in her power to prevent miscegenation. Arthur and Numè succeed in getting together in spite of Mrs. Davis, but the Western taboo that keeps white women from marrying men of color is as deeply imprinted on Cleo's mind as on the author's, so that Cleo continues to deny her love for Takashima and drives him to suicide.

Unlike Winnifred, Long made no pretense at balancing his "population types." His interest lay in the effects of the interracial encounter on his white characters. Cherry-Blossom acts as a foil. Her simple if not simple-minded chatter throws their sophistication into relief. It is the white characters who fill the book with high-society banter that Cherry-Blossom cannot follow, let alone contribute to, yet they insist on her symbolic presence in their midst. As one worldly matron puts it, "Miss Cherry-Blossom, you must come with us to give the necessary local color to the affair" (84). By contrast, Winnifred's Numè, a reincarnation of Cherry-Blossom, is allowed as much space to think and speak as are the three other lovers. Though she, like Cherry-Blossom, is infantilized and stereotyped, we are made to understand from the attention other characters pay her that her words and thoughts are as engrossing as those of Cleo or Arthur. One of Long's minor male Japanese characters, Dick Holly's disloyal secretary, splits into two men in *Miss Numè:* another minor but less odious secretary and Takashima, one of the two romantic leads. However stereotypical these characterizations of the Japanese, we need to see them in the light of Winnifred's effort to balance the ratio of Asian to white characters and redistribute agency as well as charisma among them.

In her stylized "Japan," where taboos against miscegenation are less assiduously enforced than in North America, Winnifred conducted a double experiment in sexual selection. To a contemporary reader, the novel may seem to do little more than reinforce nineteenth-century racist assumptions that while white men may possess women of color, any union between a man of color and a white women is unnatural and punishable by death. Winnifred had, to some degree, internalized this belief; of the four lovers, it is Takashima who has to die. Nonetheless, to have cast an Asian male as a romantic hero, to whom several white women are attracted and whose behavior toward Cleo is impeccable by Victorian standards, was an unprecedented step in American fiction. It is not the inappropriateness of Takashima's declaration of love but Cleo's self-absorption and cowardice that the reader is asked to condemn. The union between Arthur and Numè *is* happily consummated once Arthur overcomes his "unreasoning prejudice" toward Japanese women (83).

Were it not for the conventionality of romantic fiction and the fairy tale quality of the "Japanese" settings, it is unlikely that reviewers would have enthused over cross-racial sexual selection. And enthuse they mostly did, as the following clipping suggests: "We have a bright Japanese-American story, clear away from ordinary ruts. . . . The story is one of pathos and outlines life and love in this suddenly aroused empire in the far East. . . . It is one of the stories whose novelties must be enjoyed by reading it and catching its fine atmosphere and charming spirit." The few who gave the novel poor ratings often called into question the theme of interracial romance, in the vein of this *Philadelphia Call* reviewer: "Miss Watanna manages to carry the reader through two hundred pages of yellow and white love with a dash of crimson here and there, and, after killing off three of the most attractive characters in the book, weds the winsome little Flower Kingdom heroine to an imbecile American hero."[10] Undeniably, Winnifred relied on orientalist paradigms that her contemporaries recognized, whether they liked them or not. Her portrayal of Numè, for instance, was influenced by the popular perception of Japanese women as constitutionally childish. A contemporary reviewer had no trouble classifying Numè: "Onoto Watanna talks of a very delightful little Japanese maid who fell frantically in love with a handsome young American. . . . The colored photographs of little Japanese girls add interest to the story. They are wonderfully pretty, doll-like little creatures, these little girls of Japan. It is ridiculous to think of them as women, for mentally and morally they are as ignorant as six year old children" (*Brooklyn Eagle*, n.d. [1899]). This review projected the stereotypical characterization of Numè onto actual Japanese women in the photographs, which gives us some indication of the degree to which Winnifred was implicated in the production of racist stereotypes. But when we consider her bold treatment of miscegenation in the light of the racist language of even the most complimentary reviews, we may marvel at how resistant she actually was to such pressures.

In *Miss Numè*, Winnifred gave us a fictional study of various grades of cultural assimilation in progress, from the elderly characters of both races who are too set in their ways to accept difference, through newcomers to Japan who insist on imported foods and heavy Western furniture, to Arthur Sinclair who very nearly "goes native." Admittedly the transculturation is not quite symmetrical, for the text assumes the Japanese have more to learn from the westerners than the reverse. Numè, though she has never left Japan, has picked up many Western ideas and a little English by interacting with her father's American neighbors. She studies Western ways throughout the novel. Takashima has been following the same track when we first meet him; after eight years in American schools, he has undergone the greatest transformation of any character in the novel. He is so changed that he can no longer fit into the prescribed role of a Japanese son.

However, many racial "traits" thought to define "Americanness" and "Japaneseness" are in flux throughout the novel, and if not all attributes typically assigned to one or the other of the races are disputed, a good many are shown to be present in both. White Americans, caught up in a linear notion of civilization, claimed the apex on the grounds of intellectual development, aesthetic sensibility, and capacity for deep emotion. In nineteenth-century Western thought, a "highly developed" aesthetic sense was not just a function of being smarter than someone with "simpler" tastes. A person capable of appreciating the beauty of rugged Alpine peaks was understood to be a fundamentally better, more spiritual being.[11] Matthew Arnold's *Culture and Anarchy* and Herbert Spencer's essays "Personal Beauty" and "Progress" in his book *Progress: Its Law and Cause* talk about aesthetics in a moral and developmental framework. To question the racial hierarchy, Winnifred foregrounded the emotional and artistic sensibilities of her Japanese characters. We often see Takashima, who "like the rest of his countrymen . . . was a passionate lover of nature" (27), quietly contemplating the beauty of Mount Fuji or a sunset at sea. An articulate aesthete, Takashima holds his own in conversations with westerners. Numè, in turn, carries the story's emotional burden. She is a hyper-feminine bundle of passions—love, fear, pain, confusion, and despair—rather than the emotionless doll some of the white characters believe her to be. Several Americans stoop to base tricks and evasions, while their Japanese counterparts exhibit a strong sense of dignity and responsibility. The text thus denies that "Americanness" is any guarantee of integrity or moral superiority.

Winnifred's first three novels, *Miss Numè, A Japanese Nightingale,* and *The Wooing of Wistaria,* all tackle the problem of race from the point of view of young adults who must work around preexisting prejudices, taboos, and laws in order for sexual selection to take its "natural" course. The next two novels I discuss, *The Heart of Hyacinth* and *A Japanese Blossom,* center on the socialization of children, particularly on the ways in which certain culture-specific predispositions commonly thought to be hereditary are, in fact, learned. This was a time when Winnifred, as she herself put it, was producing "a book and a baby a year" (Price 124), writing novels to support her children and observing them as she wrote. In her life, as in both these novels, miscegenation was an accomplished fact. She now focused on its consequences.

The action of *Hyacinth* covers seventeen years, from the day of Hyacinth's birth to her marriage. Hyacinth is born in Madame Aoi's house to a dying white woman, who seeks refuge there from a faithless white husband, Richard Lorrimer. Hyacinth's development is paralleled by that of Koma, eight years her senior, son of Aoi and a wealthy Englishman who is now dead. The goal of this controlled experiment is to see the effect of a Japanese environment on a genetically white child and the effect of an English education on a Japanese-English boy raised in isolation from his Japanese peers. The narrator restudies the children's relationship with their environment and with each other at four critical stages in their lives, revealing the subtle changes that have taken place in the interim. At each point, we are asked to gauge the degree to which they have grown into or away from Japanese culture. The age and gender asymmetry between the children complicates the comparison. It makes for interesting interactions and adds variety to the otherwise predictable plot.

Madame Aoi has converted to Christianity, and English is spoken in her home, though she retains Japanese dress. She keeps her son away from Japanese children to raise him as his father's heir. Two sets of cultural influences tug at Aoi and her children. Each side is represented by a handful of character types, few of them endearing. The villagers, the schoolteacher, and the Yamashiro family, whose son wants to marry Hyacinth, stand for traditional Japan. Two English missionaries, an American lawyer and a diplomat, and eventually Hyacinth's father and his second wife descend on the Aoi household in an attempt to draw the resistant Hyacinth westward.

From Hyacinth's birth, at which point Koma is a withdrawn, lonesome child, the narrative skips about seven years, during which foster brother and sister are inseparable. The story resumes when Koma is a youth of sixteen, devouring Western literature. Hyacinth has become a naughty tomboy with no inkling of the troubles ahead. The author captures the family members in a symbolic tableau, looking at their own dim reflections in the well: "'See,' said little Hyacinth. 'There's big cherry tree in well, and little girl under it also.' Aoi looked at the reflection, lingered pensively at the three faces in the water, then drew away. 'Come,' she said. 'Listen; those temple bells already are beginning to ring'" (48). In this private moment, they are still just a family, not defined by anyone else. Hyacinth, a child deliberately raised without mirrors, does not even recognize herself at the bottom of the well. No outsider—not even the narrator—comments on the incongruity of the small group. And no one, as yet, has a stake in claiming the children's racial allegiance. But the bells interrupt their private moment, calling them to church, and the two ministers advise Aoi to send Koma to England, in accordance with his father's will.

When the West claims Koma, Hyacinth rebels against the authority of the church and turns to the Japanese community. After a time, she so thoroughly identifies with it that she "would shout strange names whenever the gaunt figure of the white missionary appeared. 'Foreign debbil! Clistian!'—such were the names this little Caucasian girl bestowed on the representatives of her race" (66). Koma claims his English roots offstage, apparently without impediments. When four years later he returns, Hyacinth shuns him too, until he changes out of his dark suit into a kimono. At twelve, Hyacinth learns from Koma that she herself is white, but the knowledge does not affect her love for Aoi and for Japan. She wears the kimono as camouflage and is not interested in trying on her mother's American dress that Aoi has kept as an heirloom. At seventeen, she accepts a marriage proposal from a strictly traditional Japanese family. The news of her father's arrival from America makes her run for the hills, and when she finally has to face him, she acts the role of a demure Japanese maiden for protection:

> With drooping head, Hyacinth softly entered the room. At first glance she seemed no different from any other Japanese girl, save that she was somewhat taller. She was dressed in kimono and obi, her hair freshly arranged in its smooth butterfly mode. Her face was bent to the floor, so that they could scarcely see more than its outline.
>
> She hesitated a moment before them; then, as though unaware of the impetuous motion towards her of the man she knew was her father, she subsided to the mats and bowed her head at his feet. (232)

Readers who have come to know Hyacinth as a vivacious, willful young woman can now see in close detail each of the elements of her Japanese persona: the clothing, hairdo, demeanor, and exaggerated performance of the ceremonial bow. In fact, the motif of dressing and undressing repeatedly draws attention to the constructedness of racial difference. Scenes of Aoi and Hyacinth coaxing their hair into appropriate styles; of Aoi, Hyacinth, and Koma practicing their English on one another; of Koma changing into and out of Western clothes; and of strangers reading contradictory meanings into Hyacinth's features depending on what they believe to be her "true" race all reinforce the message of the narrative: that heredity does not determine a subject's cultural identity. The novel's climactic moments are those in which Hyacinth and Koma make decisions concerning family and national allegiance. Paradoxically, the white Hyacinth asserts her Japaneseness by breaking the long-standing Japanese tradition of filial piety and acting in defiance of her white father. The biracial Koma, in turn, chooses to remain in Japan to marry Hyacinth and thus places love for his family over the allure of life in the West.

Because the plot of *Hyacinth* is improbable and its settings idyllic, reviewers and critics have rarely gone beyond commenting on its fairy-tale-like quality. It is important to note that the first readers of *The Heart of Hyacinth* did not necessarily see it as a story that denaturalizes race. Some quite easily read their hereditarian theories into the text, as did the reviewer who remarked on the "various racial combinations and admixtures of eastern and western temperament and modes of thought. The hereditary influences are not always known to persons subject to them, and out of this grow mysteries, griefs, and surprises, which the author has treated with considerable appreciation. It is the conflict of inherent and acquired traits that gives *The Heart of Hyacinth* its particular importance" (*Public Ledger,* September 20, 1903). This and many other reviews that neatly slotted the novel into orientalist or hereditarian paradigms provide a sobering counterpoint to overly optimistic claims about the subversive strategies of Winnifred's work. Those who read for "local color" found plenty. Even those who were fascinated by Winnifred's experiment with "racial combinations and admixtures" did not necessarily see the results in the same light as an academic reader might a century later. It is only recently that the novel has begun to draw critical attention. "Through *Hyacinth,*" wrote Najmi, "Watanna challenges prevailing notions of the 'naturalness' of blood ties and racio-cultural identity as immutable and inherited rather than acquired" (142).

Of Winnifred's novels, this one probably works hardest against Western assumptions of cultural superiority. With the exception of Hyacinth and her mother, most of the white characters in the novel are satirized. They come to "Japan" armed with penknives to chip souvenirs off sacred monuments, and they put on airs, have dreadful manners, and otherwise make nuisances of themselves. In contrast to *Miss Numè,* where the point of view is always that of a tourist, in *Hyacinth* the reader occasionally has the illusion of being an "insider" looking out, as when "two strangers to Sendai, tall and uncouth-appearing foreigners [come] walking down the main street." The illusion is only momentary, for in the second half of the sentence we encounter a cultural comparison that can come only from a "outsider" looking in: the strangers come "walking in the swift, swinging fashion peculiar to the Westerner, so totally unlike the shuffling slide of the native" (166). But though the point of view is inconsistent, Winnifred did try to decenter Western notions of beauty and civilization by writing a novel in which it is the white race that is marked.

The wearing off of cultural difference through intimacy is the theme of *A Japanese Blossom,* a fictional study of Japanese and American children brought together by chance in one household. As in *Hyacinth,* Winnifred was interested in children's reactions and adjustment to another culture depending on their age and gender. Instead of tracking two children through childhood and adolescence, here she introduced characters ranging from infancy to seventeen and compressed the action into the two years immediately before and during the Russo-Japanese War of 1904–5. While Winnifred continued to question racial determinism, she also exploited the American public's fascination with Japanese military prowess and, in effect, came close to making it a national trait. Consequently, *A Japanese Blossom* can be viewed as a transitional novel between her antideterminist early fiction and the later *Tama*, which bears traces of eugenicism.

A Japanese Blossom focuses on children's changing responses to miscegenation, cultural conflict, and war, presenting a model for resolving racial prejudice within the family. Yet even as the novel condemns brutality, the war provides a glamorous, titillating backdrop. In effect, we are left with an ambivalent text that upholds pacifism but is itself energized by war. Much has been said about the impossibility of effectively contesting a phenomenon without representing and thus reinscribing it. *A Japanese Blossom* is a peculiar case in point because it invokes Japan's victory over Russia as evidence that invalidates once and for all the claim that Asians are an "inferior" race.

Although the story of *A Japanese Blossom* was neither more nor less farfetched than Winnifred's earlier plots, it failed to enchant in the way *Wistaria* and *Hyacinth* had—perhaps because the author misjudged the mood of the times. When she began writing, Japan's popularity had reached a high point on the East Coast, but by the time the book came out voices alarmed at Japan's expansionism had begun to dominate. Winnifred had also lost sight of her intended audience: though the text dealt with adult themes, its comic elements and focus on children placed the book in the juvenile fiction category.

By this time, Winnifred, too, was tiring of Japonica and resented the fact that publishers pressed into her this niche. In 1907, she published *The Diary of Delia* in Irish brogue (analyzed later in this chapter) and published no more novels until 1910. When she resumed her career after the break, it was with another "Japanese" novel, *Tama*, a text very different from the three discussed above in terms of historical setting and characterization, as well as attitudes toward heredity and race. In sharp contrast to *Blossom*, *Tama* goes back to the end of the feudal era and the emperor's restoration in 1871, with references to the 1850s. There are also significant differences between the characters of *Tama* and those of its predecessors. In the earlier novels, the white and Japanese protagonists were ordinary rather than heroic: Arthur, Cleo, Takashima, and Numè were nice enough people but burdened with a generous share of weakness. Hyacinth's and Koma's exceptionality lay in their peculiar social positioning, not in any innate qualities, and the Kurukawa chil-

dren were quite ordinary. Each of these fictional experiments in transculturation seemed to offer the hope that, in time, racial intolerance can be overcome since history is responsible for behavioral differences commonly attributed to race. In *Tama,* that hope begins to crack. The white American teacher,
O-Tojin-san, who comes to the town of Fukui to set up a college, is a hero of
not just exceptional intellect and moral character but Herculean proportions
as well. The heroine, Tama, is a Puck-like imp, singular in every way. Child
of a Japanese priestess and an Englishman, she is blond, blue-eyed, *blind,* and
lives in the wild, hounded by her mother's people who believe her to be a fox-
woman—an evil spirit in human flesh. Tojin's mission in *Tama* is not to learn
a new way of life but to reeducate the Japanese and save Tama from them.
Tama's role is to allow herself to be tamed and saved.[12] Next to Tojin and
Tama, the other characters in the novel are dwarfed, reduced to a faceless mob
of "foreign-haters" or displayed for comic relief.

Interestingly, Tojin's character is based on a combination of two historical
figures: William Griffis and Lafcadio Hearn, both discussed in chapter 1. Griffis
worked in Japan in 1870–74, including a year in Fukui, under circumstances
similar to those described in *Tama.* Hearn came to Japan two decades later,
married a Japanese woman, and stayed permanently. Both were teachers.
Where Hearn's face had been disfigured by an eye injury, the fictional Tojin's
is marked by smallpox. Both men are extremely self-conscious about their
looks: Hearn always posed for photographs with the disfigured side of his face
away from the camera, while Tojin is afraid to let Tama see him at all, for fear
she might reject him. The myth of the fox-woman is most likely a borrowing
from Hearn, who introduced American readers to this and other legends.

Instead of doing a close reading of the novel, which has already been astutely analyzed by Rachel Lee, I focus on the shift in Winnifred's literary
approach to race and culture that led her to idealize whiteness and embrace
exceptionalism. In my analysis of the three earlier texts, I pointed out the
(imperfect) symmetries that make for awkward plots but preserve some semblance of balance between the races. *Tama,* in contrast, is remarkable for the
imbalance between the male and female protagonist; between the heroic
American and the cowardly, superstitious Japanese; between the enlightened
West and the as yet unredeemed East. Although the novel condemns racism,
bigotry, and mob violence, it firmly links these transgressions to the Japanese. It thus rationalizes any racial prejudices white readers bring to the text.

Where the earlier novels downplayed the notion of "blood" or racial affinity, *Tama* makes it crucial once more. It is because Tojin recognizes in Tama
"his own skin and blood" (107), because of "her unbound hair of gold, her
bosom and face of snow" (171), that his curiosity about her turns into a sense

of responsibility for her well-being. Tojin and Tama seek each other obsessively, through great obstacles, because each has heard of the other's whiteness. The sight of Tama's blond tresses sparks in Tojin a "revolution, mad, irresistible passion of the primitive man" (172). In declaring to Tama, "You are not Japanese" (123), Tojin assumes that since Tama has inherited her father's physical characteristics, she is also somehow culturally white. ("'Its Wavering Image'" by Edith Eaton offers an interesting parallel, though it is the villain who makes a similar pronouncement about the half-Chinese heroine: "You do not belong [in Chinatown]. You are white—white" [63]) The more time and passion Tojin invests in pursuing Tama, the less interest he takes in his students, until he abandons them altogether. To elevate whiteness, the novel must devalue the Japanese. It is tempting to say that Winnifred consciously or not managed to circumvent her publishers' injunction to "stick to [her] last" ("You Can't Run Away from Yourself" 5)—Japonica—by writing a "Japanese" romance about white people.

Except for the portrayal of a handful of Tojin's favorite students, the text repeatedly tropes the Japanese as animals, scuttling "like panic-stricken rats" (83) or "snarling" and "growling" (75) like "a whipped dog" (54). Why might such negative images of the Japanese have worked their way into *Tama*? Why are Tojin and Tama inscribed in a messianic discourse, he promising to lead her "out of the wilderness," she asserting, "You are the light" (139)? Why the "aureole" (178) around her head? Why the need to reassure readers in 1910 of white superiority?

As I suggest above, public sentiment toward Japan did start to turn after 1905. According to the historian Roger Daniels, the effects began to be felt most strongly on the West Coast, starting with the move in California to segregate Japanese schoolchildren in 1906 and to prevent "aliens ineligible for citizenship" from purchasing land. One by one, states began to extend the "Mongolian" category in pre-1902 antimiscegenation statutes to include the Japanese, and after 1909, seven states passed new legislation prohibiting Japanese from marrying whites (Sollors 402–7). On the national level, Congress passed a bill to ban Japanese immigration through Hawaii, Mexico, and Canada in 1907, and early in 1908 the Gentlemen's Agreement was negotiated with Japan, whereby the Japanese government would not issue passports to laborers bound for the United States (Daniels 38–45). The growing mistrust of Japan can best be measured by the preparations the U.S. Navy initiated for defense in case of a Japanese attack on the Philippines or the West Coast.[13] William Griffis, champion of the Japanese since the 1870s (see chapter 1), was surely responding to these alarming signals when he wrote *The Japanese Nation in Evolution* (1907), offering proof that the Japanese are racially white. Griffis claimed that since the Japanese descended from the Aryan Ainu tribes, "to-day the white man's blood is in the Japanese, for the better working of his own brain, the improvement of his own potencies, and the beautifying of his own physiognomy. The Aryan features in the Japanese body and mind are plainly discernible, and in thousands of typical instances they are striking" (26). Although he conceded the Japanese had an admixture of Malay and Mongol blood, he emphatically stated that they were unlike the Chinese in physiology, language, and customs and therefore had to be treated on par with other Caucasians. When Americans designated the Japanese the "new yellow peril," Griffis made them white.

Compounding the deteriorating image of the Japanese was the growing preoccupation with the concept of race in America. If the number and type of entries in the *Reader's Guide to Periodical Literature* is any indication, there was an explosion of popular writings on race and heredity between 1905 and 1910. Between 1890 and 1899, the *Reader's Guide* contained just seven references to articles on "race" and ten on "eugenics." In the next volume, covering 1900–1904, there are six articles listed under "race" and two under "eugenics." However, from 1905 to 1909, there are twenty-seven entries on "eugenics," sixteen on "race," forty-four on "race problems," twenty-five on "race riots" (against African Americans, Japanese, and Chinese), over a dozen on "race suicide," as well as references to such listings as "Caste; Immigration; also Chinese; Jews; Negroes; also names of countries, subheads Native races."

Although the number of published articles may not necessarily be correlated with a sudden deterioration of race relations in the United States, for those had been turbulent for centuries, it does mean that Americans were reading more than ever into race and writing about whiteness with astonishing passion. "Sexual selection," wrote Havelock Ellis in the *Eclectic Magazine* (which also published Winnifred's and her husband's work), "even when left to random influences, is still not left to chance; it follows ascertainable laws. . . . People do not tend to fall in love with those who are in racial respects a contrast to themselves; they do not tend to fall in love with foreigners" (19). Once the very notion of sexual selection between races was eradicated, one could concentrate on the "eugenic ideal," which would allow the races at a "high stage of civilization" to compensate for their dwindling numbers: "If the ideal of quantity is lost to us, why not seek the ideal of quality? . . . are we now not free to seek that our children, though few, should be at all events fit, the finest, alike in physical and psychical constitution, that the world has ever seen?" (15). It is worth considering what those powerful discourses may have meant to Winnifred, a professional writer immersed in the popular culture of the day.

Keeping the arguments of Ellis and Griffis in mind, we should give Winnifred full credit for using her fiction to explore racial intermarriage and the possibility of Asians' assimilating Western cultural values and vice versa. It does become apparent, however, that her fictional experiments with "decoupling" culture from race were contingent on the approval of her reading public. In times when the general public wanted to believe that "like is attracted to like" (Ellis 19) and that elite Western culture is a synonym for Culture, it would have been difficult to write about sexual selection across all races and to hold up cultural fluidity as an ideal even if Winnifred had been strongly invested in the cause. Cultural fluidity in Winnifred's novels is available to biracial characters whose features are ambiguous and to the refined, educated Japanese and Caucasians. Working-class characters of both races, such as the Irish nanny Nora in *Blossom* or Tojin's servants in *Tama*, seem frozen in their ethnic ways. Neither is cultural fluidity available to the black Jamaicans in *Me* (1915) or to the Chinese men in *Cattle* (1924) and *His Royal Nibs* (1925). Finally, cultural fluidity in Winnifred's fiction means, with a few exceptions, the freedom to choose Western ways and, in the case of the biracial protagonists, to marry a white person.

To point out the contradictions in Winnifred's understanding of race is not to discount the value of her texts in their own right or their value as unique historical records. On the contrary, her novels give us a rare insight into the complexities of turn-of-the-century mainstream ideology of race inflected by the agile, inquisitive mind of a biracial writer. It was the concept of race rather than knowledge of Japanese culture that absorbed Winnifred in the early years of her career. As I argued above, Winnifred found in the genre of ethnographic fiction a suitable platform from which to investigate race and redefine miscegenation. Her choice of "Japan" as a fictional space for exploring such controversial subjects was motivated precisely by its geographical and cultural "distance" from the United States and by its positive image in the United States. The American press had, for some time, been styling Japan as a sort of anti-China—a more energetic, tractable, and progressive Asian nation. The Japanese were consequently felt to be less alien than any other nonwhite people. Had Winnifred been interested in ethnography as such, she might have chosen a more easily accessible group and engaged in her own participant observation. Had she felt the need to identify with an nonwhite community, her life might have followed a course similar to her sister Edith's. Instead, like the nineteenth- and early-twentieth-century anthropologists, Winnifred based her writing on solid ethnographic homework. When Japan's exotic aura began to wane in the wake of the Russo-Japanese War, Winnifred sought difference elsewhere: inside the home where lines of class divided the kitchen from the parlor, on the closing western frontier, and in the dance halls of San Francisco's Barbary Coast.

Irish Maids, Cowboys, Indians, Illegitimate Sons, and Others

Though Winnifred's commitment to ethnography may have been superficial, her interest in difference was not. It colored most of her fiction and movie scenarios, even those with an all-white cast. Exploring the tensions between a dominant group and its "others" was more than an intellectually and psychologically satisfying practice for a writer deeply conscious of her race. Difference, whether of race, gender, or class, was and still is highly marketable—an inexhaustible source of plots. Literature feeds on stories of individuals overcoming inequality. The sense of injustice caused by social constructions of difference may serve as a rallying point for group action, or it may lead individuals to defy the oppressive ideologies, for instance by "passing," a phenomenon that, as many recent studies show, also lends itself to dramatization. Drama is thus inscribed in social constructions of difference. Whether writing a "Japanese" story for *Harper's Weekly,* or the fictional biography of her sister Sarah to be serialized in *Hearst's Magazine,* or a moving-picture scenario for Universal Studios, Winnifred balanced precariously between exploring and exploiting difference.

During her prolific Hollywood years, Winnifred was required to transpose one kind of difference into another, depending on what was in vogue at a given moment. Mexico, Russia, Shanghai, Borneo, San Francisco's Barbary Coast, and an Indian reservation are just a few of the settings with which Winnifred had to work. The degree to which she saw various types of difference as interchangeable is nowhere more apparent than in the following letter of March 5, 1930, to the filmmaker Carl Laemmle, written when Winnifred lost her position as story editor for Universal and had failed to secure other permanent work,

> If we have bought this play [*East Is West*] as the newspapers say, may I be assigned to the adaptation? This is the sort of thing I do best, and I could turn you out a corking treatment. I have any number of lyrics and jingles—Japanese—which may be transposed for a Chinese picture, and if Lupe Velez were to do the picture, she could sing them very charmingly and cutely. I think you know that I have written a great many oriental novels. . . . If we do an oriental picture, I'd like to work on it . . . when—of course—I am back on the pay roll.[14]

Several points are worth making about this passage. The letter was evidently written in a highly competitive environment by a writer anxious to get work. Her use of the first person plural pronoun in the phrases "if *we* have bought the play" and "if *we* do" marks a strong identification with Universal and its commercial interests. This identification prompted Winnifred to distance herself from things Chinese and Japanese and envisage the script from Laemmle's vantage point as a series of jingles to be sung "cutely" by a white actress passing for Chinese. At the same time, Winnifred took pride in her "oriental" novels and invoked them to demonstrate expertise in a specialized field. Finally, she used the category "oriental" in much the same way that white mainstream Americans did at the time, deliberately eliding the cultural specificities of "Chinese" and "Japanese" culture. The two function as commodities, signs of a difference that is interchangeable rather than unique.

We may wonder today at the degree to which the writer of that letter had internalized white racist attitudes. But if Winnifred was a shrewd storyteller aware of the dramatic potential and therefore the market value of difference, she was also a Eurasian preoccupied with the ways in which cultural communities produce and maintain the concept of difference. Among her most interesting and at the same time least studied works are those which "decouple culture from race" in the sense that they contrast different cultures or social groups within one racial community. To illustrate this process, I focus on two novels that have received little critical attention: *The Wooing of Wistaria* (1902), a novel with an all-Japanese cast set in Japan, and *The Diary of Delia* (1907), with an all-white cast set on Long Island. In the first case, Winnifred removed race from the narrative as the biological foundation of social difference and began to explore historical explanations. In the second, she broke away from exotica and, in a move not unlike that which Edith would make a few years later (see chapter 3), turned her ethnographic eye on the customs and manners of the (racially unmarked) white middle class. To create a cultural distance from which to view her subjects, she used a working-class Irish narrator.

The Wooing of Wistaria is a romance set on the eve of Commodore Perry's "opening" of Japan and ostensibly has nothing to do with the "race problem" since all the main characters are of the same race. Nonetheless, the narrative presents a paradigmatic case of the social construction of difference. A single word, *Eta* (denoting a difference that has no visible signifier in the way that "race" is attached to skin color),[15] wreaks havoc in the life of the heroine. Wistaria is unaware until she comes of age that she belongs to the Eta, "the despised pariah class of Japan" (108). Though she looks and feels no different from the aristocratic relatives who have been "passing" her off as one of their own, overnight, Wistaria finds herself on the social margin.

Ties of blood bind her to her deceased Eta mother and to her father, a samurai who had incurred the displeasure of his lord and was exiled to an Eta
settlement.

The central plot of *Wistaria,* the longest and most complex of Winnifred's
novels, involves an illicit romance between Wistaria and Prince Keiki, whose
families are divided by their loyalties to the shogun and the emperor, respectively. Wistaria becomes embroiled in espionage when her family discovers
the true identity of Prince Keiki, who has been courting her in disguise. Under
duress, Wistaria wrests from him information useful to her clan. To save the
prince's life when he is captured by her father, Wistaria suggests that marrying her, an Eta, would be a punishment worse than death. Prince Keiki is
indeed crushed and immediately abandons his newly wed wife. To prove
herself worthy, Wistaria enters his service in disguise and goes to war. Eventually husband and wife are reconciled, and when Japan enters the modern
era, the Eta category is erased.

There are other types of difference in the novel. Winnifred portrays a society also fractured by clan rivalry. Members of the two warring clans harbor prejudices that go back for generations, and they distinguish themselves
from the other by means of uniforms. Yet such policing is ineffective, for
lovers pass in and out of rival clans by cross-dressing. In times of war, Wistaria
uses that same strategy to escape the restrictions of gender that would keep
her away from the man she loves. Dressed as a soldier, she proves her mettle
in the battlefield, as have many legendary Chinese and Japanese women,[16] and
is eventually reconciled with her husband. At the end of the day, the gender
binary is reinstated, for Wistaria gratefully slips back into her feminine role,
but the differences of caste and clan are exposed as meaningless.

The genre of historical romance allowed Winnifred to look at specific social inequalities from a geographical and temporal distance, trace the history of their institutionalization, and erase them in the fictional world. In Japan's social castes and clans, she found an analogy to the racial lines that
fractured North American society; in Wistaria's soldiering, an analogy to
Western women's desire to collaborate and compete with men in the public
sphere. But if teasing out the possible political meanings of *The Wooing of
Wistaria* is rewarding task today, it is sobering to realize that early twentieth-
century readers were not impressed by the amount of historicizing it took
the author to make her proposition—if they saw it at all. One reviewer called
it "a chivalric romance of old Japan . . . marred by overmuch history" (*Record
Herald,* November 29, 1902). Remarking on the Japanese caste system, ven-
dettas, blood, and gore, another reader exclaimed, "What savage people the
old Japs were!" (*American Illustrator,* May 1903). No one attempted to extend

the meaning of the story beyond the shores of Japan. We can therefore conclude that the exotic location and historical distance that helped sell the book also effectively depoliticized its meaning.

Four years after *The Wooing of Wistaria,* Winnifred became disenchanted with the "long ago and far away" and wrote a comic novel, whose action takes place "here and now": in a "white" household on Long Island. Its title, *The Diary of Delia: Being a Veracious Chronicle of the Kitchen with Some Side-Lights on the Parlour,* announces that the story will turn on the contrasts of class difference. It promises the reader a peek into the kitchen to see "how the other half lives," as well as an unusual view of the parlor from below the stairs. As I explained in chapter 4, Winnifred submitted the novel to her publisher under the Irish pen name "Winnifred Mooney." Not willing to take the risk of releasing a novel by an unknown author, Doubleday decided to use the best-selling name "Onoto Watanna." The combination was not at all auspicious, for it undermined Winnifred's credibility both as the author of the new "Irish" novel and as a "Japanese author" and led to such bemused comments as "Onoto Watanna is the interpreter of a great variety of people of all sorts of nationalities. She reminds one of the quick-stepping individual who went in one prance 'from Turkey to France'" (*Pittsburgh Dispatch,* January 10, 1907).

If *Delia* is one of Winnifred's early attempts to turn the gaze away from people of color to dominant Western culture, it succeeds by a half-measure. On the one hand, the young Irish narrator does give us a mildly satirical sketch of the white middle class; on the other, she herself is the novel's true ethnographic subject, for it is her difference that the reader studies intently and compares with some preconceived Irish immigrant norm. A reviewer in the *Philadelphia Enquirer,* for instance, described Delia as "a rather typical Irish girl, with all the humor of her race, all of its shrewdness and some of its temper" (June 17, 1907). Many judged the novel's success on the basis of the verisimilitude (or lack thereof) of Delia's dialect. Since the Irish, Italians, and Slavs at the turn of the century were "not quite white" in the eyes of the culturally dominant group and since Delia's ethnicity is very pronounced in her manners as well as speech, she functions as the book's magnet. Readers who would not have bought yet another romantic comedy of errors, found a fresh interest in that same comedy of errors narrated in Irish brogue from a servant's viewpoint. Using a similar strategy but perhaps with greater success, Edith Eaton would focalize the narrative of "Mrs. Spring Fragrance" and "The Inferior Woman" through a Chinese protagonist, adding an exotic touch to her observations of the white middle class.

Winnifred wrote about that class of Long Island homeowners from experience, having lived in the suburb herself from approximately 1905 to 1908.

(Diana Birchall gives a lively account of the Babcocks' home life during this period.) In her Long Island story "A Neighbor's Garden, My Own, and a Dream One" (analyzed in chapter 4), she writes about a spunky Irish maid named Nora, and a woman who answers Nora's description was photographed with Winnifred's children in this period. It is worth noting that to write about white Americans at all was a big step for Winnifred, who was tied by her pseudonym to the Japonica niche, just as it was for Edith, who found it difficult to step out of her role of Chinatown storyteller once she had established herself in that field.

Delia's main point of contention with the Wolleys, a middle-class family of six, is work. A naive narrator who often seems unaware of the implications of what she is reporting, Delia nonetheless points up the inconsistencies of the Wolleys' attitudes toward work and money. The family has fallen on hard times and must move out of New York for the summer to economize. In the opening of the story, an enraged Delia leaves the Wolleys because they have been overworking and slighting her, but she loyally returns to take up her old position in the new home. In a scene that brings out relations within the household, Delia listens in on a family council:

> "I want you all to lissen to me," ses Miss Claire, addrissing the assimbled family in the dining-room. "Now" ses she, "if I'm to be housekeeper and we cant afford but wan girl and the works altogether too hevvy for Delia alone and shell be leaving us if—"
> "Sh!" says her mother, "spake lower. Shes in the pantry making the salad."
> "Nonsinse" ses Mr. James, "shes at the keyhole lissening."
> "Well, but do lissen all," airges Miss Claire. "Iverybody" ses she, "has got to do his indivijool share of work. The lons must be cut. A garden must be planted. Frish vigitables are absolootely nicissiry. James" ses she swately, "*You* can cut the lons." (47–48)

Although work, Delia's primary concern, is on the agenda, Delia is excluded from the debate about how it is to be delegated. But since the Wolleys know she can hear them, they perform this elaborate scene at least in part for her benefit. In this family of scholars, journalists, and women of leisure, no one has the least inclination to work, but being dependent on Delia's labor, they want her to believe they are sharing the housekeeping. The bossy young Claire assigns "juties" to the family members, leaving the "raysing of sweet flowers" for herself. In subsequent chapters, each family member, in secret from all the others, manages to talk Delia into taking over his or her "juty" (resorting to bribery if necessary). The family's vocal socialist, young Mr. James, actually hires a "dago" to cut the "lons" for him at the crack of dawn.

Living among the nation's rich and famous, the Wolleys initially make a point of dissociating themselves from "these essenshilly vulger fatheaded raskilly rich nayburs of ours," for as Mr. James says, "a man cannot make a billion onestly. I agree wid me frind Andrew Carnegie, who denies he said it, that its impossible" (50). In a comic version of the "rival clans" plot from *The Wooing of Wistaria,* two of the Wolleys fall in love with the richest of their "raskilly rich nayburs." Claire and her lover actually use Delia's basement sitting room as a meeting place. One by one, Delia's story deflates the myths of a simple life close to nature: the old Mr. Wolley, sworn enemy of the "ortemobile" and lover of horses, buys a car; the simple fare Delia cooks on a low budget is an embarrassment to the family; and the garden yields no sweet rewards.

The Wolleys, as their name suggests, are not unscrupulous exploiters of the working class; Delia knows her value and defends her rights when it suits her. Class struggle turns into a source of comedy when a more experienced domestic admonishes her, "Don't be saft. Raymimber ladies is your natrel inimies and beests of prey on poor hilpless sarvant girls" (31). Since this was a comedy, Winnifred gave her narrator a trifle more agency than a servant in her position would normally have. It could be argued that although the novel began as a satire of the middle class, since Winnifred had established herself as a member of that class and an employer, she could not be too hard on the Wolleys. Nor could she envisage Delia as a positive character without making her a devoted servant who loves her capricious employers and plays mammy to Claire ("I drors her into me arms and pets her like a baby, while she poars out into me sympathetic eers her thrubbles" [98]). The combination of mammy and bossy housekeeper comes out most clearly when, at the end of the summer, Delia turns out to be the only member of the household with substantial savings—money she unhesitatingly gives to Claire and her lover who want to elope. That the gift is really a loan and Delia expects interest on it is another matter.

Stripped of Delia's voice, the threadbare romantic intrigue that is the apparent subject of her story would not have held the reader's attention for long. The real interest and tension in the story has more to do with the intricate master-servant relations than with the resolution of the romantic subplots. Observing and criticizing the customs and manners of the middle class may be the subject of Delia's "ethnographic fieldwork," but it is Delia herself who is the reader's ethnographic subject proper.

The regional dialect that the author creatively "transcribes" to leave no phrase "uncolored" performs several important functions: it marks Delia as uneducated in contrast to the genteel Wolleys; it is an unsophisticated but effective source of comedy; and it provides an intellectual diversion as the reader tries to guess what one word or another means "in English." But beside these rather cheap effects, Delia's voice does have the unexpected result of leveling all the characters, whatever their class. When Delia narrates what Mr. Wolley or Mr. James have said, she not only is in control of the story, which would in itself be significant, but also pokes fun at "proper" speech: "'An ortermobile' ses Mr. Wolley at the brekfust table, 'is the veehicle of the moduns. It's a boom to soofering yumanity in this yumid and turribly trying of hot summers of this climut. In my opinyon' ses he, 'its the greatest of modun invinshuns'" (117). Delia may not be able to spell such words as *boon* or *humanity*, but she has no trouble understanding what they mean and rendering them in her "diary" with a fine sense of irony. The joke is thus never on Delia alone.

Winnifred constructs Delia as the Wolleys'—and the readers'—cultural other. Delia's defining feature is indiscretion, discretion presumably being a characteristic acquired with breeding. Many of Delia's chapters or diary entries open with "Aroze. Got up. Dressed. Made me bed. Imtied me slops," with such variations as "washed all over." This refrain is an effective way to establish the humdrum rhythm of a domestic's life; it also forces the reader to visualize Delia doing things a "lady" knows better than to talk about. Distressed, she throws an apron over her head and cries, "Wirrah! wirrah! wirrah!" Surprised, she shoves a dishcloth in her mouth to stifle a scream. Used to physical work, Delia is very strong: "I grabbed [Miss Claire] by the waste and hawled her up" (62). The reader involuntarily picks up these markers of class and sharpens his or her powers of discrimination. Should the reader be interested in the management of domestic servants, Delia in her indiscretion gives away some of the petty deceptions that go on in the kitchen.

There is no question that to construct Delia, Winnifred reached for popular stereotypes of Irish immigrants and the working class in general. Yet she seems to have been genuinely fond of this character, making her proud, warmhearted, and observant. With two suitors hovering about her kitchen, Delia must also be an attractive twenty-year-old. However, at least some of Winnifred's readers came away with quite a different image of the narrator—probably the one they had brought to the reading of the story. For instance, the illustrator of the 1907 Doubleday edition, May Wilson Preston, evidently conceived of Delia as belonging to a different "breed" or "tribe" than the Wolleys'. The Wolleys are sketched in the popular manner of Charles Gibson. Claire is a typical "Gibson Girl." By contrast, Delia has cartoonish features: a long fleshy nose, prominent cheekbones, disproportionately large hands with bulging knuckles, and huge feet with a strong hint of corns under the shoe leather (see figures 10 and 11). Oddly enough, Preston's Delia

Figure 10. Claire Wolley and Delia O'Malley, drawing by May Wilson Preston for *The Diary of Delia* (1907).

Figure 11. Delia O'Malley, drawing by May Wilson Preston for the frontispiece of *The Diary of Delia*.

has the (undesirable) face and figure of a middle-aged woman, even in the drawing in which a suitor comes courting. It appears that the artist, having skimmed though the novel as illustrators generally do, projected onto Delia's body the difference that the text implies mainly in her speech.

One drawing represents the "tribe" to which Delia belongs (see figure 12). In a New York job agency, seven middle-aged female domestics sit on chairs lined up against the wall. They all wear large hats with feathers jutting out in all directions. Beneath their skirts made of boldly patterned fabrics, we see—oh horror!—their knees spread wide apart. Their small, squat figures centered on the page as if on display are clones of Delia, who in the story does borrow a friend's "hat with the grand white ostrich feather" to wear to the agency. If Preston had been illustrating a travel narrative of westerners among

savages, she could not have made the physical differences between two social groups more obvious. The odd thing about this last drawing is that the
narrator does no more than mention "40 uther unforchnut girls in a room
on the sicond flure" (21). What she describes more vividly is "a grate long
room wid about twinty or thirty ladies sitting in grand drisses on sofies" on
the floor below (24). When Delia fails her first interview, a friend reassures
her, "Delia theres twinty ladies for ivery wan girl" (26). Delia is so confident
of her value on the job market that at the end of the second day she writes:
"Minnie and I interfiewed the follering ladies in regard to a position" (29).
A list of five ladies and job descriptions follows—jobs Delia has rejected.
Arguably, then, the power dynamics in the written text are reversed by Preston's drawing, which puts the (middle-class) reader in a position to choose
from the row of domestics on display.

   Besides Preston's graphic response to *Delia* and a handful of lukewarm
reviews, there is no indication of how the novel was read. It does seem, however, that Winnifred's contemporaries brought to the text a strong desire to
see Delia as one of a "tribe" marked by a set of peculiar habits, mannerisms,
and speech patterns. To some extent, Winnifred fed that desire, and in exchanging with her readers a conspiratorial wink behind Delia's back, she
established a sense of community with them. But she also complicated the
textual relations between Delia and the Wolleys by allowing her to represent

Figure 12. New York domestics, drawing by May Wilson Preston for *The Diary of Delia.*

them in a way they would never have represented themselves and by letting her speech color theirs.

I suggested earlier that Winnifred can be viewed as both exploring and exploiting difference and that *Delia* was conceived first and foremost as a marketable product. However, not all of Winnifred's work was motivated by the marketplace, and not all of it was a commercial success. One last text that I look at briefly to indicate the range of Winnifred's interests in social construction of difference is "Sins of the Fathers" (192?), an unpublished magazine-type story.[17] "I think I always knew that we were different from other people—Kit and I," are the first words of this powerful first-person narrative told by a pubescent boy, Tony, who gradually comes to understand that his mother is the mistress of the man he has known all his life as "uncle Jim." The bulk of the story describes the uneasy relations between the boy and his mother, Kit, as they move from one neighborhood to another, only to find themselves ostracized by a new set of neighbors or forced to move because the money from "uncle Jim" has run out. Each episode forces Tony to renegotiate his own perceptions of Kit and the perceptions of outsiders. Eventually, through a devastating coincidence, Tony learns that the wealthy alcoholic "uncle" is his father. In an ill-fitting, melodramatic denouement of a story written with a naturalistic attention to detail, Tony kills his father and goes to jail, his mother dies, and, upon his release from jail, he is welcomed into his father's legitimate family.

Like the naive narrator of Toni Morrison's short story "Recitatif," Tony does not fully recognize the cultural codes that distinguish him and his mother from "respectable" society. From what he tells us of her dress, lifestyle, and way of speaking, we can guess that when she first met "uncle Jim" she was an uneducated working-class girl seduced by his wealth. Maintained by him in a state of insecurity and dependence, she is not the most responsible of mothers but certainly not fundamentally "different from other people." That sense of difference is something Tony absorbs from a culture that stigmatizes extramarital sex and illegitimacy. Winnifred's ability to draw sensitive psychological portraits of the boy and his mother who try to pass into "respectable" society but always fall short seems to have originated in her own experience of alternately passing for white and Japanese. What makes "Sins of the Fathers" memorable is the careful exploration of Tony's inability to reconcile his subjective sense of self with an externally imposed identity and the tension generated by the threat of disclosure. Such paradoxes and tensions were also familiar elements of Winnifred's life.

With the growing skepticism toward all-encompassing theories or metadiscourses and with increasing attention paid to the social and historical specificities of various kinds of difference, it is not easy to make a satisfactory argument about Winnifred's strategy of transposing one type of difference, such as race, into another, such as class or moral stigma. We may have to look as far back as 1963 to the sociologist Erving Goffman's *Stigma: Notes on the Management of a Spoiled Identity* to find such labels as race, homosexuality, physical deformity, ex-convict status, and alcoholism mentioned in one paragraph (4). Though Goffman was perfectly aware of the unequal status of these various stigmatized identities and pointed out that they have vastly different material consequences for the people thus labeled, his book was an attempt to draw attention to the common experiences of stigmatized individuals. Goffman's unwritten proposition seemed to be that once we become aware of the norm against which difference is constructed and see such mechanisms as passing or internalization of the imposed identity operating in the parallel lives of a deaf person, a prostitute, and a Jew, the ground may be cleared for potential alliances.

Winnifred did not often see a possibility for such alliances. Her stigmatized characters tend to be left to fend for themselves in an unfriendly universe. They often set up a buffer between themselves and the outer margin of society. Delia distances herself from "niggers" and "dagos"; the eponymous Marion is repelled by a dark-skinned Italian suitor; and the young illegitimate narrator of "Sins of the Fathers" vents his frustration on a "nigger" maid. Although these attitudes were probably an accurate reflection of social reality, nowhere did Winnifred use irony to indicate that she did not share them. Only occasionally, as in the 1924 ranching novel *Cattle* or the 1929 treatment "Barbary Coast," are white women and people of color united against a common enemy.

But Winnifred's motives for writing about difference were far removed from Goffman's. As her family's primary breadwinner, Winnifred learned to identify and explore in her writing the differences that interested readers and moviegoers at particular historical moments. Japaneseness at the turn of the century; European immigrants and bohemian working girls in the next decade; the last true cattlemen on the vestiges of the frontier in the 1920s; reservation Indians, illegitimate children of wayward mothers, and unwed mothers of illegitimate children in the 1930s were some of Winnifred's thematic interests over the course of her career. Many failed to arouse interest; synopses, story treatments, screenplays, and continuity scripts that never made it to the screen fill more than a dozen boxes at the University of Calgary Winnifred Eaton Reeve Collection.

Because during her prolific but mostly unsuccessful Hollywood career Winnifred wrote for a popular audience and because she presumed, as did most of her fellow screenwriters, that she could write competently about anyone and anything, her constructions of difference are often crude and stereotyped. Nonetheless, to have moved out of the racially assigned slot of the writer of "Japanese romances" and to have perceived a connection in the way society stigmatized a person of color and an illegitimate child are in themselves remarkable. No matter how hackneyed her screenplays, Winnifred's experience of the psychological and practical costs of being half-Chinese continued to surface in much of her later work.

Postscript

MY WORK ON EDITH and Winnifred Eaton was done at UCLA in 1994–98. Now that I am back in Poland teaching Asian American literature, I look from a new position at this text written expressly for an American/Asian American readership and wonder how I can make the story of the Eaton sisters meaningful to my students. Where is the connection?

Introducing a volume of essays entitled *Displacing Whiteness,* Ruth Frankenberg suggested that we do not usually "undertake historical research in the absence of a set of animating concerns in the present" (3). One persistent concern I had at UCLA was my own position as a Pole in Asian American studies. The Eaton sisters allowed me to think through the contradictions of what I was doing. A Pole studying Asian American literature in Los Angeles is not unlike an ethnographer who enters another culture to become, for a time, a participant in its face-to-face relationships. As I learned from the Eaton sisters, ethnography is always written for someone as much as about someone. Traditionally, ethnographers have turned their fieldwork into formalized accounts intended for readers "back home." Before 1994, I had written papers about Asian American literature for Polish readers. Once in the United States, I found myself urgently seeking to understand the values and concerns of my Asian American colleagues and teachers in order to enter into a dialogue with them—much like Edith Eaton, who had to refocus her ethnographic eye when she left the familiar Montreal and began to write for Kingstonians.

Home again, I unloaded my notebooks, wrote up a syllabus, entered the classroom, and found myself in a position analogical to that of the traditional ethnographer with her strings of beads, feather headdress, pipes, and field notes. (Colleagues in the department refer to me as the woman who does "Chinese stuff.") And sure enough, I encountered responses that made it clear my students read literature by and about people of color primarily as ethnography. They frankly admitted they signed up because it was the most exotic-sounding class of the year. How do I temper and redirect their interest in exotica without discouraging these enthusiasts who struggle to read across race and culture in a foreign language? How much historical context do Edith's *Mrs. Spring Fragrance* and Winnifred's *Marion* require to be read productively? What exactly should a "productive reading" of an Asian American text accomplish in Poland? Surely something different than it would in the United States.

If there are answers to these questions, I suspect it will take many years to work them out. As I prepare to teach the course "Ethnography, Ethnicity, and Whiteness," I look to the Eaton sisters for lessons on the shifting, ambiguous positionings of those who do cross-racial and cross-cultural work. Ethnic American literatures will increasingly be taught outside the United States by people like me, often at universities where the politicization of literature is viewed as a passing fad at best and an assault on humanistic values at worst. According to Krzysztof Zanussi, one of Poland's leading filmmakers and cultural commentators, the job of our universities is "to pass on to the new generation a certain canon, the contents of which we have agreed on. Anyone who claims that this canon is a mere illusion opens a Pandora's box out of which will come creeping questions as to whether we ought to be paying academics to study things that are devoid of value" (105, my translation). It is Zanussi's universal "we" that is an illusion. Pandora's box has long been open. The intricacy of Edith and Winnifred Eaton's fiction and its complex engagement with history belie Zanussi's assumptions at every turn. As more of us begin to negotiate radically opposed value systems and cultural alignments, Edith and Winnifred Eaton will continue to provide us with food for thought on the power dynamics between the observer and the observed; conflicting race, class, and gender alignments; and accountability for the consequences of literary representations and our teaching practice.

Appendix: Chronology of the Eatons' Lives

Edith Eaton/Sui Sin Far

1865   Edith born in Macclesfield, England, the second child of Grace and Edward Eaton. Grace was thought to be from Shanghai, taken to London as a child, and trained to be a missionary/kindergarten teacher in the Home and Colonial School. Edward studied art in Paris and traveled to the Far East as a representative of the Eaton Silk Company.

1867   Grace and Edward Eaton immigrate to the United States, lose their money, and return to England. In 1870, the impoverished Eatons immigrate to Canada and settle in Montreal; father does clerical work and paints "potboilers" for extra income; they have fourteen children, the last of whom is born in 1887.

1889–90   Edith publishes poetry and short stories in the *Dominion Illustrated.*

1894   She begins reporting for the *Montreal Daily Star* and *Daily Witness.* Together with her mother, she joins a Chinatown mission society and teaches English in Chinese Sunday school.

1895–96   Spends six months in the Thunder Bay District on Lake Superior as a correspondent for the *Montreal Daily Star.*

1896   Edith's brother-in-law Walter Blackburn Harte publishes three of her stories in the *Fly Leaf* and *Lotus;* three other stories are accepted by Charles Lummis, editor of the Los Angeles–based *Land of Sunshine.*

1896–97   In December 1896, Edith replaces her sister Winnifred in Kingston, Jamaica as a full-time reporter for *Gall's Daily News Letter.* Covers daily legislative council proceedings and an electoral campaign; writes reports on society events, the prison, poorhouse, orphanage, charity schools, and the like, as well as short stories, reviews, and a children's column. Falls ill and returns to Montreal, probably in June 1897.

1898	Edith moves to San Francisco, then semipermanently to Seattle. Continues to seek out Chinatown missions and do volunteer work. Supports herself as a stenographer and typist while writing short stories and essays.
1898–1903	Maintains a steady correspondence with Charles Lummis of the *Land of Sunshine.* Lummis publishes nine of her stories and an article. *Overland Monthly* and *Youth's Companion* accept one story each.
1903	Spends several months in Los Angeles and writes short Chinatown articles for the *Los Angeles Express.*
1904	Writes "Wing Sing of Los Angeles on His Travels," a series of reports on railway journey from Los Angeles to Montreal, using the male persona of a merchant, Wing Sing. "A Chinese Boy-Girl" is published in *Century Magazine.*
1905	"Aluteh" is published in the *Chautauquan.*
1908–9	*Good Housekeeping* buys seven of her children's stories.
1909	*Westerner,* a Seattle magazine, commissions a series of articles on "The Chinese in America." "Leaves," her autobiographical essay, appears in the *Independent,* a New York weekly, followed by three stories.
1910	Moves to Boston and remains there until 1913. Her work appears in *Hampton's, Independent, Good Housekeeping, New England Magazine,* and *Delineator.*
1911	"The Persecution and Oppression of Me," is published anonymously in the *Independent.*
1912	*Mrs. Spring Fragrance* brought out by McClurg's.
1914	Dies in Montreal.

Winnifred Eaton/Onoto Watanna

1875	Born in Montreal, Canada, the eighth of fourteen children.
1896	Travels to Jamaica in February to work as a reporter for *Gall's Daily News Letter.* Writes news items, parliamentary reports, society column, and one poem. Leaves for the United States that spring or summer.
1897–98	Works for the *Cincinnati Commercial Tribune.*
1898	Moves to Chicago. Does secretarial work in the meatpacking industry, then breaks into the popular magazines using the pen name Onoto Watanna. Writes for *Frank Leslie's, Ladies' Home Journal, Conkey's,* and many more.
1899	Publishes her first novel, *Miss Numè of Japan.*
1901	Moves to New York. Marries Bertrand W. Babcock, a reporter. Publishes *A Japanese Nightingale.*
1901–12	Writes seven more "Japanese" romances and an "Irish" novel, *The Diary of Delia,* as well as numerous magazine stories and articles on Japanese subjects.

1902	Sues David Belasco and John Long for plagiarizing her work in their musical *Darling of the Gods.*
1903	*A Japanese Nightingale* is produced as a Broadway play.
1904	Gives birth to son Perry, followed by three more children, Bertie, Doris, and Charles. Bertie dies in 1908.
1906?	Buys a house on Long Island. Over the next nine years, her family life deteriorates as her husband slips into alcoholism and becomes physically abusive.
1914	Writes a *Chinese-Japanese Cook Book* with her sister Sarah Bosse.
1915	Anonymously publishes an autobiographical novel, *Me: A Book of Remembrance.* Begins writing movie serials. Collaborates with Sarah Bosse on *Marion,* published in 1916, a novel based on Sarah's career as an artist's model.
1916	Spends six months in Reno, Nevada, to establish residency and file for divorce. Meets and marries Frank Reeve, a Canadian farmer and entrepreneur, who is also getting divorced in Reno.
1917	The Reeves buy a farm and later a cattle ranch in Alberta, Canada. Winnifred becomes restless with domestic life and travels to New York, where in 1920 she again tries to break into the film industry. Credited for the 1921 adaptation of *False Kisses,* made by Universal.
1922	Back in Alberta, becomes chair of the Canadian Authors' Association and starts writing again. Shuttles between the ranch and a house in Calgary, where she retreats to write. Publishes her last "Japanese" novel, *Sunny-San,* followed by two western novels, *Cattle* (1924) and *His Royal Nibs* (1925).
1928–31	Makes a successful career change, becoming chief story editor for the New York branch of Universal Studios. Within months, she is transferred to Hollywood, where she remains until 1931. Authors and coauthors dozens of screenplays, including *Mississippi Gambler* and *Shanghai Lady* in 1929 and *Undertow, Young Desire,* and *East Is West* in 1930. Briefly works for MGM.
1931	Is reunited with Frank Reeve, by now a prosperous oil man, and returns to Calgary. Becomes a patron of the Calgary little theater movement.
1954	Dies in Butte, Montana, while on a trip to the States.

Notes

Introduction

1. Deciding what to call the two writers poses a problem. I cannot follow the academic usage of the last name "Eaton" when discussing them together. There is a critical tradition of referring to Edith by her pen name, Sui Sin Far, which she used fairly consistently after 1896. By the same token, I would have to call Winnifred "Onoto Watanna," but this name is a poor fit: it does not cover the author's whole career, nor was she always comfortable with it. Useful at first, by 1906 it had already become a constraining label. Winnifred aired it periodically for its market value, but when negotiating with publishers or when she wanted to extricate herself from Japonica, she fell back on her husbands' names: Babcock and Reeve. She also briefly tried out the Irish pen name Mooney and published two novels and a story anonymously. I uneasily refer to the sisters as Winnifred and Edith to avoid confusion, mark their cultural alignment with the white middle class, and preserve a distance between the writers and their literary personas.

2. For recent overviews of the question of "claiming America" versus exploring the possibilities of heterogeneous, multiple, fluid identities, see Cheung, *An Interethnic Companion* 2–10; and J. Ling 139–62.

3. Hurston trained under Franz Boas at Barnard in the 1920s. He encouraged her to collect African American folklore in the South and to make documentary films. Although her personal and emotional ties to the communities she studied made her a valuable fieldworker, the critic Fatimah Rony showed that Boas "did not seriously encourage Hurston to consider a career as a professor," finding her work unconventional and undisciplined (203). For a sensitive reading of Hurston's rarely mentioned Caribbean ethnography/memoir, *Tell My Horse,* discussed in conjunction with the amateur ethnography of Mary Austin, see Harrison 88–106.

4. While it is easy to caricature the anthropologist as I have just done, we need to keep in mind that evolutionary explanations of race, later redefined as "scientific racism" (Stepan and Gilman), emerged in reaction to potentially more dangerous theories of polygenesis that dehumanized people of color as products of a different creation than that

of westerners. How modern interracial relations would have played out without amateur and professional ethnographers as self-appointed go-betweens is impossible to say. Certainly Franz Boas was among the first to envisage a world filled with distinctive, plural, equally meaningful "cultures" (Clifford, *The Predicament of Culture* 92–93). Anthropology "fostered an ironic attitude towards one's own culture" (Marcus and Fischer 123). If its sins include the objectification of people of color, it has also played a remarkable role in promoting antiracism and self-reflexivity.

5. 1882 saw the passage of the first Chinese exclusion law, which Congress had to renew every ten years. In the years preceding the renewal of the anti-Chinese and later anti-Japanese legislation, labor organizations on the West Coast staged popular protests in cities and rural areas. Although many of the proposed anti-Asian bills did not pass at the state and federal level, such propositions were nonetheless constantly on the agenda.

6. Edgar L. Hewett's argument was ostensibly a critique of government Americanization programs and their imperialist implications. However, he seemed more concerned with the containment of Filipinos in the islands and of Native Americans on reservations—a proposition that exempted the U.S. government from granting citizenship to its subjects of color.

7. Henry Yu, in his study of the Chicago School of Sociology, for instance, pointed out that in certain historical circumstances "the possession of an 'oriental' identity became a valuable commodity" (282). For instance, students of Chinese and Japanese descent became indispensable to the sweeping surveys and in-depth studies of race and ethnicity conducted by the Chicago School from the 1920s to the 1950s.

8. The historian James Doyle in his study *The Fin de Siècle Spirit* chronicles the young Canadian literary milieu, most of whose representatives, including the well-known poet and editor Bliss Carman, the Eaton sisters, and their brother-in-law Walter Blackburn Harte, had to move to the United States in search of publishing opportunities.

Chapter 1: *Two Faces of the Oriental(ist)*

1. See, for instance, Chamberlain 237–41; Fenollosa; Simms; and Oswald.

2. For a sociohistorical background on China missions, see Hunter; Cagan; and Crouch et al.

3. Toward the end of the nineteenth century, diplomats and their wives published a good deal on China. See, for example, A. Little. Merchants, artists, and art dealers in the last quarter of the century also wrote on Japanese art in an effort to popularize the new aesthetic and cultivate a market for imported artifacts. See, for example, La Farge; and Farrar.

4. In the economic and political turmoil of nineteenth-century China, missionaries were frequently the targets of nationalistic reaction; reports of violent crimes against them and their families were common. Treated as intruders, they usually remained in China on sufferance, even when backed by the power of Britain and the United States, which were vying for economic and political influence in China. Waves of antiforeign sentiment also shook Japan in the second half of the century.

5. For detailed discussions of nineteenth-century race theorists, including Arthur Joseph de Gobineau and Henry Hotze, see Young; and Stocking, *Race, Culture, and Evolution*.

6. For a detailed account of Medhurst's career, see Leonard.

7. For a text similar in tone, see Simms. This 1897 account of a tour of Japan by a missionary and his wife is as unflattering in its treatment of the native population as Arthur Smith's *Chinese Characteristics,* a text to which Simms actually referred. *Our Life in China* by Helen Nevius, wife of a missionary, served as further proof that there was nothing inevitable about the later polarization of the Chinese and Japanese. The Neviuses had worked in China for six years when the war of 1860 forced them to move temporarily to Japan. Helen Nevius's account of the sojourn in Japan offered a series of comparisons between the Chinese and the Japanese intended to disabuse her readers of the "idea that the Japanese are vastly superior to the Chinese." Not only did she see the Japanese as immodest and prone to heavy drinking, but also her most vivid recollections were of white friends physically assaulted before an indifferent crowd of onlookers (251–64).

8. A good example of a westerner distancing herself from a stereotyped image of the missionary is the narrator of an anonymously published volume of letters entitled *The Lady of the Decoration* by Frances Little (1906). The family of the young widow from Kentucky arranged a four-year contract for her in a mission school in Hiroshima. Ever fearful of being taken for a missionary, she styled herself as a spunky, flirtatious woman of fashion.

9. William Griffis (1843–1928) was a lay Presbyterian during his stay in Japan. However, soon after his return to the United States, he enrolled at the Union Theological Seminary and entered the ministry in 1877. His biographer, Edward R. Beauchamp, described him as a man of boundless energy, with more than fifty books to his name, many of them interpreting Japan to compatriots.

10. A similar tendency to miniaturize or infantilize the Japanese can be found in *The Letters of Henry Adams, 1858–1891.* During the summer of 1886, which Adams spent in Japan, he wrote, "Everything laughs. . . . Men, women and children are taken out of fairy books. The whole show is of the nursery. Nothing is serious. . . . Life is a dream and in Japan one dreams of the nursery" (quoted in Chisolm 69).

11. Lafcadio Hearn (1850–1904) came to Japan disenchanted with Christianity, modernity, and industrial progress. Starting as a correspondent for *Harper's,* he quickly improved his social status in Japan, where he rose from the post of provincial high school teacher to lecturer at the Imperial University. He married a Japanese woman, changed his citizenship, and continued publishing a book a year on Japanese subjects until his death.

12. Alice Mabel Bacon (1858–1918) was an American writer and high school teacher.

13. For further examples of women's narratives of exploration, see Pratt, *Imperial Eyes.*

Chapter 2:   A Journalistic Mission

1. Several of Edith's anonymously published journalistic pieces I refer to here have not been reprinted; my reasons for attributing them to Edith are provided in the endnotes. I shared these findings with Amy Ling and Annette White-Parks, who accepted my speculative identifications.

2. The review was one of several covering recent publications on Chinese religions and customs. It was inserted among drawings of stone axes and photographs of Indian cave dwellings and skulls.

3. In lieu of issuing transit visas, in the 1890s Canada and the United States enforced

immigration regulations that required Chinese to travel to the country of their destination in locked, guarded compartments.

4. "Chinese Entertainment" (1896). I attribute this anonymous article to Edith because its opening sentences describing Chinese musicians are almost identical with a passage from her story "Sweet Sin" (1898). Thematically and stylistically, the piece is consistent with Edith's prose.

5. Racial identity was the decisive factor here: Grace, being from Shanghai, would have known little or no Cantonese, while Edith spoke only English and French. According to surviving relatives, Grace Eaton was taken to England at a young age by the Matheson family and placed in the Home and Colonial School in London. In correspondence with Diana Birchall, the school archivist James Mann suggested that Grace was probably trained as a missionary/kindergarten teacher.

6. See, for example, "Extraordinary Finger-Nails"; Ng Poon Chew; and Percival.

7. Though I refrain from using the term *tragedy* here, I am uncomfortable with the traditional distinction between melodrama and tragedy as defined by Robert Bechtold Heilman in *Tragedy and Melodrama*. If tragedy requires that the fatal flaw be inscribed within—not without—the protagonist and that he or she be fully aware of this predicament, then any literary effort to locate the problem outside the self, in the society at large, is relegated to the inferior realm of melodrama.

8. This anonymous article was clearly Edith Eaton's because she recycled parts of it in "The Chinese in America" (1909). In contrast to the bulk of *Daily Star* journalism, this piece is marked by empathy toward the Chinese and a focus on the domestic sphere.

9. In this, missionaries to China were not exceptional. As Renato Rosaldo explained, most ethnographers to this day "prefer to study events that have definite locations in space with marked centers and outer edges. Temporally, they have middles and endings. Historically, they appear to repeat identical structures by seemingly doing things today as they were done yesterday. Their qualities of fixed definition liberate such events from the untidiness of everyday life so that they can be read like articles, books, or, as we now say, texts" (12).

10. My predecessors had difficulty accessing *Gall's Daily News Letter* because, for reasons of privacy, the Eaton sisters referred to the paper either by an incomplete or a fictional name. Unfortunately, the issues to which Winnifred contributed in the spring and summer of 1896 are now lost, though one February 1896 issue does carry a short poem signed "Winnifred Eaton," marking the beginning of her work on the newspaper staff. Edith's stay in Jamaica is, however, easy to trace.

11. For more information on the Jamaican political system, see Brereton 91–95; and Rogozinski 193.

12. In her fictionalized autobiography *Me: A Book of Remembrance*, Winnifred Eaton recalled that she replaced a young Canadian woman who had contracted malaria. The editor "could not afford to pay a man's salary, and being very loyal to Canada, he had been accustomed to send there for bright and expert young women reporters to do virtually all the work of running his newspaper" (25).

13. King-Kok Cheung suggested in a conversation that the source of this byline may be a traditional Chinese folktale, perhaps retold by Grace Eaton, in which a poor but exceptionally studious boy reads late into the night by the light of a jar filled with fire flies. The

choice of a night insect seems appropriate for a writer who frequently identified with the night and the moon in her *Dominion Illustrated* poems.

14. I assume that culturally the Eatons identified with the dominant majority. No matter how alienated the biracial children may have felt from the white middle class, that was their broader community. As a journalist, Edith Eaton took on a mediatory role between the dominant majority and her "mother's own people," but the mediation was asymmetrical: it usually involved explaining to the dominant group the position of the minority.

15. I borrow the term *exploratrice sociale* from Mary Louise Pratt, who used it with reference to the "specifically exploratory activity identified with urban middle-class women in the early nineteenth century. The political work of social reformers and charity workers included the practice of visiting prisons, orphanages, hospitals, convents, factories, slums, poorhouses, and other sites of social management and control" (*Imperial Eyes* 244).

16. *Chickabiddy*, a Scottish word for child, is apparently no relation to the racially marked *pickaninny*. *Coolie* in this case may mean Chinese but is more likely to refer to the child of Indian immigrants, since British India provided most Jamaican plantation labor after the abolition of slavery on the island in 1838.

17. Among the most politically engaged of her articles is a February 8, 1897, commentary on the widely publicized trial of Mr. Nunes, a white customs officer, and Mr. Moulton, a lower-ranking black officer. Mr. Nunes assaulted Mr. Moulton with racist slurs, a fight ensued in which both were injured, and both were charged with assault. The judge found both parties guilty but fined the white man one shilling and the black man ten. Though Edith did not challenge the judge's decision, she used this opportunity to interrogate racist attitudes in Jamaica ("A Veracious Chronicle of Opinion").

Chapter 3: Subjects of the Gaze

1. "Onoto Watanna," *Frank Leslie's Popular Monthly* 54 (August 1902): 370, a biographical note accompanying a photograph of her, three years after her first story was published in the journal.

2. Interestingly, only children in Sui Sin Far's work are permitted to physically and verbally express their fury at racist treatment. For instance, "Sweet Sin" opens with a street fight; in "O Yam—A Sketch" (November 1900), a Chinese girl holds her own in a screaming match against a group of white children; and the protagonist of "A Chinese Boy-Girl" (April 1904) comes up with a variety of strategies to protest racism. Adult characters are often rendered powerless by social conventions.

3. To avoid confusion, I use the name *Land of Sunshine* throughout, although in December 1901 Lummis finally changed the name to one of his choosing: *Out West*. The editorial goals, however, remained unchanged.

4. Starting in about 1903, images of miners, fieldworkers, and other working people did begin to appear occasionally in the *Land of Sunshine*. Chinese, however, were present in it as far back as October 1894 (Ng Poon Chew). Edith's stories stand out as the most sympathetic and committed, but numerous illustrated accounts of Chinatown tourism by Anglo-American writers also appeared in the magazine (see note 15).

5. I use the term *progressive* rather loosely, following William Deverell and Tom Sitton, who caution against situating California progressives rigidly between the two other ma-

jor groups, "big business" and "big unions." As Deverell and Sitton argue, progressives engaged in a "weird amalgam of self-defense and selfless reform." The progressive movement "could seemingly tilt left and right at the same time," forming complex alliances that cut across class interests (6–7).

6. This is how the historian Mike Davis encapsulated the labor situation of the period: "After the collapse of the railroad-engineered land rush [of the late 1880s and early 1890s], Colonel Otis—representing the toughest of the new settlers—took command of the city's business organizations on behalf of the panic-stricken speculators. To revive the boom, and to launch a reckless competition with San Francisco (the most unionized city in the world), he militarized industrial relations in Los Angeles. Existing unions were locked out, picketing was virtually outlawed, and dissidents were terrorized" (25).

7. Few of Lummis's studies fall under the rubric of physical anthropology, yet the first *Land of Sunshine* issue published under his editorship carried his illustrated article on biracial women in the Americas. The article blended the rhetoric of imperialism with race theory. Lummis particularly admired the Spaniard who "mastered every country between here and Patagonia" and "wrote across it his racial autograph in a hand so virile and characteristic that neither time nor change can efface it" ("The Spanish American Face" 21–22).

8. This was the title of a column written by Lummis in 1899–1900.

9. For a dramatic account of South California's booster era (1885–1925), see Davis.

10. Mary Austin's literary theory, particularly her manifesto for American poetry, evolved from the same assumption. See *The American Rhythm*.

11. For discussions of nineteenth-century evolutionary theories of racial progress versus degeneration, see Stocking, *Race, Culture, and Evolution* 65–74; and Young.

12. An example of a Native American voice is an anonymous essay entitled "Lame Dancing-Masters."

13. The *Overland Monthly,* published out of San Francisco, was *Land of Sunshine*'s rival literary magazine, better-endowed and thus in a position to solicit the work of best-selling authors. It, too, featured a fair amount of Chinatown fiction and in October 1901 published a protest against anti-Chinese discrimination by the Chinese consul-general in San Francisco, Ho Yow.

14. Letter to Charles Lummis, September 16, 1900, Charles Lummis Collection, Southwest Museum and Library, Pasadena. Fourteen of these letters (1897–1912) were preserved in the Charles Lummis Collection. All the letters to Lummis referred to in the text are in this collection.

15. That Lummis held fairly stereotypical views about the Chinese is suggested by the quality of Chinatown writings by white writers that he periodically published in the *Land of Sunshine.* See Connor; Hartnell; W. Wood; Van Denburgh; Percival; and Deering.

16. See Lummis's tributes to Bandelier: "A Hero in Science"; and "In Memory."

17. Introduction to her *Mules and Men* 3. For valuable interpretations of Hurston's ethnographic practice, see Rony; Sánchez-Eppler; Harrison; and Carby.

18. Edith's habit of belittling own literary skills and applying the adjective *little* to everything associated with her person would make for interesting comparisons with a similar pattern in Sarah Orne Jewett's writings. Brodhead analyzed the way Jewett positioned her work in relation to high-culture definitions of "major" and "minor" writing and tempered her aspirations in return for privileged membership in the literary elite (142–76).

19. Edith might have come across literature of the British colonial experience in the Far East, but these writings dehumanized the Chinese in their effort to justify the ideology of empire. Retellings of Chinese folktales constituted another potential model, and a number of Edith's stories for children do tap into this tradition.

20. Among the most absorbing and informative studies of the staging of otherness are Thomson; Moy; Rony; and Hinsley.

21. The article's episodic structure is very similar to that of "Leaves from the Mental Portfolio of an Eurasian." Like the narrator of "Leaves," the anonymous speaker makes no secret of her Chinese descent and has a policy of "coming out" when faced with "bitter prejudice against the Chinese people" ("Persecution" 421). Three of her stories explore the perils of excessive intimacy between white female Sunday school teachers and Chinese men, an issue raised on the last page of the article. Between 1909 and 1913, the *Independent* published five of Edith's most overtly political pieces. It is likely that a friendly editor would publish an anonymous article upon Edith's request. Geographical references to the West Coast, Massachusetts, and French Canadians coincide with what we know of Edith's movements. In addition, the narrator describes herself as a small woman, weighing less than ninety-four pounds; the *Boston Globe* essay also gives the author's weight ("Sui Sin Far" 293). Taken separately, these details would be inconclusive; it is unlikely, however, that there was more than one diminutive half-Chinese woman writing autobiographical criticism for the *Independent* at that time.

22. Malinowski's *Diary in the Strict Sense of the Term* has been the subject of much attention within and outside anthropology. For critiques, see Torgovnick 227–35; and Minh-ha, *Woman, Native, Other* 74–76.

23. Other examples of this genre include Hartnell; W. Wood; and Inkersley.

24. As Annette White-Parks noted, Edith grew up surrounded by English culture and could not have been ignorant of Tennyson's nationality (168). Edith probably allowed her protagonist to make this slip to show that there are many levels of cultural proficiency and that Mrs. Spring Fragrance is not as thoroughly "Americanized" as her husband believes.

25. For a discussion of "'Its Wavering Image'" as a case of irresponsible journalistic intrusion into a Chinatown community, see Lee 249–73.

26. Since its establishment in 1848, the *Independent*, a New York weekly, was known for its staunch support of abolitionism, woman suffrage, and coeducation. Racial issues became the editors' major concern at the turn of the century, while in the years 1909–11 their gaze was more frequently turned east than west. Fostering good relations between the United States, China, and Japan was one of the most apparent editorial goals in this period.

Chapter 4: Strategies of Authentication

1. For further thoughts on "being there," see Clifford, *The Predicament of Culture* 22; and Behdad 100.

2. *Shabono* is a self-reflexive novel of extended cross-cultural interaction. The narrator is a young woman anthropologist studying Indian healing practices in Venezuela. An elderly tribeswoman asks the narrator to follow her to a *shabono* (village) in the interior. A year-long ritual of initiation into the Yanomama culture follows. The narrator leaves

part of her ethnographic equipment behind and loses the rest; unable to write up her experience as a scholarly text, she decides to tell it as a novel.

3. The fin de siècle was not the only time when claiming an exotic ancestry made political and economic sense. For instance, the anthropologist Susan Stewart discussed the fascinating case of Psalmanazar, a man of French-German descent, who in the late 1600s chose to pass for a Formosan. A canny forerunner of Onoto Watanna, Psalmanazar invented not only an elaborate autobiography for himself but also a complete ethnography of "Formosa," a rudimentary language system, and an alphabet. He became a celebrity in England, and even after his imposture was exposed, he continued to write for a living, "subject to pressures and demands of printers" (49). A more recent example of imposture is that of the popular white rapper Robert Van Winkle (aka Vanilla Ice), who impersonated what the critic Tricia Rose called "ghetto-blackness" to validate his presence in rap music circles. These two cases of white men constructing nonwhite identities to promote themselves give some idea of the marketability of a racial or cultural essence.

4. The book reviews I refer to are selected from several hundred preserved in the University of Calgary Archives. My generalizations are based on a sample of over one hundred, covering most of Winnifred's career but concentrating on 1903–4, the peak of her popularity. That there are more reviews from this period than from any other may mean that Winnifred, who paid clippings agencies to collect them, was most interested in the public response at the time or that she simply earned enough to afford the service.

5. Yone Noguchi, born in Japan in 1875, immigrated to the United States at the age of eighteen. He studied poetry under Joaquin Miller and had his first five poems accepted by the *Lark*, a small San Francisco literary magazine. Alternately praised and derided, Noguchi went on to become a widely published critic and propagator of the Japanese aesthetic in art and literature.

6. The Japanese-German writer Sadakichi Hartmann (1850–1904), born in Japan but reared in Germany, turned the Japanese half of his racial heritage into an asset when writing art criticism. His *A History of American Art* (1902) and *Japanese Art* (1904) were well received, and in the 1910s Hartmann was still publishing magazine articles on Japanese poetry, fiction, and drama. See Weaver; *Dictionary of Literary Biography* 54; and Quartermain 154–63.

7. Gish Jen in her novel *Typical American* (1991) explored a similar relationship between members of a Chinese immigrant family and their white middle-class neighbors in a New York suburb half a century later. Gardening still plays a similar role, with neighbors performing for one another and making casual contacts.

8. According to L. H. Bailey's *The Standard Cyclopedia of Horticulture* (1914), *rudbeckia* is the umbrella term for thirty-one species of plants, most of them weeds, that thrive in the poorest soil. Folk names for rudbeckia are "black-eyed Susan" and "nigger heads." The gift could not have been intended as a compliment.

9. Another text by Winnifred that explored a similar theme is "The Japanese Drama and the Actor" (1902), a well-researched historical piece. Among the anecdotes she cited is one on a famous seventeenth-century actor-playwright duo: "Takemoto would keep his eyes and ears alert for sensational occurrences. As soon as he heard one that pleased him, he forthwith went to Chickamatsu, who used the subject before it became commonly known, and thus it was presented to the people as something fresh and novel. Chicka-

matsu excelled in his domestic plays rather than in historical, as in the latter he was forced to subordinate his genius to the popular traditions of historical characters" (232). Several elements of this story resonate with Winnifred's literary practice. She was, at the time, beginning to collaborate with her husband, who also acted as her literary agent. Writing for a broad readership, she knowingly pursued subjects that were novel and sensational. And finally, she had chosen a field where she would not have to "subordinate [her] genius" to the literary canon of high culture.

10. As the critic Valerie Smith pointed out, "[A]ccording to the one-drop rule, individuals are classified as black if they possess one black ancestor; the 'hypo-descent' rule, acknowledged historically by the federal courts, the U.S. census bureau and other agencies of the state, assigned people of mixed racial origin to the subordinated racial group" (43–44).

11. In the novel, the one exception to this rule is a group of wealthy female painters, among whom Marion recognizes the wife of the president of the United States. They have Marion "posing in gypsy costume" and talk to her occasionally "in a patronizing way, as if I were a little poodle" (199). The gypsy costume may simply reflect a nineteenth-century fad, yet it is also a way the painters have Marion perform difference where there is none to create a distance between them and the woman they objectify.

12. "These travelers who have made a study of Japanese life tell us that sexual morality is at its lowest ebb. . . . Prostitution exists to an alarming extent and is regarded with a high degree of favor as a legitimate occupation. We are informed by one authority that it is not an uncommon experience for a Japanese farmer to bring his daughters into a city and put them into a house of prostitution for a stipulated time, and then return and take away his daughters with their nefarious earnings back to his farm." See facsimile of Japanese and Korean Exclusion League proclamation and address by Frank MacGowan cited in Ichihashi 274.

Chapter 5: Decoupling Race and Culture

1. The idea of reading Winnifred's "Japanese" novels through the rhetoric of Mendelian genetics occurred to me at a joint talk by the biologist Banu Subramian and the rhetorician Michael Whitmore, "Tropes in the Field: A Rhetoric of Science in Action," given at UCLA in May 1998. In a subtle, self-reflexive way, the speakers explored the intersection of the humanities and the sciences to make language visible in scientific description and to probe the ideological entanglements of rhetorical studies. Examining Subramian's dissertation on the hybridization of morning glories, Whitmore pointed out the continuing indebtedness of Mendelian genetics to the discourse of struggle, balance, and domination, as well as to the evolutionary discourse of race. This chapter reverses Subramian and Whitmore's strategy in that it borrows scientific terms to elucidate literary texts.

2. See Stocking, *Race, Culture, and Evolution* 46–49, 61–76; Clifford, *Predicament of Culture* 92–93; and Degler 139–211. The title of this chapter is an adaptation of Degler's chapter heading, "Decoupling Behavior from Nature."

3. I thank Jean Lee Cole for this piece of information.

4. For a discussion of the influence of Darwin and Spencer on Wharton's work, see Howard. Winnifred Eaton and Edith Wharton wrote for some of the same magazines, and

there is archival evidence that they were acquainted. They were exposed to the same scientific and popular discourses of heredity and race, though Winnifred's race and class background gave her a somewhat different perspective on these matters.

5. Subsequent to writing this chapter, I became aware of Shea's article, which covers some of the same ground that I do here. Although I also examine the impact of sexual and racial environment on Winnifred's fiction, I reach different conclusions.

6. The adjective *Japanned* was used to describe Western imitations of Japanese decorative art. Here I am referring to a review entitled "Novels Japanese and Japanned" (1904). This is perhaps the most scathing exposition on Winnifred's historical and ethnographic blunders. The reviewer found enough inaccuracies to fill two pages and suggested that Winnifred's "description of life at the present Japanese court comes as near to the facts as do the 'shilling-shockers' and 'penny dreadfuls'" (1446).

7. Writing against the Madame Butterfly paradigm according to which Asian women invariably fall for white blackguards, David Henry Hwang in his play *M. Butterfly* tried to make his audience imagine the reverse: "Consider it this way: what would you say if a blonde homecoming queen fell in love with a short Japanese businessman?" (17). It is remarkable that Winnifred tackled the same racist stereotype as far back as 1906.

8. It is not my intention to deny that the Japanese harbored prejudices against westerners. Akira Iriye's study *Mutual Images* made it clear that in their encounters with Americans the Japanese were often guided by racist assumptions. Also Benedict Anderson suggested that Japan's transformation into a nation-state after 1854 was, in part, facilitated by racist sentiment. I merely suggest that Winnifred's rendition of Japanese prejudices was not based on firsthand knowledge but instead reflected the situation in the United States, where a stronger majority exercised its power over a disenfranchised minority.

9. Ironically, it was Winnifred who sued John Long and David Belasco in 1903 for plagiarizing two of her novels in their musical *The Darling of the Gods,* staged on Broadway a few months before *A Japanese Nightingale.* For details of the conflict with Belasco, see Birchall 79–84. Once Winnifred became a celebrity, she attempted to deflect attention from her first novel by dismissing it as juvenilia. In December 1903, *Harper's Weekly* wrote, "She has written a number of Japanese stories . . . and a Chicago firm had published a short novel written when she was only nineteen, which, with pardonable pride, she is now anxious to forget" ("Onoto Watanna" 1959).

10. Undated newspaper clippings, Winnifred Eaton Reeve Fonds, Special Collections, University of Calgary Library. Though decidedly unheroic, Arthur does nothing to deserve the adjective "imbecile" except marry a woman the reviewer disapproves of.

11. Theories of a parallel aesthetic and moral development were popularized by such prominent figures as Professor Grant Allen, who in 1881 wrote in *Popular Science Monthly* that "it is only among the most cultivated classes of the most advanced types that the aesthetic faculty reaches [its] highest and most disinterested stage" (351).

12. Rachel Lee interpreted the symbolic aspect of Tama's blindness: if Tama stands for a Japan infused with Western ideas but still resistant to them, Tojin's power to bring to Fukui a white surgeon who removes the cataracts from Tama's eyes parallels his own role as civilizing agent to the Japanese.

13. Daniels as well as Tupper and McReynolds showed that diplomatic considerations led President Taft and Congress to temper the rampant racism of California legislators

and labor unionists. Certainly not all Americans were swayed by the "yellow peril" rhetoric, but, as Daniels demonstrated, even the East Coast was rocked by war scares in 1907 and 1912–13.

14. Correspondence with Carl Laemmle, Winnifred Eaton Reeve Fonds, Special Collections, University of Calgary Library. Quoted with permission from Paul Rooney.

15. Griffis described the Eta caste in *The Mikado's Empire* 279–80; other historians refer to it as one of the darker manifestations of Japanese feudalism. Though theoretically the caste was eradicated during the Restoration period, the stigma of Eta ancestry persists to this day. I thank King-Kok Cheung for alerting me to this fact and Mizuho Murayama for confirming the muted presence of a caste system in present-day Japan.

16. Alice Mabel Bacon (discussed in chapter 1) recounted a visit to the home of a Japanese noblewoman who showed her the armor worn by a female relative. Bacon learned that in times of war, when the men went to battle, Samurai women stayed to defend the castles. I suspect that the idea for Wistaria's cross-dressing comes from Bacon rather than from the Chinese folk tradition of Fa Mulan.

17. Winnifred Eaton Reeve Fonds, Special Collections, University of Calgary Library. Quoted with permission from Paul Rooney. The front page bears a Calgary address, and the story was probably written in the mid-1920s, before Winnifred went to work for the film industry in New York and then Hollywood.

Selected Bibliography

Archives/Special Collections

Lummis, Charles. Collection. Southwest Museum and Library, Pasadena, Calif.
Reeve, Winnifred Eaton. Fonds. Special Collections, University of Calgary Library, Calgary, Alberta, Canada.

Selected Writings by Edith Eaton (Listed Chronologically)

"The Origin of a Broken Nose." *Dominion Illustrated* 2 (May 11, 1889): 302.
"Robin." *Dominion Illustrated* 2 (June 22, 1889): 394–95.
"Lines." *Dominion Illustrated* 4 (April 5, 1890): 223.
"Spring Impressions: A Medley of Poetry and Prose." *Dominion Illustrated* 4 (June 7, 1890): 358–59.
"In Fairyland." *Dominion Illustrated* 5 (October 18, 1890): 270.
"Girl Slave in Montreal: Our Chinese Colony Cleverly Described." *Montreal Daily Witness,* May 4, 1894.
"Half-Chinese Children." *Montreal Daily Star,* April 20, 1895.
"Thrilling Experience." *Montreal Daily Star,* July 9, 1895.
"Chinamen with German Wives." *Montreal Daily Star,* December 13, 1895.
"The Chinese and Christmas." *Montreal Daily Star,* December 21, 1895.
"The Gamblers." *Fly Leaf* 1 (February 1896): 14–18.
"Ku Yum." *Land of Sunshine* 5 (June 1896): 29–31.
"The Story of Iso." *Lotus* 2 (August 1896): 117–19.
"A Plea for the Chinaman." Letter to the Editor. *Montreal Daily Star,* September 21, 1896.
"A Love Story of the Orient." *Lotus* 2 (October 1896): 203–7.
"A Chinese Feud." *Land of Sunshine* 5 (November 1896): 236–37.
"The Woman about Town." *Gall's Daily News Letter,* December 14, 1896.
"As Others See Us." *Gall's Daily News Letter,* December 16, 1896.
"The Races as Seen by Fire Fly: First Day." *Gall's Daily News Letter,* December 16, 1896.

"Impressions of the Races." *Gall's Daily News Letter,* December 17, 1896.

"The Races as Seen by Fire Fly: Second Day." *Gall's Daily News Letter,* December 19, 1896.

"Among the Stores." *Gall's Daily News Letter,* December 19, 1896.

"The Baby Show." *Gall's Daily News Letter,* December 23, 1896.

"The Fire Fly and Rum." *Gall's Daily News Letter,* December 23, 1896.

"Fire Fly's Christmas Budget." *Gall's Daily News Letter,* December 24, 1896.

"Christmas Eve at the Post Office." *Gall's Daily News Letter,* December 28, 1896.

"The Woman about Town." *Gall's Daily News Letter,* December 29, 1896.

"The Woman about Town: The Horse Car, Sarah Bernhardt." *Gall's Daily News Letter,* December 30, 1896.

"Chinese Entertainment." *Montreal Daily Star,* December 31, 1896.

Letters to Charles Lummis, 1897–1912. Charles Lummis Collection, Southwest Museum and Library, Pasadena, Calif.

"The Chinese Woman in America." *Land of Sunshine* 6 (January 1897): 60–65.

"The Woman about Town." *Gall's Daily News Letter,* January 2, 1897.

"The Woman about Town." *Gall's Daily News Letter,* January 4, 1897.

"Fire Fly's Wanderings Up and Down." *Gall's Daily News Letter,* January 11, 1897.

"The Girl of the Period: The Projectographe, Lawyers." *Gall's Daily News Letter,* January 13, 1897.

"The Girl of the Period: The Theatre." *Gall's Daily News Letter,* January 28, 1897.

"The Girl of the Period: At Alpha Cottage." *Gall's Daily News Letter,* February 2, 1897.

"Reviews: Magazines." *Gall's Daily News Letter,* February 3, 1897.

"The Girl of the Period: A Talk with Tommy Talker." *Gall's Daily News Letter,* February 5, 1897.

"A Veracious Chronicle of Opinion." *Gall's Daily News Letter,* February 8, 1897.

"Reviews: 'Marm Lisa' by Kate Douglas Wiggin." *Gall's Daily News Letter,* February 9, 1897.

"The Girl of the Period: Tommy Tattler Again." *Gall's Daily News Letter,* February 10, 1897.

"Just What Jamaica Wants: An Industrial Farm School." *Gall's Daily News Letter,* February 16, 1897.

"The Girl of the Period: At Church." *Gall's Daily News Letter,* February 16, 1897.

"The Union Poor House." *Gall's Daily News Letter,* February 26, 1897.

"Woman's Gossip: Victoria Order of Home Helpers." *Gall's Daily News Letter,* March 6, 1897.

"Woman's Gossip: Don't Tax Bicycles; Civil Service Examinations." *Gall's Daily News Letter,* March 17, 1897.

"Another Pleasure Party: Interview with John Jacob Astor." *Gall's Daily News Letter,* April 5, 1897.

"The Busy Bee." *Gall's Daily News Letter,* April 9, 1897.

"An Easter Story." *Gall's Daily News Letter,* April 24, 1897.

"The Children's Column." *Gall's Daily News Letter,* May 29, 1897.

"Sweet Sin." *Land of Sunshine* 8 (April 1898): 223–26.

"A Chinese Ishmael." *Overland Monthly* 34 (July 1899): 43–49.

"The Story of Tin-A." *Land of Sunshine* 12 (December 1899): 100–103.

"The Smuggling of Tie Co." *Land of Sunshine* 13 (July 1900): 100–104.

"O Yam—A Sketch." *Land of Sunshine* 13 (November 1900): 341–43.

"The Coat of Many Colors." *Youth's Companion* 76 (April 24, 1902): 208–9.

"In Los Angeles Chinatown." *Los Angeles Express,* October 2, 1903.

"Betrothals in Chinatown." *Los Angeles Express,* October 8, 1903.

"Chinatown Needs a School." *Los Angeles Express,* October 14, 1903.

"Chinatown Boys and Girls." *Los Angeles Express,* October 15, 1903.

"Leung Ki Chu and His Wife." *Los Angeles Express,* October 22, 1903.

"Chinese in Business Here." *Los Angeles Express,* October 23, 1903.

"The Horoscope." *Out West* 19 (November 1903): 521–24.

"Chinese Laundry Checking." *Los Angeles Express,* November 3, 1903.

"Wing Sing of Los Angeles on His Travels." *Los Angeles Express,* February 4, 5, 6, 10, and 24 and March 9, 1904.

"A Chinese Boy-Girl." *Century Magazine* 67 (April 1904): 828–31.

"Aluteh." *Chautauquan* 42 (December 1905): 338–42.

"The Puppet Show." *Good Housekeeping* 46 (January 1908): 95.

"The Wild Man and the Gentle Boy." *Good Housekeeping* 46 (February 1908): 179–80.

"What about the Cat?" *Good Housekeeping* 46 (March 1908): 290–91.

"The Heart's Desire." *Good Housekeeping* 47 (May 1908): 514–15.

"Tangled Kites." *Good Housekeeping* 47 (July 1908): 52–53.

"Leaves from the Mental Portfolio of an Eurasian." *Independent* 66 (January 21, 1909): 125–32. Reprinted in Sui Sin Far, *Mrs. Spring Fragrance and Other Writings,* edited by Amy Ling and Annette White-Parks, 218–30. Urbana: University of Illinois Press, 1995.

"Ku Yum and the Butterflies." *Good Housekeeping* 48 (March 1909): 299.

"The Half-Moon Cakes." *Good Housekeeping* 48 (May 1909): 584–85.

"The Chinese in America: Intimate Study of Chinese Life in America, Told in a Series of Short Sketches." *Westerner* 10–11 (May–August 1909).

"In the Land of the Free." *Independent* 67 (September 2, 1909): 504–8.

"Mrs. Spring Fragrance." *Hampton's* 24 (January 1910): 137–41. Reprinted in Sui Sin Far, *Mrs. Spring Fragrance and Other Writings,* edited by Amy Ling and Annette White-Parks, 17–28. Urbana: University of Illinois Press, 1995.

"A White Woman Who Married a Chinaman." *Independent* 68 (March 10, 1910): 518–23.

"The Inferior Woman." *Hampton's* 24 (May 1910): 727–31. Reprinted in Sui Sin Far, *Mrs. Spring Fragrance and Other Writings,* edited by Amy Ling and Annette White-Parks, 28–41. Urbana: University of Illinois Press, 1995.

"The Sugar Cane Baby." *Good Housekeeping* 50 (May 1910): 570–72.

"An Autumn Fan." *New England Magazine* 42 (August 1910): 700–702.

"Her Chinese Husband." *Independent* 69 (August 18, 1910): 358–61.

"The Bird of Love." *New England Magazine* 43 (September 1910): 25–27.

"The Persecution and Oppression of Me." *Independent* 71 (August 24, 1911): 421–26.

"A Love Story from the Rice Fields of China." *New England Magazine* 45 (December 1911): 343–45.

"Who's Game." *New England Magazine* 45 (February 1912): 573–79.

"Sui Sin Far, the Half Chinese Writer, Tells of Her Career." *Boston Globe,* May 5, 1912. Reprinted in Sui Sin Far, *Mrs. Spring Fragrance and Other Writings,* edited by Amy Ling and Annette White-Parks, 288–96. Urbana: University of Illinois Press, 1995.

"The Moon Harp." *Independent* 72 (May 23, 1912): 1106.

"Chan Hen Yen, Chinese Student." *New England Magazine* 45 (June 1912): 462–66.
"'Its Wavering Image.'" In *Mrs. Spring Fragrance.* Chicago: A. C. McClurg, 1912. Reprinted in *Mrs. Spring Fragrance and Other Stories,* edited by Amy Ling and Annette White-Parks, 61–66. Urbana: University of Illinois Press, 1995.
Mrs. Spring Fragrance. Chicago: McClurg, 1912. Reprinted in Sui Sin Far, *Mrs. Spring Fragrance and Other Writings,* edited by Amy Ling and Annette White-Parks, 17–166. Urbana: University of Illinois Press, 1995.
Mrs. Spring Fragrance and Other Writings. Edited by Amy Ling and Annette White-Parks. Urbana: University of Illinois Press, 1995.

Reviews and Biographical Notes on Edith Eaton (Listed Chronologically)

Harte, Walter Blackburn. "Bubble and Squeak." *Lotus* 2 (October 1896): 216–17.
[Lummis, Charles.] "In Western Letters." *Land of Sunshine* 13 (November 1900): 336.
"Edith Eaton." *Chautauquan* 45 (July 1906): 446.
"A New Note in Fiction: Mrs. Spring Fragrance." *New York Times Book Review,* July 7, 1912, 405.
"Mrs. Spring Fragrance." *American Antiquarian and Oriental Journal* 35 (July–September 1913): 181–82.

Selected Writings by Winnifred Eaton (Listed Chronologically)

"A Poor Devil." *Metropolitan Magazine,* n.d. [189?]. Winnifred Eaton Reeve Fonds, Special Collections, University of Calgary Library.
"Sneer Not." *Gall's Daily News Letter,* March 10, 1896.
"A Rhapsody on Japan." *American Home Journal,* n.d. [189?]. Winnifred Eaton Reeve Fonds, Special Collections, University of Calgary Library.
"The Half Caste." *Conkey's Home Journal,* November 1898. Winnifred Eaton Reeve Fonds, Special Collections, University of Calgary Library.
"The Life of a Japanese Girl." *Ladies' Home Journal* 16 (April 1899): 7.
"A Half Caste." *Frank Leslie's Popular Monthly* 48 (September 1899): 489–96.
Miss Numè of Japan: A Japanese-American Romance. Chicago: Rand McNally, 1899.
"Where the Young Look Forward to Old Age." Clipping from *Ladies' Home Journal,* n.d. [1899?]. Winnifred Eaton Reeve Fonds, Special Collections, University of Calgary Library.
"New Year's Day in Japan." *Frank Leslie's Popular Monthly* 49 (January 1900): 283–86.
"The Two Converts." *Harper's Monthly,* September 1901, 585–89. Reprinted in *Nineteenth-Century American Women Writers: An Anthology,* edited by Karen L. Kilcup, 571–76. Cambridge, Mass.: Blackwell, 1997.
"Kirishima-San." *Idler* 20 (November 1901): 315–21.
"Margot." *Frank Leslie's Popular Monthly* 53 (December 1901): 202–9.
A Japanese Nightingale. New York: Harper and Brothers, 1901.
"Eyes That Saw Not" (with Bertrand W. Babcock). *Harper's Monthly,* June 1902, 30–38.
"A Contract." *Frank Leslie's Popular Monthly* 54 (August 1902): 370–79.

"The Japanese Drama and the Actor." *Critic* 41 (September 1902): 231–37.

The Wooing of Wistaria. New York: Harper, 1902.

"The Loves of Sakura Jiro and the Three-Headed Maid." *Century Magazine* 65 (March 1903): 755–60. Reprinted in *Nineteenth-Century American Women Writers: An Anthology,* edited by Karen L. Kilcup, 576–81. Cambridge, Mass.: Blackwell, 1997.

"Miss Lily and Miss Chrysanthemum." *Ladies' Home Journal* 20 (August 1903): 11–12.

"The Flight of Hyacinth." *Current Literature* 35 (October 1903): 437–40.

The Heart of Hyacinth. New York: Harper and Brothers, 1903.

"Every-Day Life in Japan." *Harper's Weekly,* April 2, 1904, 500–503, 527–28.

"The Marvelous Miniature Trees of Japan." *Woman's Home Companion,* June 1904, 16.

"The Love of Azalea." *Bookman* 19 (August 1904): 58–95; 20 (September 1904): 65–79; 21 (October 1904): 161–68.

The Daughters of Nijo: A Romance of Japan. New York: Macmillan, 1904.

The Love of Azalea. New York: Dodd, Mead, 1904.

"The Wrench of Chance." *Harper's Weekly,* October 20, 1906, 1494–96, 1505, 1531.

A Japanese Blossom. New York: Harper and Brothers, 1906.

"The Japanese in America." *Eclectic Magazine* 148 (February 1907): 100–104.

The Diary of Delia: Being a Veracious Chronicle of the Kitchen with Some Side-Lights on the Parlour. New York: Doubleday, 1907.

"The Manœuvres of O-Yasu-san." *Saturday Evening Post,* January 25, 1908, 9–11, 22.

"A Neighbor's Garden, My Own, and a Dream One." *Good Housekeeping* 46 (April 1908): 347–53; 46 (May 1908): 484–90.

"Delia Dissents." *Saturday Evening Post,* August 22, 1908, 22–23.

"An Unexpected Grandchild." *Lippincott's Monthly* 84 (December 1909): 684–700.

Tama. New York: Harper and Brothers, 1910.

The Honorable Miss Moonlight. New York: Harper and Brothers, 1912.

Chinese-Japanese Cook Book (with Sara Bosse). Chicago: Rand McNally, 1914.

Me: A Book of Remembrance. New York: Century, 1915.

Marion: The Story of an Artist's Model. New York: W. J. Watt, 1916.

"Lend Me Your Title." *MacLean's Magazine,* February 1919, 13–14, 72–74; March 1919, 16, 18–19, 66–69.

"Other People's Troubles: An Antidote for Your Own." *Farm and Ranch Review,* February 5, February 20, April 5, April 21, May 5, May 20, June 5, June 20, July 21, and August 5, 1919. Winnifred Eaton Reeve Fonds, Special Collections, University of Calgary Library.

"Starving and Writing in New York." *MacLean's Magazine,* October 15, 1922, 66–67.

Sunny-San. Toronto: McClelland and Stewart, 1922; New York: George H. Doran, 1922.

"Elspeth." *Quill,* January 1923, 23–30.

"The Canadian Spirit in Our Literature." *Calgary Daily Herald,* March 24, 1923.

Cattle. New York: W. J. Watt, 1924.

His Royal Nibs. New York: W. J. Watt, 1925.

"Sins of the Fathers." Typescript, n.d. [192?]. Winnifred Eaton Reeve Fonds, Special Collections, University of Calgary Library.

"You Can't Run Away from Yourself." Typescript, n.d. [192?]. Winnifred Eaton Reeve Fonds, Special Collections, University of Calgary Library.

"Because We Were Lonely." *True Story Magazine,* April 1933, 28–30, 92–96.

Reviews and Biographical Notes on Winnifred Eaton (Listed Chronologically)

"Onoto Watanna, the Japanese Woman Writer." *Current Literature* 24 (October 1898): 306.

"A Japanese Novelist: Now Chicago Boasts of a Japanese Woman Writer Who Is Destined to Make a Hit." *Detroit Free Press*, n.d. [1898]. Scrapbook, Winnifred Eaton Reeve Fonds, Special Collections, University of Calgary Library.

"A Charming Japanese Tale." *New York Times Book Review*, August 19, 1899, 559.

"Onoto Watanna." *Frank Leslie's Popular Monthly* 48 (September 1899): 553–54.

"A Japanese Girl's Novel." *New York Times Book Review*, November 9, 1901, 819.

"Notes of a Bookman." *Harper's Weekly*, December 21, 1901, 1300.

Howells, William Dean. "A Psychological Counter-Current in Recent Fiction." *North American Review* 173 (December 1901): 872–88.

"General Gossip of Authors and Writers." *Current Literature* 32 (February 1902): 236.

"Onoto Watanna." *Frank Leslie's Popular Monthly* 54 (August 1902): 370.

"The Heart of Hyacinth." *New York Times Book Review*, October 3, 1903, 685.

Dale, Alan. "A Japanese Nightingale Is Drury Lane Melodrama Set to Light of Lanterns." *New York American*, November 21, 1903.

"Japanese Nightingale Suffers from Locomotor Ataxia and Influenza." Newspaper clipping, November 21, 1903. Winnifred Eaton Reeve Fonds, Special Collections, University of Calgary Library.

"Jap Artist Sees 'A Japanese Nightingale.'" *Sunday Telegraph*, November 29, 1903.

"Onoto Watanna." *Harper's Weekly*, December 5, 1903, 1959–60.

"Natural Fighters, She Says of Japs: Daughter of Japanese Mother Says Natives Are Natural Fighters as Descendants of Famous Samurai." Clipping from *Evening Telegraph*, February 12, 1904. Winnifred Eaton Reeve Fonds, Special Collections, University of Calgary Library.

"Tale of a Sonnet: Dispute about the Origin of a Certain Descriptive Passage in Onoto Watanna's Book 'A Japanese Nightingale.'" *New York Times Book Review*, February 20, 1904, 116.

"Love in Japan: Daughters of Nijo." *New York Times Book Review*, April 30, 1904, 301.

"Novels, Japanese and Japanned." *Independent* 56 (June 23, 1904): 1445–46.

"Children of Two Worlds: A Japanese Blossom." *New York Times Book Review*, January 12, 1907, 17.

"The Kitchen's Viewpoint: The Diary of Delia." *New York Times Book Review*, June 15, 1907, 386.

"The Diary of Delia." *New York Times Book Review*, June 29, 1907, 418.

"Tama." *New York Times Book Review*, January 14, 1911, 16.

"A Japanese Story: The Honorable Miss Moonlight." *New York Times Book Review*, October 27, 1912, 628.

"Is Onoto Watanna Author of the Anonymous Novel 'Me'?" *New York Times Book Review*, October 10, 1915, 869+.

Price, Elizabeth Bailey. "Onoto Watanna Has Written a New Book." *Canadian Bookman*, April 1922, 123–25. Winnifred Eaton Reeve Fonds, Special Collections, University of Calgary Library.

"Onoto Watanna Decries 'Yellow Peril' in Talk on Women of East and West." Newspaper clipping, [192?]. Winnifred Eaton Reeve Fonds, Special Collections, University of Calgary Library.

Lang, Naomi. "Alberta Women Who Make News." *Calgary Herald,* September 6, 1941.

Rooney, Doris. "Souvenir from the Past." *Field, Horse and Rodeo,* July 1963, 45–47.

Books, Articles, and Dissertations

Ackerman, Jessie. *Through a Woman's Eyes.* Chicago: Rand McNally, 1896.

Allen, Grant. "Aesthetic Evolution in Man." *Popular Science Monthly* 18 (January 1881): 339–56.

Anderson, Benedict. *Imagined Communities: Reflections on the Origin and Spread of Nationalism.* London: Verso, 1983.

Apter, Emily, "Acting Out Orientalism: Sapphic Theatricality in Turn-of-the-Century Paris." In *Performance and Cultural Politics,* edited by Elia Diamond, 15–34. New York: Routledge, 1996.

Arnold, Edwin. *Japonica.* 1891. Reprint, New York: Scribner's, 1892.

———. *Seas and Lands.* 1891. Reprint, London: Longmans, 1892.

Arnold, Matthew. *Culture and Anarchy.* New York: Macmillan, 1896.

Austin, Mary. *The American Rhythm.* New York: Harcourt, Brace, 1923.

———. "The Basket Maker." In *The Land of Little Rain,* by Mary Austin. Boston: Houghton, Mifflin, 1903. Reprinted in Mary Austin, *Stories from the Country of Lost Borders,* edited by Marjorie Pryse, 93–99. New Brunswick, N.J.: Rutgers University Press, 1987.

"The Awakening World." *Independent* 49 (October 21, 1910): 906.

Bacon, Alice Mabel. *Japanese Girls and Women.* Boston: Houghton, Mifflin, 1891.

———. *A Japanese Interior.* Boston: Houghton, Mifflin, 1893.

Bailey, L. H., ed. *The Standard Cyclopedia of Horticulture.* 6 vols. New York: Macmillan, 1914–17.

Bandelier, Adolf. *The Delight Makers.* 1890. Reprint, New York: Dodd, Mead, 1960.

Banta, Martha. Introduction to *The House of Mirth,* by Edith Wharton, vii–xxxi. Oxford: Oxford University Press, 1994.

Barnett, Suzanne Wilson, and John King Fairbank, eds. *Christianity in China: Early Protestant Missionary Writings.* Cambridge, Mass.: Harvard University Press, 1985.

Beard, George M. *American Nervousness: Its Causes and Consequences.* New York: Putnam, 1881.

Beauchamp, Edward R. *An American Teacher in Early Meiji Japan.* Honolulu: University Press of Hawaii, 1976.

Beer, Gillian. *Darwin's Plot: Evolutionary Narrative in Darwin, George Eliot, and Nineteenth-Century Fiction.* London: Routledge, 1983.

Behdad, Ali. *Belated Travelers: Orientalism in the Age of Colonial Dissolution.* Durham, N.C.: Duke University Press, 1994.

Bhabha, Homi. *The Location of Culture.* London: Routledge, 1994.

Bingham, Edwin R. "Charles F. Lummis and His Magazine." Ph.D. diss., University of California, Los Angeles, 1950.

Birchall, Diana. *Onoto Watanna: The Story of Winnifred Eaton*. Urbana: University of Illinois Press, 2001.

Bird, Isabella. *Unbeaten Tracks in Japan*. 2 vols. 1880. Reprint, New York: Putnam's, 1881.

Blanch, Lesley. *Pierre Loti: The Legendary Romantic*. New York: Harcourt, Brace, 1983.

Botshon, Lisa M. "Cautious Pluralism: Ethnic Women Writers and Early Twentieth-Century United States Popular Culture." Ph.D. diss., Columbia University, 1997.

Bowler, Peter. *The Mendelian Revolution: The Emergence of Hereditarian Concepts in Modern Science and Society*. Baltimore: Johns Hopkins University Press, 1989.

Brereton, Bridget. "Society and Culture in the Caribbean: The British and French West Indies, 1870–1980." In *The Modern Caribbean*, edited by Franklin Knight and Colin A. Palmer, 85–110. Chapel Hill: University of North Carolina Press, 1989.

Broca, Paul. *On the Phenomena of Hybridity in the Genus Homo*. London: Longman, 1864.

Brodhead, Richard H. *Cultures of Letters: Scenes of Reading and Writing in Nineteenth-Century America*. Chicago: University of Chicago Press, 1993.

Brooks, Margaret. "Japan, the Youngest Born." *Overland Monthly* 33 (April 1899): 313.

Cagan, Rosemary R. *A Sensitive Independence: Canadian Methodist Missionary Women in the Orient, 1881–1925*. Montreal: McGill-Queen's University Press, 1992.

Carby, Hazel. "The Politics of Fiction, Anthropology and the Folk: Zora Neale Hurston." In *History and Memory in African-American Culture*, edited by Geneviève Fabre and Robert O'Meally, 28–44. New York: Oxford University Press, 1994.

Cary, Otis. *A History of Christianity in Japan*. Rutland, Vt.: Tuttle, 1976.

"Celestials Going Home." *Montreal Daily Star*, September 12, 1894.

"The Celestials in Montreal: How the Chinese Employ Their Leisure Time." *Montreal Daily Star*, September 8, 1894.

Chamberlain, Basil Hall. *Things Japanese*. London: Kelly and Walsh, 1891.

Chan, Jeffery Paul, Frank Chin, Lawson Fusao Inada, and Shawn Wong, eds. *The Big Aiiieeeee! An Anthology of Chinese American and Japanese American Literature*. New York: Meridian, 1991.

Chan, Sucheng. *This Bittersweet Soil: The Chinese in California Agriculture*. Berkeley: University of California Press, 1986.

Cheung, King-Kok. "The Woman Warrior versus the Chinaman Pacific: Must a Chinese American Critic Choose between Feminism and Heroism?" In *Conflicts in Feminism*, edited by Marianne Hirsch and Evelyn Fox Keller, 234–51. New York: Routledge, 1990.

———, ed. *An Interethnic Companion to Asian American Literature*. Cambridge: Cambridge University Press, 1997.

———. *Words Matter: Conversations with Twenty Asian American Writers*. Honolulu: University of Hawaii Press, 2000.

Chin, Frank, Jeffery Paul Chan, Lawson Fusao Inada, and Shawn Wong, eds. *Aiiieeeee! An Anthology of Chinese-American Writers*. Washington, D.C.: Howard University Press, 1974.

"Chinamen at Sunday School: An Afternoon at St. Gabriel Presbyterian Church." *Montreal Daily Star*, November 24, 1894.

China Mission Handbook. Shanghai: American Presbyterian Mission, 1896.

"The Chinese Land of Promise." *Montreal Daily Star*, June 23, 1894.

Chisolm, Lawrence W. *Fenollosa: The Far East and American Culture*. New Haven, Conn.: Yale University Press, 1963.

Clement, Ernest W. *A Handbook of Modern Japan.* Detroit: McClurg, 1903.

Clifford, James. "On Ethnographic Allegory." In *Writing Culture: The Poetics and Politics of Ethnography,* edited by James Clifford and George E. Marcus, 98–121. Berkeley: University of California Press, 1986.

———. *The Predicament of Culture: Twentieth-Century Ethnography, Literature, and Art.* Cambridge, Mass.: Harvard University Press, 1988.

Cole, Jean Lee. "Guided by Voices: The Strange Career of Winnifred Eaton Reeve." Ph.D. diss., University of Texas at Austin, in progress.

Connor, Torrey. "Only John." *Land of Sunshine* 4 (February 1896): 111–16.

Crapanzano, Vincent. *Hermes' Dilemma and Hamlet's Desire: On the Epistemology of Interpretation.* Cambridge, Mass.: Harvard University Press, 1992.

Crouch, Archie R. et al., eds. *Christianity in China: A Scholar's Guide to Resources in the Libraries and Archives of the United States.* Armonk, N.Y.: M. E. Sharpe, 1989.

Culin, Stewart. "Social Organization of the Chinese in America." *American Anthropologist* 4 (October 1891): 347–52.

Daniels, Roger. *The Politics of Prejudice: The Anti-Japanese Movement in California and the Struggle for Japanese Exclusion.* New York: Atheneum, 1968.

Darden, Lindley. *Theory Change in Science: Strategies from Mendelian Genetics.* New York: Oxford University Press, 1991.

Davidson, Cathy. *Revolution and the Word: The Rise of the Novel in America.* New York: Oxford University Press, 1986.

Davis, Mike. *The City of Quartz.* New York: Random House, 1992.

Deering, M. "The Daughters of Ah Sum." *Out West* 18 (July 1903): 21–25.

Degler, Carl. *In Search of Human Nature: The Decline and Revival of Darwinism in American Social Thought.* New York: Oxford University Press, 1991.

DeHolmes, Rebecca B. "Is *Shabono* a Scandal or Superb Social Science?" *American Anthropologist* 85 (July–September 1983): 664–67.

De Kay, Charles. "Painting Racial Types." *Century Magazine* 60 (June 1900): 163–69.

Dennett, Andrea Stulman. "The Dime Museum Freak Show Reconfigured as Talk Show." In *Freakery: Cultural Spectacles of the Extraordinary Body,* edited by Rosemarie Garland Thomson, 315–26. New York: New York University Press, 1996.

Denning, Greg. "The Theatricality of Observing and Being Observed." In *Observers Observed: Essays on Ethnographic Fieldwork,* edited by George Stocking Jr. Madison: University of Wisconsin Press, 1983.

Deverell, William, and Tom Sitton, eds. *California Progressivism Revisited.* Berkeley: University of California Press, 1994.

Dictionary of American Biography. Edited by Allen Johnson. New York: Scribner's, 1928–58.

Dictionary of Literary Biography. Detroit: Gale Research Group, 1978.

Donner, Florinda. *Shabono.* New York: Delacorte, 1982.

Doolittle, Justus. *Social Life of the Chinese.* 2 vols. New York: Harper and Brothers, 1865.

Doyle, James. *The Fin de Siècle Spirit: Walter Blackburn Harte and the American/Canadian Literary Milieu of the 1890s.* Toronto: ECW, 1995.

———. "Sui Sin Far and Onoto Watanna: Two Early Chinese-Canadian Authors." *Canadian Literature* 140 (Spring 1994): 50–58.

Drake, Fred W. "Protestant Geography in China: E. C. Bridgman's Portrayal of the West." In *Christianity in China: Early Protestant Missionary Writings*, edited by Suzanne Wilson Barnett and John King Fairbank, 89–106. Cambridge, Mass.: Harvard University Press, 1985.

Dwight, Henry Otis, H. Allen Tupper, and Edwin Munsell Bliss, eds. *The Encyclopedia of Missions.* 2d ed. New York: Funk and Wagnalls, 1904.

Editorial. "The American Sentiment concerning Russia and Japan." *Century Magazine* 68 (September 1904): 815–17.

Editorial. *Independent* 46 (January 14, 1909): 108.

Ellis, Havelock. "Eugenics and St. Valentine." *Eclectic Magazine* 147 (July 1906): 14–20.

"Extraordinary Finger-Nails." *Dominion Illustrated* 110 (August 9, 1890): 94.

Fairbank, John K. "Introduction: The Place of Protestant Writings in China's Cultural History." In *Christianity in China: Early Protestant Missionary Writings*, edited by Suzanne Wilson Barnett and John King Fairbank, 1–18. Cambridge, Mass.: Harvard University Press, 1985.

Farrar, Reginald J. *The Garden of Asia: Impressions from Japan.* London: Methuen, 1904.

Fenollosa, Ernest. "Chinese and Japanese Traits." *Atlantic Monthly* 69 (June 1982): 769–74.

Ferens, Dominika. "Tangled Kites: Sui Sin Far's Negotiations with Race and Readership." *Amerasia Journal* 25 (Summer 1999): 87–115.

Fischer, Michael J. "Ethnicity and the Post-Modern Arts of Memory." In *Writing Culture: The Poetics and Politics of Ethnography*, edited by James Clifford and George E. Marcus, 194–233. Berkeley: University of California Press, 1986.

Frankenberg, Ruth. Introduction to *Displacing Whiteness: Essays in Social and Cultural Criticism*, edited by Ruth Frankenberg, 1–33. Durham, N.C.: Duke University Press, 1997.

Furner, Mary O. *Advocacy and Objectivity: A Crisis in the Professionalization of American Social Sciences, 1865–1905.* Lexington: University Press of Kentucky, 1975.

Georgi-Findlay, Brigitte. *The Frontiers of Women's Writing: Women's Narratives and the Rhetoric of Westward Expansion.* Tucson: University of Arizona Press, 1995.

Ginsberg, Elaine, ed. *Passing and the Fictions of Identity.* Durham, N.C.: Duke University Press, 1996.

Goffman, Erving. *Stigma: Notes on the Management of a Spoiled Identity.* 1963. Reprint, New York: Touchstone, 1986.

Griffis, William Elliot. *The Japanese Nation in Evolution.* London: Harrap, 1907.

———. *The Mikado's Empire.* New York: Harper and Brothers, 1877.

Harris, Cheryl I. "Whiteness as Property." *Harvard Law Review* 106 (June 1993): 1709–91.

Harris, Neil. "All the World a Melting-Pot: Japan at American Fairs, 1876–1904." In *Mutual Images: Essays in American-Japanese Relations*, edited by Akira Iriye, 24–54. Cambridge, Mass.: Harvard University Press, 1975.

Harrison, Beth. "Zora Neale Hurston and Mary Austin: A Case Study in Ethnography, Literary Modernism, and Contemporary Ethnic Fiction." *MELUS* 21 (Summer 1996): 89–106.

Hartmann, Sadakichi. *Sadakichi Hartmann: Critical Modernist. Collected Art Writings.* Edited by Jane Calhoun Weaver. Berkeley: University of California Press, 1991.

Hartnell, E. "Some Little Heathens." *Land of Sunshine* 5 (September 1896): 153–57.

Hearn, Lafcadio. *Glimpses of Unfamiliar Japan.* Boston: Houghton, Mifflin, 1894.

The Heath Anthology of American Literature. Edited by Paul Lauter. Lexington, Mass.: D. C. Heath, 1990.

Heilman, Robert Bechtold. *Tragedy and Melodrama: Versions of Experience.* Seattle: University of Washington Press, 1968.

Hewett, Edgar L. "Ethnic Factors in Education." *American Anthropologist* 7 (January–March 1905): 1–16.

Hinsley, Curtis. "Zunis and Brahmins: Cultural Ambivalence in the Gilded Age." In *Romantic Motives: Essays on Anthropological Sensibility,* edited by George W. Stocking Jr., 169–207. Madison: University of Wisconsin Press, 1989.

Hood, George A. *Mission Accomplished? The English Presbyterian Mission in Lingtung, South China: A Study of the Interplay between Mission Methods and Their Historical Context.* New York: Peter Land, 1986.

Howard, Maureen. "The House of Mirth: The Bachelor and the Baby." In *Cambridge Companion to Edith Wharton,* edited by Millicent Bell, 137–56. Cambridge, Mass.: Cambridge University Press, 1995.

Howells, William Dean. *Criticism and Fiction and Other Essays.* Edited by C. M. Kirk and R. Kirk. New York: New York University Press, 1959.

Hunter, Jane. *The Gospel of Gentility: American Women Missionaries in Turn-of-the-Century China.* New Haven, Conn.: Yale University Press, 1894.

Hurston, Zora Neale. *Mules and Men.* 1935. Reprint, Bloomington: Indiana University Press, 1978.

Huxley, Thomas H. *Evidence of Man's Place in Nature.* New York: Appleton, 1886.

———. *Evolution and Ethics and Other Essays.* New York: Appleton, 1894.

Hwang, David Henry. *M. Butterfly.* 1988. Reprint, New York: Penguin, 1989.

Ichihashi, Yamato. "Emigration from Japan and Thence Their Immigration into the State of California." Ph.D. diss., Harvard University, 1913.

Ichioka, Yuji. *The Issei: The World of the First Generation Japanese Immigrants, 1885–1924.* New York: Free Press, 1988.

Inkersley, Arthur. "The Chinaman in the United States." *Frank Leslie's Popular Monthly* 55 (February 1903): 359–70.

Iriye, Akira. "Japan as Competitor, 1895–17." In *Mutual Images: Essays in American-Japanese Relations,* edited by Akira Iriye, 73–99. Cambridge, Mass.: Harvard University Press, 1975.

James, Henry. "Pierre Loti." In *Essays in London and Elsewhere,* by Henry James, 151–85. New York: Harper and Brothers, 1893.

Jansen, Marius B. "The 1911 Revolution and the United States East Asian Policy." In *The 1911 Revolution in China,* edited by Eto Shinkichi and Harold Z. Schiff. Tokyo: University of Tokyo Press, 1984.

Jen, Gish. *Typical American.* Boston: Houghton Mifflin, 1991.

Kawakami, Kiyoshi K. "How California Treats the Japanese." *Independent* 74 (May 8, 1912): 1019–23.

Keane, A. H. *Ethnology.* Cambridge: Cambridge University Press, 1895.

———. *Man, Past and Present.* Cambridge: Cambridge University Press, 1899.

Kim, Elaine H. *Asian American Literature: An Introduction to the Writings and Their Social Context.* Philadelphia: Temple University Press, 1982.

Kinnosuke, Adachi. "The Beautiful and the Necessary," *Overland Monthly* 41 (January 1903): 3–9.

Kondo, Dorinne. *About Face: Performing Race in Fashion and Theater.* New York: Routledge, 1997.

La Farge, John. *An Artist's Letters from Japan.* New York: Century, 1897.

"Lame Dancing-Masters: An Indian View of Government Schools." *Land of Sunshine* 12 (May 1900): 356–58.

Lape, Noreen Groover. "West of the Border: Cultural Liminality in the Literature of the Western American Frontiers." Ph.D. diss., Temple University, 1996.

Larson, Ruth. "Ethnography, Thievery, and Cultural Identity: A Reading of Michel Leiris's *L'Afrique fantome*." *PMLA* 112 (March 1997): 229–42.

Latourette, Kenneth Scott. *A History of Christian Missions in China.* New York: Macmillan, 1929.

Lee, Rachel. "Journalistic Representations of Asian Americans and Literary Responses, 1910–1920." In *Interethnic Companion to Asian American Literature,* edited by King-Kok Cheung, 249–73. Cambridge: Cambridge University Press, 1997.

Leonard, Jane Kate. "W. H. Medhurst: Rewriting the Missionary Message." In *Christianity in China: Early Protestant Missionary Writings,* edited by Suzanne Wilson Barnett and John King Fairbank. Cambridge, Mass.: Harvard University Press, 1985.

Leroy-Beaulieu, Pierre. "The Chinaman: A Character Study from Life." *McClures* 15 (December 1900): 134–40.

Ling, Amy. *Between Worlds: Women Writers of Chinese Ancestry.* New York: Pergamon, 1990.
———. "Creating One's Own Self: The Eaton Sisters." In *Reading the Literatures of Asian America,* edited by Shirley Lim and Amy Ling, 305–18. Philadelphia: Temple University Press, 1992.
———. "Winnifred Eaton: Ethnic Chameleon and Popular Success." *MELUS* 11 (Fall 1984): 5–15.

Ling, Jinqi. *Narrating Nationalisms: Ideology and Form in Asian American Literature.* New York: Oxford University Press, 1998.

Lionnet, Françoise. "Autoethnography: The An-Archic Style of *Dust Tracks on a Road.*" In *African American Autobiography: A Collection of Critical Essays,* edited by William L. Andrews, 113–37. Englewood Cliffs: Prentice Hall, 1993.

Little, Alicia Helen. *Intimate China: The Chinese as I Have Seen Them.* Philadelphia: Lippincott, 1901.

Little, Frances. *The Lady of the Decoration.* Toronto: Musson, 1906.

"The Living Races of Mankind: Review." *American Anthropologist* 4 (April–June 1902): 305–6.

Long, John Luther. *Madame Butterfly.* 1895. Reprint, New York: Century, 1904.
———. *Miss Cherry-Blossom.* Philadelphia: Lippincott, 1895.

Loti, Pierre. *Madame Chrysanthème.* 1888. Translated by Laura Ensor. Reprint, London: KPI, 1985.

Lowe, Lisa. *Critical Terrains: British and French Orientalisms.* Ithaca, N.Y.: Cornell University Press, 1991.

Lummis, Charles. "Catching Our Archaeology Alive." *Land of Sunshine* 22 (January 1905): 35–48.

———. "A Hero in Science." *Land of Sunshine* 13 (August 1900): 158–65.

———. "In the Lion's Den." *Land of Sunshine* 12 (December 1899): 49–52.

———. "In the Lion's Den." *Land of Sunshine* 12 (January 1900): 378–79.

———. "In the Lion's Den." *Land of Sunshine* 12 (February 1900): 188–96.

———. "In Memory." Introduction to *The Delight Makers*, by Adolf Bandelier, i–iv. 1890. Reprint, New York: Dodd, Mead, 1916.

———. "My Brother's Keeper." *Land of Sunshine* 11 (August 1899): 139–47.

———. "The Spanish American Face." *Land of Sunshine* 2 (January 1895): 21–22.

MacFarlane, Charles. *Japan: An Account Geographical and Historical.* New York: Putnam, 1852.

MacGillivray, D., ed. *A Century of Missions in China (1807–1907).* Shanghai: Christian Literature Society for China, 1907.

Malinowski, Bronislaw. *A Diary in the Strict Sense of the Term.* Translated by Norbert Guterman. 1967. Reprint, Stanford, Calif.: Stanford University Press, 1989.

Marcus, George E., and Michael J. Fischer. *Anthropology as Cultural Critique: An Experimental Moment in the Human Sciences.* Chicago: University of Chicago Press, 1986.

Matsukawa, Yuko. "Cross-Dressing and Cross-Naming: Decoding Onoto Watanna." In *Tricksterism in Turn-of-the-Century American Literature: A Multicultural Perspective,* edited by Elizabeth Ammons and Annette White-Parks, 106–25. Hanover, N.H.: University Press of New England, 1994.

Medhurst, W. H. *China: Its State and Prospects.* Boston: Crocker and Brewster, 1838.

Meech, Julia, and Gabriel P. Weisberg. *Japonisme Comes to America: The Japanese Impact on the Graphic Arts, 1876–1925.* New York: Harry N. Abrams, 1990.

Meissenburg, Karin. *The Writing on the Wall: Socio-Historical Aspects of Chinese American Literature, 1900–1980.* Frankfurt-am-Main: Verlag für Interkulturelle Kommunikation, 1987.

Meyerowitz, Joanne. "Sexual Geography and Gender Economy: The Furnished-Room Districts of Chicago, 1890–1930." In *Unequal Sisters: A Multicultural Reader in U.S. Women's History,* 2d ed., edited by Vicki L. Ruis and Ellen Carol Dubois, 186–202. New York: Routledge, 1994.

Minh-ha, Trinh T. *Framer Framed.* New York: Routledge, 1992.

———. *Woman, Native, Other: Writing, Postcoloniality, and Feminism.* Bloomington: Indiana University Press, 1989.

Moser, Linda Trinh. Afterword to *Me: A Book of Remembrance,* by Winnifred Eaton. Jackson: University Press of Mississippi, 1997.

Moy, James. *Marginal Sights: Staging the Chinese in America.* Iowa City: University of Iowa Press, 1993.

Najmi, Samina. "Representations of White Women in Works by Selected African American and Asian American Authors." Ph.D. diss., Tufts University, 1997.

Nevius, Helen. *Our Life in China.* New York: Robert Carter, 1869.

Ng Poon Chew. "The Chinese in Los Angeles." *Land of Sunshine* 1 (October 1894): 102–3.

Noguchi, Yone. "The American Diary of a Japanese Girl." *Frank Leslie's Popular Monthly* 53 (November 1901): 68–82; 53 (December 1901): 192–201.

———. *Selected English Writings of Yone Noguchi: An East-West Literary Assimilation.* Edited by Yoshinobu Hakutani. London: Associated University Press, 1992.

"Novels Japanese and Japanned." *Independent* 56 (June 23, 1904): 1445–47.

Oswald, F. L. "Modern Mongols." *Popular Science Monthly* 57 (October 1900): 618–23.

Palumbo-Liu, David. "The Minority Self as Other: Problematics of Representation in Asian American Literature." *Cultural Critique* 28 (Fall 1994): 80–99.

Parsons, Alfred. *Notes in Japan*. New York: Harper, 1896.

Pascoe, Peggy. *Relations of Rescue: The Search for Female Moral Authority in the American West, 1874–1939*. New York: Oxford University Press, 1990.

Pecora, Vincent. "The Sorcerer's Apprentices: Romance, Anthropology, and Literary Theory." *Modern Language Quarterly* 55 (December 1994): 345–82.

Peery, R. B. *The Gist of Japan*. New York: Fleming H. Revell, 1897.

Percival, Olive. "An Afternoon in Chinatown." *Land of Sunshine* 12 (October 1899): 50–52.

Pott, F. L. Hawks. *The Emergency in China*. Cincinnati: Methodist Book Concern, 1913.

Pratt, Mary Louise. "Fieldwork in Common Places." In *Writing Culture: The Politics and Poetics of Ethnography*, edited by James Clifford and George E. Marcus, 27–50. Berkeley: University of California Press, 1986.

———. *Imperial Eyes: Travel Writing and Transculturation*. New York: Routledge, 1992.

Prus, Robert. *Symbolic Interpretation and Ethnographic Research: Intersubjectivity and the Study of Human Lived Experience*. Albany: State University of New York Press, 1996.

Quartermain, Peter, ed. *American Poets, 1880–1945*. Detroit: Gale Research, 1986.

Quintana, Alvina. "Ana Castillo's *The Mixquiahuala Letters*: The Novelist as Ethnographer." In *Criticism in the Borderlands: Studies in Chicano Literature, Culture, and Ideology*, edited by Héctor Calderón and José David Saldívar, 72–83. Durham, N.C.: Duke University Press, 1991.

Review of Frank Putnam's *Love Lyrics*, with an introduction by Onoto Watanna. Scrapbook, Winnifred Eaton Reeve Fonds, Special Collections, University of Calgary Library.

Rogozinski, Jan. *A Brief History of the Caribbean*. New York: Meridian, 1992.

Rony, Fatimah Tobing. *The Third Eye: Race, Cinema, and the Ethnographic Spectacle*. Durham, N.C.: Duke University Press, 1996.

Rosaldo, Renato. *Culture and Truth: The Remaking of Social Analysis*. Boston: Beacon, 1989.

Rose, Tricia. *Black Noise: Rap Music and Black Culture in Contemporary America*. Hanover, N.H.: University Press of New England, 1994.

Said, Edward. *Orientalism*. New York: Pantheon, 1978.

Sánchez-Eppler, Benigno. "Telling Anthropology: Zora Neale Hurston and Gilberto Freyre Disciplined in Their Field-Home-Work." *American Literary History* 4 (Fall 1992): 464–88.

Saxton, Alexander. *The Indispensable Enemy: Labor and the Anti-Chinese Movement in California*. Berkeley: University of California Press, 1971.

Scharnhorst, Gary. "'Ways That Are Dark': Appropriations of Bret Harte's 'Plain Language from Truthful James.'" *Nineteenth-Century Literature* 51 (December 1996): 377–99.

Shea, Pat. "Winnifred Eaton and the Politics of Miscegenation in Popular Fiction (Popular Literature and Film)." *MELUS* 22 (Summer 1997): 19–35.

Simms, J. "In the Empire of the Mikado." *Frank Leslie's Popular Monthly* 44 (August 1897): 174–81.

Smith, Arthur H. *Chinese Characteristics*. New York: Fleming H. Revell, 1894.

———. *The Uplift of China.* 1907. Reprint, New York: Missionary Education Movement, 1912.

Smith, Valerie. "Reading the Intersections of Race and Gender in Narratives of Passing." *Diacritics* 24 (Summer–Fall 1994): 43–57.

Solberg, S. E. "Sui Sin Far/Edith Eaton: First Chinese-American Fictionist." *MELUS* 8 (Spring 1981): 27–29.

———. "Sui, the Storyteller." In *Turning Shadows into Light: Art and Culture of the Northwest's Early Asian/Pacific Community,* edited by Mayumi Tsutakawa and Alan Chong Lau, 85–90. Seattle: Young Pine, 1982.

Sollors, Werner. *Neither Black nor White: Explorations in Interracial Literature.* Cambridge, Mass.: Harvard University Press, 1997.

Spaulding, Carol Vivian. "Blue-Eyed Asians: Eurasianism in the Work of Edith Eaton/Sui Sin Far, Winnifred Eaton/Onoto Watanna, and Diana Chang." Ph.D. diss., University of Iowa, 1996.

Spencer, Herbert. *Progress: Its Law and Cause.* New York: J. Fitzgerald, 1881.

Spooner, Brian. "Weavers and Dealers: The Authenticity of an Oriental Carpet." In *The Social Life of Things: Commodities in Cultural Perspective,* edited by Arun Appadurai, 195–235. Cambridge: Cambridge University Press, 1986.

Stepan, Nancy Leys, and Sander Gilman. "Appropriating the Idioms of Science: The Rejection of Scientific Racism." In *The Bounds of Race: Perspectives on Hegemony and Resistance,* edited by Dominick LaCapra, 159–78. Ithaca, N.Y.: Cornell University Press, 1991.

Stewart, Susan. "Antipodal Expectations: Notes on the Formosan 'Ethnography' of George Psalmanazar." In *Romantic Motives: Essays on Anthropological Sensibility,* edited by George W. Stocking Jr., 44–73. Madison: University of Wisconsin Press, 1989.

Stocking, George W., Jr. *The Ethnographer's Magic and Other Essays in the History of Anthropology.* Madison: University of Wisconsin Press, 1992.

———. *Race, Culture, and Evolution: Essays in the History of Anthropology.* New York: Macmillan, 1968.

———, ed. *Colonial Situations: Essays on the Contextualization of Ethnographic Knowledge.* Madison: University of Wisconsin Press, 1991.

———. *Observers Observed: Essays on Ethnographic Fieldwork.* Madison: University of Wisconsin Press, 1983.

———. *Romantic Motives: Essays on Anthropological Sensibility.* Madison: University of Wisconsin Press, 1989.

Stuart, J. L. "Women's Conference on the Home Life of Chinese Women." *Chinese Recorder and Missionary Journal* 32 (January 1901): 31–34.

Szyliowicz, Irene L. *Pierre Loti and Oriental Women.* London: Macmillan, 1988.

Tate, Claudia. *Domestic Allegories of Political Desire.* New York: Oxford University Press, 1992.

Taylor, Frank Fonda. *To Hell with Paradise: A History of the Jamaican Tourist Industry.* Pittsburgh: University of Pittsburgh Press, 1993.

"Theatres Next Week." *Montreal Daily Star,* March 2, 1895.

Thomson, Rosemary Garland, ed. *Freakery: Cultural Spectacles of the Extraordinary Body.* New York: New York University Press, 1996.

Tompkins, Jane. *Sensational Designs: The Cultural Work of American Fiction, 1790–1860.* New York: Oxford University Press, 1985.

Torgovnick, Marianna. *Gone Primitive: Savage Intellects, Modern Lives.* Chicago: University of Chicago Press, 1990.

Tracy, Arthur. *Rambles through Japan without a Guide.* London: Samson Low, 1892.

Tupper, Eleanor, and George E. McReynolds. *Japan in American Public Opinion.* New York: Macmillan, 1937.

Van Denburgh, M. "The Doll of the White Devils." *Land of Sunshine* 10 (February 1899): 131–33.

Weaver, Jane Calhoun. Introduction to *Sadakichi Hartmann: Critical Modernist. Collected Art Writings.* Edited by Jane Calhoun Weaver. Berkeley: University of California Press, 1991.

Webster, Jean. *Daddy Long-Legs.* 1915. Reprint, New York: Bantam Books, 1982.

White-Parks, Annette. *Sui Sin Far/Edith Maude Eaton: A Literary Biography.* Urbana: University of Illinois Press, 1995.

"Will Montreal Have a Chinatown?" *Montreal Daily Star,* December 14, 1895.

Williams, Patricia J. *The Alchemy of Race and Rights.* Cambridge, Mass.: Harvard University Press, 1991.

Williams, Teresa Kay. "Race-ing and Being Raced: The Critical Interrogation of 'Passing.'" *Amerasia Journal* 23, no. 1 (1997): 61–65.

Wong, Sau-ling Cynthia. "Sugar Sisterhood: Situating the Amy Tan Phenomenon." In *The Ethnic Canon: Histories, Institutions, and Interventions,* edited by David Palumbo-Liu, 174–210. Minneapolis: University of Minnesota Press, 1995.

Wood, J. G. *The Uncivilized Races; or, Natural History of Man.* 2 vols. Boston: G. M. Smith, 1870.

Wood, James Playsted. *Magazines in the United States.* New York: Ronald, 1956.

Wood, Willard. "A Chinese New Year." *Land of Sunshine* 9 (June 1898): 12–16.

Yin, Xiao-Huang. "Between the East and West: Sui Sin Far—the First Chinese-American Woman Writer." *Arizona Quarterly* 47 (Winter 1991): 49–84.

———. *Chinese American Literature since the 1850s.* Urbana: University of Illinois Press, 2000.

———. "Gold Mountain Dreams: Chinese American Literature and Its Sociohistorical Context, 1850–1963." Ph.D. diss., Harvard University, 1991.

Young, Robert J. C. *Colonial Desire: Hybridity in Theory, Culture, and Race.* London: Routledge, 1995.

Yu, Henry. "Thinking about Orientals: Modernity, Social Science, and Asians in Twentieth Century America." Ph.D. diss., Princeton University, 1995.

Zanussi, Krzysztof. "Shakespeare politycznie niepoprawny." *Polityka* 48 (November 28, 1998): 105.

Index

DOMINIKA FERENS received her Ph.D. from the University of California at Los Angeles and now teaches American literature at the University of Wrocław in Poland. She specializes in Asian American literature, popular fiction, and travel narratives.

The Asian American Experience

The University of Illinois Press
is a founding member of the
Association of American University Presses.

Composed in 10.5/13 Minion
with Minion display
by Jim Proefrock
at the University of Illinois Press
Manufactured by Thomson-Shore, Inc.

University of Illinois Press
1325 South Oak Street
Champaign, IL 61820-6903
www.press.uillinois.edu